Roe

ROE

THE HISTORY OF A NATIONAL OBSESSION

MARY ZIEGLER

Yale

\textbf{UNIVERSITY PRESS}

New Haven and London

Yale University Press books may be purchased in quantity for educational,
business, or promotional use. For information, please e-mail sales.press@
yale.edu (U.S. office) or sales@yaleup.co.uk (U.K. office).

Set in Adobe Garamond and Gotham types by IDS Infotech Ltd.
Printed in the United States of America.

Library of Congress Control Number: 2022938461
ISBN 978-0-300-26610-8 (hardcover : alk. paper)

A catalogue record for this book is available from the British Library.

This paper meets the requirements of ANSI/NISO Z39.48–1992
(Permanence of Paper).

10 9 8 7 6 5 4 3 2 1

To Dan, forever

Contents

Preface

In the fall of 2021, when the Supreme Court heard a case that might eliminate abortion rights in the United States, *Roe v. Wade* again led the news cycle. The case before the justices, *Dobbs v. Jackson Women's Health Organization*, involved a Mississippi ban on abortion at fifteen weeks, well before *Roe*'s cutoff at viability, the point at which survival is possible outside the womb. Reporters across the world questioned why the United States was rolling back protection for abortion just as nations from Argentina and Mexico to Kenya and South Korea were liberalizing their rules. At oral argument that December, the Court's conservative majority seemed poised not only to uphold Mississippi's law but also to repudiate the idea of a right to choose.

Dobbs was big news, but *Roe* is never out of the headlines for long. The decision overshadows Supreme Court nominations, inspires acts of political violence, and helps to decide presidential elections.[1]

But anyone reading about U.S. constitutional law and politics is left with a nagging question: why *Roe*? Why, for nearly five decades, has *Roe* had such a magnetic pull? Scholars question its reasoning, some feminists criticize it, and most Americans are indifferent to the workings of the Supreme Court. There are other culture wars—around guns, race, and the rights of same-sex couples—in which the Court has intervened. Some major decisions, like *Citizens United v. Federal Election Commission*, which freed up corporations to spend more on federal elections, are both relatively well known and unpopular. Yet *Roe* is uniquely visible.

Many of the best-known Supreme Court decisions receive attention because Americans appear to agree on them. Scholars have identified a constitutional canon—a set of crucial decisions that the entire political spectrum largely agrees were correctly decided—and an anticanon, a body of opinions that are universally derided. For example, Americans from left to right agree that the *Dred Scott v. Sandford*, which held that people of African descent could never be citizens, was terrible. Everyone says that *Brown v. Board of Education*, a decision invalidating the racial segregation of schools, should not be overruled. Canonical and anti-canonical cases are important because they offer shared reference points for disagreement about law, politics, and culture. There are some decisions that we all think are good or bad, and this allows for a more coherent dialogue even as we hotly contest the lessons these cases offer. *Roe*'s attraction is radically different: Americans disagree intensely about whether it was right or wrong.[2]

Perhaps *Roe*'s hold on us reflects the divisiveness of abortion itself. Debates about abortion in the United States were deeply polarized well before 1973, when the Court issued its decision. Any major Court decision on abortion in the United States might have been iconic, but *Roe* swept away most existing laws and proclaimed a new right to choose.

But if *Roe*'s allure is about abortion alone, it is hard to explain why more recent—and legally central—abortion decisions have not had the same cultural resonance. In 1992, the Court partially overruled *Roe* and grounded abortion rights in concerns about equality as well as the ideas about privacy articulated in 1973. Yet that decision, *Planned Parenthood of Southeastern Pennsylvania v. Casey*, has never been the kind of lightning rod that *Roe* is. Many Americans may not even recognize the name *Casey*.[3]

This book suggests that *Roe* has remained so salient for so long because it has been used to express nuanced, complicated ideas about abortion that the Supreme Court supposedly put out of reach in 1973. Since the battle to reform abortion laws began, the discussion has often seemed binary: abortion will be legal or criminal; abortion rights are a constitutional imperative or a mockery of human rights; the American public is pro-life or pro-choice. Yet in reality, abortion in America has been defined as much by complexity as by bright lines.

Roe has become the repository for the contradictions of the American abortion war. By infusing it with so many complex ideas, those contesting the abortion wars can preserve the façade of a black-and-white debate. But by telling the story of how we have redefined *Roe*, I hope to illuminate the paradoxes of our abortion politics and show that the pro-choice/pro-life binary has captured only a small part of how Americans think, talk, and fight about abortion.

Of course, Americans have reinterpreted decisions beyond *Roe*. Jamal Greene, Sanford Levinson, Ken Kersch, Jack Balkin, and others have done important work on how politics can change the way we interpret major Supreme Court rulings. But the history considered here tells us something important about how this meaning-making happens. *Roe* is perhaps the best example of a highly salient judicial decision that fits in neither the canon nor the anti-canon. Like canonical cases, it takes on a range of meanings that reflect differences over national values. But its power is not that we agree on whether it was rightly decided. It captures our imaginations because it has become both a meta-symbol of our many political and cultural *disagreements* and a shorthand for their inherent contradictions.

Staking out a position on *Roe* may seem like a helpful shortcut, a quick way to distinguish political friend from foe. But when discussing *Roe*, many people raise questions or arguments that do not fit the left/right, Democrat/Republican, pro-choice/pro-life categories that often define discussion. On the surface, *Roe* appears to reflect our profound polarization, but the ways we discuss it suggest that our views are neither simple nor diametrically opposed. Americans discussing *Roe* raise complex questions about sexual consent, sexual violence, and sexual harassment, about the role of the judiciary in American democracy, about the needs of working parents, about the role of science in politics, about racial justice, and about religious liberty. A symbol of everything that divides us, *Roe* reflects the degree to which Americans do not fall into cleanly drawn categories when it comes to abortion or many of our other most divisive issues.

That this symbol of our disagreements is a Supreme Court decision carries its own contradictions. Our constitutional canon—and *Roe*, the clearest shorthand for our political disagreements—involve decisions rendered by judges. Yet there is a disconnect between the unique legitimacy of judicial interpretation that such a practice assumes and the way Americans actually rethink precedent. Invoking a decision as a touchstone of debate suggests deference to the judiciary, but the free and frequent reinterpretation of opinions like *Roe* suggests that the courts are only one voice in a broader dialogue about rights.

At the time of this writing, the Court's public standing has taken a hit, especially as more citizens across the political spectrum consider it a partisan institution. The more the justices convince Americans of their partisanship, the more we may consciously untether our ideas about the Constitution and national identity from what the justices say. The reinterpretation of *Roe* suggests that a robust popular constitutionalism is already possible. If belief in the Court's impartiality continues to nosedive, the practice of popular constitutionalism may become more openly independent of the Court.[4]

Activists' repurposing of *Roe* also tells us something important about how social movements frame their arguments. Sociologists, political scientists, and legal scholars have studied the importance of the framing strategies used by social movements, the messaging tactics that shape how other actors understand and even react to an issue. The raw material for movements' meaning-making can come from a wide variety of places, including other political or cultural struggles (the civil rights movement, for example, has been an important inspiration for organizations across ideological lines). Social movement scholars, however, have paid particular attention to the influence that a movement's messaging has on its opponent. Studies have described the back-and-forth between competing movements as an "interactive evolution," a process in which movements and countermovements "seek to offset the moves of the other."[5]

The many interpretations of *Roe* offer a powerful example of how the strategic exchanges between movements unfold. Battles centered on the meaning of *Roe* often followed a distinctive pattern. Rarely did either movement respond to a point made by the opposition by changing the subject; more often, each side acknowledged the importance of whatever issue had been tied to *Roe*, from religious freedom to racial justice. But each movement insisted that its opponents were actually trying to subvert the very value they claimed to defend. This dynamic created a kind of fun-house mirror effect: while claiming to embrace the same values, each side distorted or entirely changed the point that the other was trying to make.

This process seems at first to limit the kinds of ideas that movements can articulate: advocates often responded to the opposition rather than taking the conversation in a new direction. In practice, however, within these apparent limits, both movements managed to address a wide variety of crucial issues—many of them only tangentially related to the claims made by the opposition. When discussing equality for women, for example, anti-abortion activists turned the conversation from career and education to claims about health. Later, when right-to-lifers made claims about *Roe* and religious liberty, supporters of abortion rights raised the same issues to spotlight prochoice faith-based communities. As these examples suggest, the limits involved in responding to the opposition's arguments were less strict than it first appeared.

Understanding how we talk about *Roe* also helps us make sense of both *Dobbs* and the future of U.S. abortion law. The Supreme Court has a conservative supermajority poised to undo abortion rights. The history of debates around *Roe* tells us what it would mean if the Court redefined or reversed it. Some argue that abortion access is already almost gone in conservative states, and that those most likely to be affected by criminalization already cannot get abortions.

Something serious will still be lost if the Court reverses the decision. Many states will likely criminalize not only the conduct of doctors performing abortions within their own borders but also out-of-state procedures or self-managed abortion. But the legacy of *Roe* goes beyond abortion. *Roe* has such tremendous resonance partly because in popular conversation, it can stand in for the entirety of the Court's jurisprudence on sex and equality, and much else as well. By taking it on, the Court signals a willingness to rethink more of our constitutional framework than the justices deciding *Dobbs* would likely admit.

The *Dobbs* opinion may present itself as the end of *Roe* and of the Court's involvement with abortion. We should not believe a word of that. *Roe* has always had a hold on the popular imagination for reasons well beyond controlling what state lawmakers can do. *Dobbs* will not end efforts to see *Roe*—whatever we mean by it—written into American law.

Of course, making visible the contradictions embodied by *Roe* will not resolve the American abortion divide any more than overturning *Roe* would. Nevertheless, the history of *Roe*'s changing meanings shows that the pro-choice/pro-life binary has never fully captured the complexity of the American abortion wars. The history of how we talk about *Roe* illuminates the inconsistencies and unsettled issues in our abortion politics; identifying them gives us a better chance to escape the well-worn ruts into which the abortion debate has fallen. In this book, I hope to recapture some of the nuance in our fights about abortion. It has long resided where we would least expect to find it—in the meaning of *Roe* itself.

Acknowledgments

I could not have completed this book without the support of many people. Thanks to the staff at libraries at Harvard University, Catholic University, Columbia University, Duke University, the Concordia Seminary of the Lutheran Church Missouri Synod, the George H. W. Bush Presidential Library and Museum, the William J. Clinton Presidential Library and Museum, the Gerald Ford Presidential Library and Museum, the Ronald Reagan Presidential Library and Museum, the University of California–Berkeley, the Southern Baptist Historical Society, Liberty University, Barnard College, Smith College, the University of Wyoming, Northwestern University, the University of Missouri–St. Louis, and the Wilcox Collection at the University of Kansas.

Many wonderful people have shared comments on the ideas advanced in the book, including Aziza Ahmed, Susan Appleton, David Cohen, Deborah Dinner, Gillian Frank, Michele Goodwin, Joanna Grossman, Karissa Haugeberg, Jennifer Holland, Courtney Joslin, Laura Kalman, Andrew Lewis, Kristin Luker, Kimberly Mutcherson, Rachel Rebouché, Carol Sanger, Logan Sawyer, Dan Sharfstein, Geoffrey Stone, David Strauss, Robert Tsai, and Daniel K. Williams.

I thank my editor at Yale University Press, Bill Frucht, for taking such care with the book, and my agent, Chris Calhoun, for his advocacy of my work. Others at Yale University Press, including Amanda Gerstenfeld, have been unfailingly helpful. Katrina Miller and the library staff at Florida State have done more than I could have asked to keep the project on track. I also thank my tremendous research assistants, Matt Michaloski, Sahara Williams, Bradyn Shock, Savannah Harden, and Rachelle Hollinshead, for helping me sort through a ridiculous amount of archival material. I am grateful to James Bopp Jr., Karen Mulhauser, Linda Wharton, and Myrna Gutiérrez for access to their papers.

Finally, I thank my husband, Dan, my daughter, Layla, and my mom and dad, all of whom made this book possible.

Roe

1

The Making of *Roe*

Conversations about abortion in the United States often begin with *Roe v. Wade*, but debates about the procedure reach much further back. Techniques to end pregnancy were known to native peoples, enslaved Americans, and Europeans immigrating to the United States. The subject came up when people in colonial America faced criminal prosecution for fornication, and in medicinal guides advising women what to do about "blocked menses," a term colonial Americans used for early pregnancy. The common law did criminalize some of these abortions, but most clearly at quickening, the point at which a patient could feel fetal movement, between sixteen and twenty weeks after a person's last menstrual period. Historians have debated the extent to which states adopted the quickening doctrine. What is clear is that states introduced new abortion regulations in the 1820s, initially focusing on prohibiting the sale of poisons marketed as abortion drugs. In the 1840s, newspapers fed a seemingly endless public appetite for salacious stories about black market abortions. In the wake of this surge of coverage, more states formalized their rules, often retaining quickening as a dividing line: most treated abortion as a felony only after that point in pregnancy.[1]

In the 1850s, physicians leading the recently founded American Medical Association led a fight for more stringent laws. Horatio Storer, still often viewed as the founding father of gynecology in the United States, was at the forefront of the campaign. A Boston Brahmin with a

Harvard degree and a famously difficult personality, Storer believed that human life began at fertilization, not at quickening. He insisted that only properly trained physicians like himself could understand abortion's ethical dimensions. But he was not focused just on the nature of life in the womb. At a time of great emigration from Germany and Ireland, he argued that abortion was sapping the nation's strength. Women of Anglo-Saxon descent, he believed, had used abortion to limit their families while immigrant birth rates were exploding. Worse, these women were damaging their marriages by shirking their natural duties as wives and mothers. Some physicians disapproved of Storer's crusade, but others recognized that his approach gave so-called regular doctors, mostly white men like Storer, a competitive advantage over midwives and practitioners of alternative medicine, many of whom were women and/or people of color.[2]

Storer gradually won over most state legislatures, with many criminalizing abortion throughout pregnancy by 1880 (with narrow exceptions for situations when a pregnancy was life-threatening). Enforcement of the laws remained lax, however, with few prosecutions unless a patient died.[3]

With the coming of the Great Depression, this settlement no longer seemed tenable. The abortion rate spiked as Americans delayed marriage, lost jobs, and struggled to support large families. Although the spread of antibiotics in the 1930s began to reduce deaths in childbirth, abortion was still dangerous; in 1930, physicians attributed nearly one-fifth of all maternal deaths to the procedure. The more often women showed up in doctors' offices with post-abortion complications, the harder it was for physicians to deny that many were ending their pregnancies.[4]

Nor, in the 1940s and 1950s, were prosecutors willing to tolerate abortion so long as doctors did not kill the women who came to get them. Instead, state attorneys general more often equated abortion with gambling and prostitution, vices in which the unscrupulous exploited the ignorant. In 1941, John Harlen Amen, a special prosecutor for Kings County (Brooklyn), denounced an "abortion racket" for producing nothing but "disability and death."[5]

Concerned about legal liability, physicians working in some non-Catholic hospitals created therapeutic abortion committees to regulate the procedure. These committees initially cut down on the number of abortions, but over time, different physicians reached conflicting conclusions about when a procedure was needed to protect a patient's life. A growing number began to sign off on procedures for patients who claimed to be suicidal; a study of six leading hospitals conducted between 1951 and 1960 showed that doctors cited mental health justifications for nearly half of all abortions they performed. Some doctors believed the law itself had become a problem.[6]

In the 1960s, Dr. Alan Guttmacher and a handful of other physicians, authors, and feminists launched a movement to reform abortion laws. The reformers first seized on a model law proposed by the American Law Institute (ALI), a group of judges, lawyers, and academics charged with recommending improvements to the law. In 1962, when the final version of its Model Penal Code came out, the ALI proposed legislation making abortion legal in cases of rape, incest, grave fetal defects, or a serious threat to the patient's physical or mental health. Five years later, Colorado became the first state to pass a version of ALI's model law. By 1970, more than ten others had followed suit (Florida, Michigan, Maine, and Arizona had rejected the ALI model). Some politicians in both parties saw the law as a sensible compromise; Republicans and Democrats both voted for the bill, with conservative governors from Ronald Reagan of California to Spiro Agnew of Maryland signing versions into law. Some Jews and mainline Protestants backed reform, with one group founding the Clergy Consultation Service on Abortion in 1967 to give patients reliable information about the procedure and referrals to doctors who could safely perform it.[7]

An emerging right-to-life movement viewed the ALI law as a betrayal of moral principle. "The state," wrote anti-abortion scholar and ALI member Eugene Quay, "cannot authorize medical men to do what is beyond its own authority—to destroy an innocent life."[8] Catholic dioceses led the early opposition to the law, and in 1968, the Family Life Division of the National Conference of Catholic Bishops founded the National Right to Life Committee (NRLC) to relaunch the anti-abortion movement as a secular struggle for human rights. The early movement had been burdened with an explicitly religious message and a willingness to link opposition to abortion with opposition to contraception; NRLC broke with that pattern. James McHugh, the left-leaning young priest in charge of the organization, instead wanted to frame abortion as a matter of constitutional rights.[9]

Rank-and-file right-to-lifers, most of them white and middle class, compared their cause to the fight to abolish slavery. Constitutionally, they relied on the Fourteenth Amendment, a provision passed in the aftermath of the Civil War that created powerful protections for people of color and recognized citizens' rights to due process and equal protection of the law. Anti-abortion lawyers insisted that the framers of the Fourteenth Amendment viewed an unborn child as a person and thus entitled to constitutional protection. Anti-abortion leaders compared unborn children to enslaved Americans—both fetuses and people of color, the movement suggested, had their humanity denied by others who perpetrated acts of unspeakable violence against them. This argument fell flat with some who argued that relatively few right-to-lifers had joined the civil rights movement that sought equality and protection from violence for people of color, but as a constitutional strategy, the effects of personhood would be hard to understate. If the law recognized it, that would make abortion un-

4

constitutional everywhere in the United States. Right-to-life organizations used this constitutional rhetoric in their efforts to stop ALI bills across the country.[10]

But increasingly, it was not just abortion foes who disapproved of the ALI law. The abortion rights movement was losing patience with reform laws. By the late 1960s and early 1970s, new voices had joined the call to legalize abortion. Some sympathized with a population control movement that had influenced national politics since World War II. Population control appealed to some refugees of the eugenics movement, which had successfully championed compulsory sterilization laws in the early twentieth century. These activists believed that reducing the total population would almost certainly require that "undesirables" have fewer children. But population control had a broader appeal. Some Cold Warriors thought spiraling birth rates were causing poverty and famine. The resulting instability in the developing world, they suggested, might push other nations into the arms of the Soviet Union. Curbing population would help the United States preserve its edge in the conflict with Communism. Others tied population growth to the depletion of scarce environmental resources or the liberation of women.[11]

Some population controllers opposed the legalization of abortion; others were sympathetic to the idea but did not want to publicly endorse something that was still so controversial. Others, like the college students who founded chapters of Zero Population Growth, Inc., described legal abortion as a tool in the fight to save the environment and enrich women's lives.[12]

While arguments about public health and population control might have enjoyed bipartisan support, much of the energy in the legalization movement came from those fighting for women's liberation. The National Organization for Women, one of the nation's largest feminist organizations, called for the complete repeal of abortion restrictions in 1967. Socialist feminists and radical feminists also championed repeal. Many supporters of women's rights justified abortion not as a means to an end but as a fundamental right. "The [criminal] abortion statutes," explained abortion rights litigator Roy Lucas in 1970, "curtail a woman's freedom of choice."[13]

The new members of the legalization movement were fed up with the ALI law, which had done little to expand abortion access, and they lobbied legislatures to remove all restrictions on legal abortion: New York, Hawaii, Washington, and Alaska eliminated almost all such restrictions. In addition to the twelve states that had passed ALI-style laws by 1970, Alabama and Massachusetts allowed for abortion when a pregnant person faced certain threats to physical health, and Mississippi permitted abortion in cases of sexual assault. The remaining states allowed abortion only when a patient's life was at risk. It was no surprise that some repeal proponents also pursued change in the courts.[14]

The repeal movement drew on a line of precedents recognizing a right to privacy, starting with *Griswold v. Connecticut*, a case about a Connecticut law that prohibited married couples from using birth control. The justices in that case voted 7-2 that the statute violated a constitutional right to privacy. Repeal proponents insisted that the decision to have an abortion, just like the right to contraception recognized in *Griswold*, involved the critical matter of when or whether to have a child. Feminists also contended that abortion regulations denied women equal protection under the law, limited their economic independence, subjected them to medical risks and social stigma, and required them to live up to the government's ideas about proper gender roles.[15]

Members of the growing right-to-life movement, meanwhile, felt confident about their chances to keep abortion a crime. State anti-abortion organizations developed effective lobbying techniques and attracted a more religiously diverse membership. New anti-abortion recruits took heart from an ambiguous 1971 Supreme Court decision, *United States v. Vuitch*, that upheld a Washington, DC, abortion ordinance. Dr. Milan Vuitch, a vocal repeal proponent, had argued that the ordinance was unconstitutionally vague and did not give doctors enough guidance about when abortion was allowed. The Court rejected Vuitch's argument, saying that the law's health exception clearly applied to both physical and mental well-being. Interpreted in this way, the Court reasoned, the ordinance did not violate the due process clause.[16]

Right-to-lifers thought the courts might even upend state laws that expanded access to abortion. Robert Byrn, a law professor at Fordham, petitioned the New York courts to name him guardian for all children scheduled for abortion in the city. Other anti-abortion lawyers similarly sought to be appointed guardians. The guardianship gambit generally failed, but some state and federal courts also rejected constitutional challenges to abortion regulations. In the early 1970s, right-to-lifers defeated referenda on abortion in Michigan and North Dakota and persuaded the New York state legislature to reimpose abortion restrictions before Republican governor Nelson Rockefeller vetoed the proposal.[17]

Abortion rights supporters also had reason for optimism after the Supreme Court issued an opinion in another contraception case, *Eisenstadt v. Baird*, in 1972. Bill Baird, a self-described contraceptive crusader, did his best to get arrested on the campus of Boston University for distributing contraceptive foam. At the time, Massachusetts law allowed anyone to get a contraceptive device or drug to prevent sexually transmitted diseases, but when it came to using the same articles for preventing conception, only married people could obtain contraceptives—and only after receiving a prescription from a licensed physician. During his criminal trial, Baird argued that Massachusetts's law violated the right to privacy established by *Griswold*. The Court agreed. The justices found no rational basis for the distinction the state had drawn between married and unmarried people. Massachusetts had argued that it had an interest in limiting birth control because contraceptives themselves were immoral. In response, the *Eisenstadt* majority stressed that however far the right to privacy extended to birth control, it did so equally for unmarried as well as married people. "If the right of privacy means anything," wrote Justice William Brennan, "it is the right of the individual . . . to be free from unwarranted governmental intrusion into matters so fundamentally affecting a person as the decision whether to bear or beget a child."[18]

Abortion rights supporters saw *Eisenstadt* as a sign that the Court might strike down abortion bans. There were already two such cases pending before the justices. *Roe v. Wade* involved a Texas law banning abortion unless a patient's life was at risk. A companion case, *Doe v. Bolton*, addressed Georgia's version of the ALI law. At the time it issued the *Eisenstadt* ruling, the Court had already heard oral argument once in *Roe*; Harry Blackmun had originally planned to write a majority opinion holding that the law was too vague because doctors could not know when a procedure should be deemed life-saving. But several of Blackmun's liberal colleagues pushed for a more expansive ruling, and the case was scheduled for reargument.[19]

In January 1973, by a vote of 7-2, the Court struck down both Texas's and Georgia's laws. Before writing the *Roe* decision, Blackmun had spent a great deal of time at the Mayo Clinic, an elite Minnesota hospital he had represented in the 1950s. His focus on medicine showed in his majority opinion in *Roe*, which canvassed medical attitudes about abortion from ancient Greece to the present. Blackmun presented abortion as a medical matter best left to doctors and their patients. The right to privacy recognized in *Griswold* and *Eisenstadt*, he wrote, was broad enough to encompass a patient's decision to end her pregnancy. He also detailed the consequences of denying a patient that liberty: threats to mental and physical health, the burdens of childrearing, and the stigma of unwed motherhood made the abortion decision particularly consequential. But if pregnancy and parenting disproportionately affected women, the *Roe* Court unmistakably assigned abortion rights at least partly to doctors.[20]

The determination that there was an abortion right did not decide the case. Texas argued that the interests of the unborn child trumped any liberty that patients could identify. The Court also considered the idea that the state might regulate abortion to protect patients, but Blackmun's opinion stressed that abortion had become safer over time, and at least before the second trimester, it posed relatively little risk to patients. Texas responded that the state had a compelling interest in protecting life from fertilization onward. Blackmun's majority opinion acknowledged that some faith traditions and physicians believed that human life gained value at fertilization, but he stressed that this conclusion was far from universal. If disagreement ran this deep, he reasoned, the state could not impose its own view.[21]

Texas's last chance was to argue that an unborn child was a rights-holding person under the Fourteenth Amendment. Right-to-lifers had made the same argument in friend-of-the-court briefs; some framed personhood as a biological fact. Others contended that states had criminalized abortion during the same years that the Fourteenth Amendment was written and ratified—and that the framers of that amendment meant to include an unborn child within its protections. This argument had a textual component—the Fourteenth Amendment protected "persons," a term that right-to-lifers claimed unambiguously included all human beings, before or after birth. Anti-abortion lawyers also stressed that in the lead-up to 1868, when Congress ratified the Fourteenth Amendment, states were not only criminalizing abortion but also treating it as a crime against a "person." But there arguably were holes in the argument: states, when banning abortion, did not invoke the Constitution as a justification or argue that the procedure violated federal rights. The framers of the Fourteenth Amendment, who were focused on the treatment of free people of color, likely gave little thought to abortion. Later, progressive scholars even suggested that the original public meaning of the Fourteenth Amendment, which called for equality under the law, *ensured* a right to abortion for women rather than establishing that abortion was unconstitutional.[22]

Blackmun's opinion instead treated personhood as a question of textual interpretation: when "person" appeared in the Constitution, he wrote, it always applied postnatally, and there was no reason to think the framers of the Fourteenth Amendment had broken with that convention.[23]

But Blackmun also stressed that the constitutional right to abortion had limits. The state had little power to regulate in the first trimester, but in the second trimester, it could regulate abortion to protect maternal health. Only at fetal viability—at the time, roughly twenty-four to twenty-six weeks after a woman's last menstrual period—did the state's interest in protecting fetal life become compelling. At one point, Blackmun had thought of drawing the line at the end of the first trimester, but other justices suggested that viability was more logical: at that point, there was no longer a zero-sum choice between protecting life and a patient's desire not to be pregnant.[24]

The parallel decision, *Doe*, struck down Georgia's law at the same time. The effect of the two decisions is hard to overstate: with the stroke of a pen, the vast majority of the nation's abortion laws were made unconstitutional.

The *Roe* decision cast a shadow over the lives of the people most closely tied to it. Sandra Cano had led a tumultuous life before be-

coming Mary Doe in *Doe v. Bolton*. With a husband in and out of
prison and two children in and out of foster care, she had just relin-
quished a third child for adoption when she found herself pregnant
again. She later said that she went to an attorney hoping to divorce
her husband and get her children back; her attorney later claimed that
Cano had come to her seeking an abortion. Whatever the truth, Cano
did not terminate her pregnancy, but after her husband went to jail
for kidnapping and molesting three other young children, she did end
her marriage. Cano would later argue that she never felt comfortable
with abortion and never wanted to have one; in 1988, she denounced
the right to choose. In 2003, as a plaintiff in a bid to reopen her case
(and *Roe*), she asserted that she had been lied to about what abortion
really was.[25]

By the time she died, Cano had been through five marriages, cervical cancer, and a stroke. She spent much of her time championing
the cause of her son, Joel Lee, who, she claimed, had been wrongfully
convicted of murder. In the eyes of many, however, the *Doe* case still
defined her. "I speak," she told the *Atlanta Journal-Constitution* in
2003, "to let people know I never believed in abortion."[26]

Harry Blackmun, the author of *Roe*, never doubted his position
on the matter either. After 1973, he watched support for legal abortion
on the Court gradually erode. In *Roe* itself, only two justices dissented
from Blackmun's opinion recognizing abortion rights. In 1986, by
contrast, only four other justices joined him in striking down a Pennsylvania abortion law. Three years later, when a conservative majority
upheld a Missouri abortion restriction, Blackmun accused his colleagues of overruling the *Roe* decision without having the courage to
say so. He stayed on the Court long enough to see the justices turn
away a 1992 request to reverse *Roe*. "Just when so many expected the
darkness to fall," he wrote then, "the flame has grown bright." When
Blackmun passed away in 1999, many celebrated his long and storied

legal career, but most accounts began by describing him as the author of *Roe v. Wade*. His *New York Times* obituary described him as the "author of the abortion right."[27]

Norma McCorvey, the Jane Roe of *Roe v. Wade*, made a living from her connection to *Roe*. McCorvey never had an abortion, instead relinquishing her three children for adoption, and she never saw the abortion issue in black and white. She believed for many years that abortion should be legal until the twelfth week but not after. Her complex views did not stop her from being a poster child for the pro-choice movement for a time, the headliner of dinners and marches, and then a pro-life convert. After she died of heart failure in 2017, opposing sides of the abortion issue continued to debate whether McCorvey was really pro-choice or pro-life. The truth—that she had never fit neatly into either camp—was harder to acknowledge.[28]

When we think of *Roe*, we often pay the most attention to people like Blackmun or McCorvey, those most closely involved in the 1973 Supreme Court decisions. In the past half-century, however, a diverse group of activists, lawyers, lobbyists, politicians, judges, and ordinary Americans put forth their own ideas of what *Roe* stood for. Some shared Sandra Cano's aversion to legal abortion. Others reflected Norma McCorvey's ambivalence. In national conversations about consent, the role of the judiciary, the needs of working parents, and the politics of science, racism, and religious liberty gave *Roe* a dizzying range of meanings.

As I write this, the Court again seems ready to reverse *Roe*. Six conservatives, handpicked for judicial philosophies that hold *Roe* to be wrongly decided, now sit on the Court. Among the many abortion cases available, these judges chose to hear a case in which upholding a disputed regulation would be impossible without reversing *Roe,* or else rewriting it so extensively that it would amount to a reversal. There is every reason to think the Court will do this.

But a look at the people who redefined *Roe* shows how little the Court has controlled what the decision means, or why it resonates. The Supreme Court may change the rules that govern access to abortion, but *Roe*—as a cultural symbol or a rallying cry—will almost certainly remain.

2

Choice and Consent

Describing *Roe* as a symbol of the right to choose made perfect sense to Karen Mulhauser. In 1975, she was a young mother new to the nation's capital, starting a job as the executive director of the Washington, DC, office of the nation's leading abortion rights organization, the National Abortion Rights Action League (NARAL). She sometimes found it surreal that she had the job. As a child, she had imagined that she would be a scientist like both her parents. Even after two years in medical school, she could not see herself in front of a microscope.[1]

But anyone who looked at Mulhauser's résumé could see why NARAL chose her. After dropping out of medical school, she started teaching science at a Massachusetts boarding school, and students began flooding her with questions about sex. She married a fellow teacher, moved to Boston, and volunteered at a pregnancy counseling service that helped people find abortions—for the well-off, chartered flights to England, where abortion was legal; for those with less money, the Clergy Consultation Service, which referred patients to safe but illegal providers. After New York repealed its restrictions on abortion, she organized carpools there. NARAL's board of directors thought she was perfect. But Mulhauser did not tell her new bosses that she had self-induced an abortion in 1964. She had never told anyone; her parents and then-boyfriend went to their graves without knowing.[2]

The summer she got pregnant, Mulhauser's life had seemed idyllic. She was a student at Antioch College, fresh off a year abroad in Nigeria, Italy, and other parts of the Mediterranean. She had a summer job at Tufts University School of Dental Medicine, a boyfriend of six months, and an adorable sublet in Cambridge. But then her period was a month late, then two. She waited until no one else was home and found a long knitting needle. Everything seemed to go well until, while on her way back to college, she collapsed at the bus station and woke up in the station's office. She felt lucky that she had not suffered long-lasting consequences from the abortion, and she thought her parents and boyfriend would have supported her decision to end her pregnancy, but she could never bring herself to tell them. In the 1960s, it seemed that no one, including Karen Mulhauser, thought abortion was a legitimate choice.[3]

Mulhauser was part of a generation of activists who made *Roe v. Wade* a symbol of choice for women. But those activists inadvertently raised a much harder issue: Was genuine reproductive choice possible at a time when the right to say no to sex was more an idea than a reality? If women had a right to make choices in the 1970s and early 1980s, few agreed on the criteria for believing, much less respecting, those decisions. With the rules on sexual assault and sexual harassment very much up for grabs, discussions of *Roe* and choice exposed questions about what reproductive autonomy for women would really require.

When the *Roe* decision came down, both sides of the abortion debate had to flesh out what it meant—and how to talk about it. The anti-abortion movement found itself at a crossroads. In February 1973, the movement's largest national organization, the National Right to Life Committee, then just five years old, hosted a strategy session.[4] Most of those present had no doubt about what to do next. Several members of Congress had already proposed constitutional amendments establishing fetal personhood, and for right-to-lifers, the question was not whether to back this strategy but which amendment to support. Although their details varied, every version would not just overturn *Roe v. Wade* but also criminalize abortion from coast to coast. Passing any constitutional amendment required supermajority support in both Congress and the states, but the constitutional amendment campaign set the terms of the abortion debate in the immediate aftermath of *Roe*.[5]

At first, the leaders of major abortion rights organizations responded that the constitutional amendment campaign was out of step with modern medicine. Presenting *Roe* as a decision about doctors' prerogatives certainly suited NARAL's mostly white and white-collar leadership. Larry Lader and Betty Friedan, two NARAL luminaries, moved in the same high-end social circles. Bea Blair, who served as executive director before Mulhauser, had an ancestor who advised Andrew Jackson, while another served as postmaster general under Abraham Lincoln (the family later donated their home, Blair House, to the federal government, which used it to house visiting dignitaries).[6]

The best chance of defeating an amendment, NARAL leaders believed, was to enlist the support of the nation's medical and legal elite. Some also worried about complacency among abortion rights supporters. Linking *Roe* to the medical elite, NARAL leaders hoped, would reinforce that abortion was a normal, respectable procedure without reopening a broader political debate about it. "The Court has spoken," wrote Blair's predecessor, Lee Gidding, to her colleagues in 1974, "and the case is closed."[7]

Anti-abortion advocates also began describing *Roe* as a decision protecting the rights of doctors. Many of the movement's early leaders were physicians angry that organizations like the American Medical Association backed the legalization of abortion. The movement's most popular spokesperson, a charismatic Black graduate of Harvard Medical School named Mildred Jefferson, crisscrossed the country giving speeches linking *Roe* to rights for doctors. "The highest court in the land," she told Congress in 1974, "undermined respect for the medical profession by giving doctors a nearly unlimited license to kill the unborn child."[8]

With Dr. Jefferson's guidance, NRLC stressed that *Roe* gave rights to abortionists—and insisted that abortion providers were nothing like ordinary doctors. Of course, botched abortions—and incompetent providers—had existed before 1973, but Jefferson used stories about bad doctors operating after *Roe* as evidence that the Supreme Court's decision would "foster sloppy practice on the part of doctors performing abortions, free them from accountability, and endanger the lives and health of pregnant women." Identifying *Roe* with "abortionists" made perfect sense to a movement that wanted to stop abortion from being considered an ordinary part of medical care.[9]

But the new generation of abortion rights leaders, including Karen Mulhauser, found it absurd to define *Roe* as a decision about doctors' rights. There had always been feminists in the abortion rights movement; before 1973, arguments about women's equality and autonomy were made on marches, in speak-outs, in the media, and in court. But large organizations like NARAL sometimes pushed these arguments to the side, fearing that a focus on women's rights would fall flat with (mostly male) legislators and judges.[10]

By the mid-1970s, the women leading abortion rights organizations, many of whom had experience with abortion, miscarriage, or stillbirth, believed that *Roe* should stand for a woman's right to make her own decisions. Mulhauser certainly felt that way. Four years after her abortion, she had lost a daughter in stillbirth. Just as much as her abortion, losing a child reinforced her commitment to a woman's right to choose; she believed that only women understood the experience of pregnancy, abortion, or stillbirth, and the law should honor their decisions.[11]

In the mid-1970s, organizations like NARAL began reframing *Roe* as a decision involving women's freedom of choice, especially when abortion foes campaigned to ban Medicaid funding for abortion. Medicaid, a joint federal and state program that provided free or low-cost health care to low-income Americans, had transformed abortion in the United States after *Roe*. Before 1973, people of color had far fewer legal abortions than white patients but at least twice as many illegal terminations. Between 1972 and 1974, the percentage of legal abortions obtained by people of color rose nearly 7 percent. Between 1976 and 1977, the abortion rates for Medicaid recipients (61.5 per 1,000 women versus 20.7 per 1,000) and people of color (58 per 1,000 versus 19 per 1,000) were higher than those for other women.[12]

For this reason, right-to-lifers in Congress believed that a national Medicaid ban would put a serious dent in the national abortion rate. It was Henry Hyde, a Republican from a district near the Chicago O'Hare International Airport, who succeeded in writing the ban into an appropriations bill for the Department of Health, Education, and Welfare in 1976.[13]

The Hyde Amendment forced groups like NARAL to rethink how they talked about *Roe*. The amendment did not obviously strip doctors of any right to perform abortions; indeed, the number of abortions rose 12 percent in 1977, with over 1.3 million procedures performed that year (the per capita rate also continued to increase, rising from 16.6 to 27.5 per 1,000 women between 1973 and 1978). But the ban had a stark effect on the ability of Medicaid-eligible patients to get an abortion: the Guttmacher Foundation, the research arm of Planned Parenthood, estimated that immediately after the Hyde Amendment went into effect, at least 100,000 women seeking an abortion had not been able to afford one because of the law.[14]

The Medicaid funding led NARAL and other abortion rights groups to begin describing *Roe* as a decision about a woman's right to choose. A 1977 NARAL letter to Congress explained that supporting *Roe* meant standing up "for the health and welfare of millions of American women, and for their ability to make difficult decisions about abortions for themselves."[15] At rallies against the Hyde Amendment, movement leaders proclaimed, "Freedom Is the Right to Choose" and "Freedom to Choose Is the American Way."[16]

It might seem odd that abortion rights groups focused on self-determination rather than equality, given that feminists were then waging a war to write the federal Equal Rights Amendment (ERA) into the Constitution. The ERA would have prohibited discrimination on the basis of sex. First drafted by feminists in the 1920s, it had passed Congress in the early 1970s and been sent to the states for ratification (anti-feminists led by Phyllis Schlafly ultimately defeated the ERA in the 1980s). In the 1970s, some ERA proponents wanted to treat abortion as a separate issue, since connecting it too closely to sex discrimination seemed likely to jeopardize ratification of the amendment. But abortion rights advocates had their own reasons for firmly tying *Roe* to freedom of choice. A choice framework resonated with feminists who had launched the anti-rape movement of the 1970s. Rape had been the least reported violent crime for centuries, and laws against it were rarely enforced. States made it legal for married men to rape their wives, and prosecutors rarely pursued convictions when a woman was assaulted by an acquaintance or had a reputation for being sexually active.[17]

But in the late 1960s an invigorated feminist movement began defining rape as an act of violence. In 1971, Susan Griffin published an essay in the radical feminist press describing rape as a "daily part of every woman's consciousness."[18] Several years later, Susan Brownmiller's best-selling *Against Our Will: Men, Women, and Rape* brought a new awareness of sexual violence to millions of readers. In the 1970s, feminists across the country set up rape crisis centers and hotlines, offered social services, legal support, and counseling, and hosted Take Back the Night marches to protest the widespread acceptance of assault.[19]

The National Organization for Women (NOW) launched a Rape Task Force in 1973 with an eye to changing state laws. NOW advocated that any unchosen sex be considered rape and insisted that a survivor's reputation or sexual past was "irrelevant for the purpose of establishing consent."[20] By 1975, thirteen states had enacted rape shield laws that limited the admission of such information as evidence; many more would follow. Meanwhile, advocates like Catharine MacKinnon and Lin Farley theorized a right to be free of sexual harassment at work. For activists like Mulhauser, linking *Roe* to both choice and consent made sense as part of a broader approach to women's sex, sexuality, and reproduction. A right to choose, rooted in *Roe*, was part of women's freedom to say yes or no, without penalty, to sexual activity.[21]

By the mid-1970s, even the Supreme Court was describing *Roe* as recognizing a woman's right to choose, rather than liberty for doctors. In 1976, the Court framed *Roe* this way in *Singleton v. Wulff*, a landmark case on who could challenge the constitutionality of abortion laws. Missouri had changed its Medicaid scheme in 1975 to exclude reimbursement for elective abortions. Two doctors challenged the constitutionality of the law, arguing that Missouri had deprived them of their "right to practice medicine." The Supreme Court refused to say whether such a right existed and held instead that doctors had standing to assert the rights of their patients.[22] The following year, in *Maher v. Roe*, the Court upheld a Connecticut Medicaid ban, insisting that *Roe* was about a "woman's decision to terminate her pregnancy." Legally, by the late 1970s, *Roe* seemed to stand for women's choice.[23]

A Pro-Choice Majority

Linking *Roe* to choice for women also seemed politically imperative. NARAL leaders were still shell-shocked by the passage of the
Hyde Amendment; shortly after the bill went into effect, Mulhauser
warned her colleagues that members of Congress being viewed "pro-
choice as a political liability in an election year." It did seem that lawmakers, like many Americans, were growing increasingly uncomfortable
with the idea of abortion. That was no accident: abortion opponents
were having considerable success stigmatizing abortion providers.[24]

The anti-abortion movement benefited from changes to the delivery of abortion services. In 1973, over 50 percent of abortions were
done in hospitals, but three years later, hospital abortions comprised a
little over 35 percent of the annual total. The hospitals were replaced
by freestanding clinics. Four years after abortion became legal, over
five hundred such clinics were operating across the country. By 1982,
over 80 percent of abortions were performed in freestanding clinics.
Some offered everything from prenatal care to deliveries; feminist
women's health centers combined birth control and abortion services
with counseling intended to demystify women's bodies. But most
clinics created a different image of abortion—physically and symboli-
cally separating it from other medical services or framing it as a matter
of liberation for women. The further abortion seemed from the rest of
medicine, the easier it was for NARAL and others to link *Roe* to wom-
en's rights rather than those of doctors.[25]

These changes in the delivery of abortion services coincided with
a massive shift in the health care market. In the 1970s, the number of
new physicians spiked, but most chose to specialize. Primary care
doctors, those with whom patients were the most familiar, clustered
in urban areas or along highways, setting up shop in strip malls already packed with podiatrists, chiropractors, and massage therapists.
These "docs in a box" reinforced the idea that medical services were

just another commodity. Describing abortion as a choice—a fundamental right as well as a consumer option—reflected most Americans' experience of the health care system. Mulhauser and her colleagues would later recognize that these changes came at a tremendous cost. The physical and symbolic separation of abortion clinics from other medical facilities made it easier for anti-abortion groups to mount pickets and stigmatize a procedure that they described as lucrative for doctors and dangerous for women. But identifying *Roe* with patient choice increasingly reflected the real-world practice of abortion in the 1970s.[26]

For Mulhauser and her colleagues, linking *Roe* to a right to choose also made political sense, especially after anti-abortion political action committees made an impact in the 1978 midterms. Immediately after 1973, neither political party staked out a consistent position on abortion, and the 1976 presidential election hardly clarified things. The Democratic standard-bearer, Jimmy Carter, a former peanut farmer who loved to show off his Christian faith, wanted neither to criminalize nor fund abortion—a position that put him at odds with advocates on both sides of the debate. His opponent, Gerald Ford, supported a constitutional amendment that would leave abortion regulation to each state—a measure no right-to-lifers actually liked. The 1978 midterms, on the other hand, were a game changer—partly courtesy of a trio of pranksters whom no one had taken seriously.[27]

Robert Morton Downey Jr. thought of himself as a minor celebrity. The chain-smoking son of a show business family, he had summered near the Kennedy compound as a child, then grown up to record country and pop songs that reached the top 100 on the *Billboard* chart. His friend Paul Brown was the husband of a prominent pro-life activist. Brown had spent most of his career at the Kmart corporation, but he instinctually understood Downey's loudmouth style. The final member of the trio, California attorney Bob Sassone, was fond of railing against the dangers of falling birth rates in the United States.[28]

The three men founded the Life Amendment Political Action Committee in 1977 and quickly made it a household name. LAPAC, as it called itself, pledged to take down several incumbents, including Democratic senator Dick Clark of Iowa.[29] It received crucial assistance from the leadership of the New Right, a group of conservative activists who coalesced after Barry Goldwater's failed presidential bid in 1964. Paul Weyrich, a former radio host, created the New Right's ecosystem, helping to found a think tank, the Heritage Foundation; the Committee for the Survival of a Free Congress, a political action committee to fundraise for conservative candidates; and the American Legislative Exchange Council, an organization that promoted right-wing laws in state legislatures. Richard Viguerie, a direct mail wizard, helped to raise money for preferred candidates. The New Right was ultraconservative, populist, and committed to purging moderates and establishment figureheads from the GOP. Some moderate figures in the GOP establishment, including Ford's vice president, Nelson Rockefeller, and his wife, Betty, were pro-choice. Right-to-lifers could upend the party, and that is precisely what the New Right intended to do.[30]

In 1978, both New Right and anti-abortion organizations felt that their money was well spent. The right-to-life vote caused the seemingly unbeatable Dick Clark to lose his Senate seat to Roger Jepsen, a pro-life evangelical with a penchant for flip-flopping and verbal gaffes, by a little more than twenty-six thousand votes.[31] Though Brown and his colleagues claimed credit for the defeat of Clark and several other incumbents, it was not clear how much abortion politics affected the results. Even in Iowa, where right-to-lifers' influence seemed the clearest, the *Des Moines Register* claimed that "the abortion issue was not decisive."[32]

Whatever the truth was, the media ran with the story of the anti-abortion swing vote. Brown and his colleagues fed reporters juicy tidbits to stoke interest, declaring a hit list for the 1980 race, then dangling Downey as a presidential candidate. The National Right to Life Committee launched its own PAC in 1979. Abortion rights leaders felt that to catch up with the pro-life message they had to redefine *Roe*—and their cause.[33]

In January 1980, Mulhauser laid out plans to increase "the number of single-issue, pro-choice votes on the abortion issue." But NARAL leaders recognized the growing stigma around the idea of abortion.[34] Defining *Roe* as a symbol of choice for women would appeal to a broader cross-section of voters, particularly those who did not want the government interfering in their private lives. As important, tying *Roe* to liberty for women would legitimize the idea that women had the right to say no (or yes) to parenthood and pregnancy as well as to sex. "We do not shrink from the difficulties inherent in a woman's decision to abort," NARAL explained in talking points. "That being the case, we must never let our viewpoint—be it that of a few individuals or a religious denomination—to be imposed on all citizens."[35]

In 1980, NARAL announced a new political initiative to identify a cohort of single-issue pro-choice voters. In launching this project, called Impact 80, Mulhauser worked with advocates with political organizing experience, many of whom were far more progressive than the society ladies who had once dominated NARAL's board. One of the newcomers was Kay Harrold, who had first read about the Hyde Amendment at a hippie farm in Berkeley Springs, West Virginia. At the farm, she had to make each copy of the *Washington Post* last a week, so she began each morning with old news and coffee. Shocked when Congress passed the Hyde Amendment, Harrold asked Mulhauser about volunteering at NARAL and later became her deputy director.

Another activist who worked closely with Mulhauser, Heather Booth, had helped launch the Jane Collective, a group that performed illegal abortions for women in the Chicago area, in 1969. Four years later, Booth started the Midwest Academy, a national training institute for causes related to social, racial, and economic justice. Booth contracted with NARAL to train activists and expand the organization's chapters. Among those she trained as community organizers was Jean Weinberg, a native of Hartsdale, New York. After Weinberg moved to Massachusetts, she became the executive director of NARAL's affiliate in the state, and later worked as a community director and oversaw the organization's affiliates. Booth, Weinberg, and Harrold saw grassroots organizing as the movement's future.[36]

Although they now had a Supreme Court decision on their side, Mulhauser and her colleagues felt that the anti-abortion movement was outcompeting them in state and national elections. A hostile Senate might consider passing a constitutional amendment. Anti-abortion legislators would pass more restrictions. Mulhauser's staff increasingly believed the reason NARAL had fallen behind politically was that the abortion rights movement had little presence in the states, and the states were where the action was. "We are not outnumbered," Mulhauser told the *Washington Post* in 1979. "We are being out-organized."[37]

To make a difference, NARAL would have to convince politicians that pro-choice voters were both numerous and dedicated. The blizzard of February 1978, a catastrophic nor'easter that hit New England, New Jersey, Pennsylvania, and New York, trapped Weinberg and Pam Lowry, the head of NARAL's executive committee, at a Holiday Inn on their way home to Boston from Washington, DC. While pacing the hotel halls, Weinberg convinced Lowry of the importance of political organizing. NARAL gave Weinberg $1.5 million to work with. She and other organizers went from state to state, hosting "house parties" at supporters' homes and then asking those present to volunteer for political campaigns. The guests then hosted their own coffee meetings and recruited even more volunteers. Weinberg counseled her recruits to mention abortion only once—when querying candidates about their positions. She thought there was a silent majority that might be willing to get into abortion politics in order to get the abortion issue out of politics. "Many of our supporters would not choose abortion themselves," she explained, "but they see it as an individual choice."[38]

Like Weinberg, Mulhauser believed state policy would determine the future of the abortion debate. States would decide whether an anti-abortion constitutional amendment became law (thirty-eight of the fifty states would have to ratify one). Before 1979, no anti-abortion amendment had made progress in Congress, but Mulhauser worried that the 1980 election would change that.[39]

NARAL staff also believed it made sense to focus on state law even if a constitutional amendment was dead in the water. States had begun introducing a wide range of abortion restrictions, and Mulhauser and her allies saw that these laws could eliminate abortion access even if *Roe* was still on the books. Maximizing influence in the states required a message with broad appeal.[40]

A License to Licentiousness

The anti-abortion movement's embrace of a new interpretation of *Roe* reflected the movement's changing composition. In the 1960s and much of the 1970s, when it first got underway, most of the movement's members were Catholic, with members holding a wide range of views on women's rights.[41]

But in the later 1970s, the political mobilization of conservative evangelical Protestants began to reshape the anti-abortion movement. Evangelical Protestants had always voted, but not for one party in particular, and before 1978, there was no consistent evangelical opposition to abortion, at least officially. Northern evangelicals, some affiliated with the National Association of Evangelicals, had taken a stand against abortion starting in 1971. But the Southern Baptist Convention, the world's largest Baptist denomination and the second-largest Protestant denomination in the United States, had opposed both abortion on demand and the criminalization of the procedure throughout much of the 1970s.[42]

Paul Weyrich, the wunderkind of the New Right, increasingly saw evangelical voters as the linchpin of his plan for a hostile takeover of the GOP. In 1978 he gave office space at the Heritage Foundation to Robert Grant, a pastor from Southern California who had been fighting pornography and gay rights since 1974 and encouraged other conservative luminaries to help Grant launch his new organization, Christian Voice, to mobilize conservative Christian voters. The following year, Weyrich persuaded Jerry Falwell, the pastor of a Virginia megachurch, to found the Moral Majority, which soon became synonymous with the religious right.[43]

The Moral Majority got another boost in 1980 when Larry Lewis, a Missouri pastor, successfully lobbied the Southern Baptist Convention (SBC) to denounce legal abortion and embrace a right to life. This shift by the SBC energized evangelicals who were already uncomfortable with the idea of legal abortion.[44]

So did the increasing visibility of evangelicals in popular culture. Pollster George Gallup found that half of American Protestants surveyed claimed to have been born again—an eye-popping number that led *Newsweek* magazine to declare 1976 "the year of the evangelical." Evangelicals more often moved to Sunbelt states, where they could theoretically punch above their political weight by voting as a bloc. As the nation's evangelical movement grew, right-to-lifers gained a powerful group of allies.[45]

Falwell was all too happy to link *Roe v. Wade* to both the women's movement and a right to choose. He routinely described *Roe* as a "decision legalizing abortion on demand." The language of "abortion on demand" had circulated in the anti-abortion movement since the late 1960s; originally, right-to-life leaders had used it to signal their opponents' extremism (and the reasonableness of their own position).[46]

Falwell meant something different when he invoked abortion on demand. The right to choose, as he saw it, was a frivolity, a sign that women had "murdered thirteen million little babies" for no reason at all.[47] His rhetoric of abortion on demand painted some women as shrewish and demanding—barely feminine enough to count as women. A right to choose, as Falwell saw it, was a sign of everything wrong with feminism and with American culture—a "license to licentiousness," a symptom of a "pleasure-mad, sin-sick society that wants to sin without penalty."[48]

Identifying *Roe* with a right to choose also suited an emerging group of anti-abortion litigators. Well into the mid-1970s, anti-abortion leaders had largely given up on the Supreme Court. Seven justices had just voted that the Constitution recognized a right to choose abortion, and only one new justice, John Paul Stevens, had joined the Court in the years since. But in 1976, in *Planned Parenthood of Central Missouri v. Danforth*, the Court upheld a law requiring women to give written informed consent before having an abortion. *Danforth* convinced some right-to-life litigators that the Supreme Court might sign off on enough restrictions to make *Roe* increasingly incoherent.[49]

In the late 1970s, a group of anti-abortion professors, lawyers, and government employees revisited their movement's legal strategy, and many of them saw *Danforth* as the starting point for a sweeping set of abortion restrictions. Anti-abortion lawyers went well off the beaten path in finding a place for their experiment: Akron, Ohio, a rustbelt city along the Little Cuyahoga River. Akron passed a comprehensive anti-abortion bill in 1978, including a sweeping informed consent requirement.[50]

Journalists descended on the city, packing courtrooms and breath-lessly reporting on the doings of the local government. They were not wrong to pay attention: the Akron ordinance seemed destined for the Supreme Court. Informed consent laws like Akron's made it tempting for right-to-lifers to talk about *Roe* as a decision involving a right to choose. "The so-called 'right to choose,' " wrote James Bopp, one of the attorneys defending the Akron law, "is meaningless if a woman is not informed about alternatives to abortion." Like his colleagues, Bopp thought *Roe* was wrongly decided, but rather than get it over-turned, he planned to redefine the right to choose to make it easier to restrict abortion. If the Supreme Court recognized a right to choose, he suggested, the justices should also know that *Roe* did not "protect women from exploitation by abortion profiteers."[51]

Defining Choice

Making *Roe* a symbol of choice did not answer the difficult ques-tion of what reproductive choice required at a time when women of-ten lacked the ability to say no to sex. Karen Mulhauser experienced this ambiguity firsthand. In 1978, she worked into the early hours of the morning almost every day, afraid she would miss some detail that would change the course of the abortion struggle. One hot August night, when her husband was away on business, she let her seven-year-old son sleep in the basement to keep cool and opened the kitchen door to let in the breeze. When she looked up from her com-puter screen, she saw a man with a gun. He forced her into the garage where another man was waiting, then told her to take off her clothes. They took turns raping her for two and a half hours, stole everything of value they could carry away, bound her with her husband's neck-ties, and drove off in her car.[52]

At first, Mulhauser struggled to process what had happened. She had to decide whether to move to a new home and accept that none of her stolen family heirlooms would ever be recovered. She had to ask her son if he knew what the word *rape* meant. But by 1979, when the Hyde Amendment battle heated up again, Mulhauser believed that her experience helped make sense of why *Roe* should stand for a right to choose. If she had become pregnant, she could afford an abortion. She felt strongly that victims of sexual assault who had fewer resources should have the ability to make the same choice.[53]

The passage of the Hyde Amendment began a congressional tradition of yearly free-for-alls to determine the scope of its exceptions. Starting in 1978, supporters of abortion rights, led by Democratic senator Ted Kennedy of Massachusetts, argued that Medicaid should fund abortions in cases of rape, incest, and certain severe health threats. Henry Hyde and his allies argued against this exception—not because anti-abortion lawmakers dismissed the seriousness of sexual assault (although one congressman made a joke about how much women enjoyed rape), but because, Hyde insisted, most women who claimed to be victims of sexual assault were lying to get the money to terminate a pregnancy. He complained that women had only to allege rape and they would be believed; "no additional accountability," he said, "is required of them."[54]

In 1979, Mulhauser decided to use her experience of sexual assault to illustrate the need for an exception by addressing the media and giving congressional testimony. "There is no way," she stated, "that I would be twice victimized by such a forced pregnancy." She denounced those who argued that the "rape clause is a loophole that allows a woman who wants an abortion to claim she was raped." Recognizing a right to choose meant nothing if lawmakers did not trust women. "If a male Congressman or Senator believes that a woman enjoys rape," Mulhauser wrote, "he might also believe that a woman would enjoy the pregnancy that results from rape."[55]

It was not easy for everyone to believe women like Mulhauser. Judie Brown, Paul's wife and a prominent pro-life activist in her own right, suggested that Mulhauser had made the whole thing up.[56] She sent a staffer to question Tom Kelly, the detective who investigated Mulhauser's case, about her story. Had Mulhauser really been raped by two men, as she claimed? Had she even been raped at all?[57]

Paul Brown went further, allegedly opining that Mulhauser was too unattractive for any man to want to assault her. "Karen is not the most beautiful creature in the world," he told *New York* magazine in 1980. "So when I hear her say she had been raped, my response is, 'you wish.' " The Browns later argued that they had been misrepresented. Judie stressed that right-to-lifers had compassion for everyone, particularly victims of sexual assault, while Paul maintained that the reporter who quoted him was "lying through his teeth."[58]

This discussion of rape reflected a deeper problem with how Americans thought of choice. In November 1980, Ronald Reagan, the first major-party presidential candidate to run on a pro-life platform, rolled over incumbent Jimmy Carter, winning all but a handful of states and the District of Columbia.[59] In office, Reagan disappointed anti-abortion leaders who had expected an immediate push for a constitutional amendment, but he acted quickly to shut down a rape and incest exception to the Hyde Amendment.[60]

In 1981, when Congress went along with Reagan's proposal, several of the Democratic senators who cast the deciding votes to eliminate the exception questioned whether women could even get pregnant from a sexual assault. Suggesting that women would lie to get what they wanted, Nevada Democrat Howard Cannon called the exception "a solution to a problem that doesn't exist."[61]

Having a right to choose abortion meant something different at a time when Cannon's attitude toward sexual consent was still widespread. The consistent support for a rape exception suggested that even those who favored abortion bans saw pregnancy as a risk that came with the choice to have sex; women forced into sex had made no such choice, the argument went, and should not be compelled to continue a pregnancy.[62]

But what did it mean to be coerced into sex? Did women threatened with the loss of a job, housing, or child custody "consent" to sex? What about women who were heavily intoxicated? Those financially dependent or in abusive relationships? It was far easier to link *Roe* to choice in the abstract than it was to build support for the choices women actually made.

Mulhauser soon realized how little agreement existed on what "choice" for women meant. In the early 1980s, the NARAL Board of Directors voted to dedicate more resources to the fight against an anti-abortion constitutional amendment, particularly in states that seemed less likely to ratify one—only thirteen states were needed to block an amendment. Yet as Mulhauser and her staff began to execute this plan, the board began complaining that they were neglecting the needs of conservative states, especially those with clinics facing escalating anti-abortion pickets—clinics whose owners were on the board of directors. They began pressing her to fire her staff, but she refused; the staffers were carrying out plans the board had endorsed. During a 1982 board meeting, after she again defended her staff, the board gave her two days to clean out her office (only a plurality on the board voted to fire her because several members abstained). Based on her relationship with the man leading the charge, Mulhauser believed the complaints were more personal than strategic.[63]

That man, Bob McCoy, had been involved in the movement before abortion was legal. In 1973, he opened the first legal abortion clinic in the state of Minnesota and routinely debated abortion opponents on college campuses and local television. He always held a powerful position in NARAL, but Mulhauser had avoided him for years because of what happened in 1975 in Mexico City.[64]

Mulhauser, like many Americans, had traveled there that summer. The city was celebrating the 650th anniversary of its founding, but she did not go for the disco nights and rooftop feasts that drew most of the tourists. She was there to represent NARAL at the World Conference on Women, the first international summit focused on women's rights. She had been pleasantly surprised when McCoy offered to travel to Mexico City to help staff NARAL's exhibit booth. Even though she did not know him well, she had heard about his appearances on *The Tonight Show* with Johnny Carson. McCoy liked to display his collection of medical oddities for television audiences. He had a phrenology machine that could do a personality reading on a pineapple and print out the results.[65]

When Mulhauser arrived in Mexico City, she did not find McCoy at the NARAL booth. She did not see him at all until she was closing the booth at the end of the day. When he arrived, McCoy suggested that they go up to his hotel room to strategize about the best way to tell NARAL's story in the days that followed. When they got to the room, he sat on the bed and began explaining that he and his wife had an understanding and could sleep with other people. Mulhauser managed to blurt out that she and her husband had no such understanding before slamming the door behind her. McCoy never showed up the next morning; he had left early.[66]

Beyond telling a few of those closest to her, Mulhauser said nothing about the incident. When she confided in Jean Weinberg, Weinberg shared the story of Mary Heffernan, a young NARAL activist who had faced sexual harassment from Oregon senator Bob Packwood, one of the pro-choice movement's strongest allies in Congress. In 1981, Mulhauser could not shake the feeling that Bob McCoy campaigned to get her fired because she had turned him down six years earlier.[67]

Having been forced out of NARAL, Mulhauser decided not to be run out of the house where she had been sexually assaulted. She and her family stayed there; Mulhauser headed up an organization that battled nuclear proliferation, and she consulted for politicians and nonprofits. She became something of a legend among Democratic women, the person who had seemingly mentored everyone. In 2018, during Brett Kavanaugh's confirmation hearings for a seat on the Supreme Court, she hosted a watch party for survivors of sexual assault. The following year, she and her husband finally moved to a smaller place. She held a downsizing party and gave away four decades' worth of treasures while serving mimosas. By then her name had literally become synonymous with mentoring: the liberal Women's Information Network gave out an annual Karen Mulhauser Award for helping and supporting young pro-choice women. Into her seventies, she coordinated a community of over one thousand progressive consultants.[68]

A few years after Mulhauser left NARAL, Bob McCoy was forced to resign his position as director of his clinic, the Midwest Health Center, after the Minnesota Department of Human Rights found probable cause that he had sexually harassed female colleagues.[69] Before long, however, it seemed this history was largely forgotten. In his later years, he was known for the Museum of Questionable Medical Devices that he opened in Minneapolis and for his appearances on *The Late Show* with David Letterman. Most women at NARAL had heard stories about people who said no to Bob McCoy, but when he died in 2010, many still described him as a man who cared about women's right to choose.[70]

3

The Judiciary in American Democracy

No one would have predicted that Northwestern University law professor Victor Rosenblum would help make *Roe v. Wade* a symbol of judicial activism. Few professors had the following he commanded: a lecturer with a voice so powerful that he rarely needed a microphone, a father who could be a strict disciplinarian or sit in the dunk tank of his daughters' backyard carnivals, a brilliant thinker whom few students forgot.[1]

Rosenblum had a hero of his own: Earl Warren, the chief justice of the United States Supreme Court. Warren, a Republican, first became a household name when serving as California's attorney general. After Dwight Eisenhower nominated him to be chief justice in 1953, the Court handed down a series of decisions that would redefine civil rights, voting rights, protections for criminal defendants, and much more. The Warren Court became a symbol of American liberalism, and Warren, the erstwhile Republican governor, became public enemy number one to American conservatives. To Rosenblum, he embodied the transformative power of the law. Rosenblum had eight children, and he named his second youngest Warren to honor the legacy of a man he greatly admired. (Warren had also offered Rosenblum a position as clerk of court at the Supreme Court, which he declined.)[2]

The basis of this admiration was Rosenblum's belief in limitless possibilities. He grew up in the central Bronx; his father struggled to make a go of it in the fur business; his mother had managed to get out of Russia one day after World War I broke out. Victor admired his parents, but he most wanted to be like his grandfather, a patriarch with a big family, ready to help anyone who needed it.[3]

Rosenblum met his wife, Louise, at a friend's sweet sixteen party when both were fifteen years old. They married at the age of twenty; Victor went to law school at Columbia, they crossed the country so he could get a PhD in political science at Berkeley, and they started a family. Many who crossed their paths found something idyllic in the Rosenblum family: Victor's graduate students buzzing in and out, the intellectual jousting at the dinner table, Louise maintaining a career as a psychiatric social worker even with a house full of children.[4]

Victor was a passionate advocate for the rights of people of color and the poor, and he felt equally strongly about fighting against abortion. He believed that the push to legalize it reflected a desire to prevent women of color from reproducing. "If we believe [our] problems can be solved by cutting down the birth of children," he told reporters in 1969, "we are modern Malthusians, not the humanitarians we think we are." He was proud that his wife aided "unwed mothers" at the Cradle, an adoption agency in Evanston that helped childless couples and counseled women who got pregnant out of wedlock. But the birth of the Rosenblums' youngest son, Joshua, in 1969 was arguably the most significant reason for his pro-life convictions. When Joshua was born, the family learned he had Down syndrome. Their relatively new community in Portland, Oregon, where Rosenblum was briefly president of Reed College, reacted awkwardly, with some viewing the birth of their eighth child more as a misfortune than a cause for celebration. Despite the shock of Joshua's diagnosis, he was welcomed into the family, and Rosenblum grew even more sure that any abortion was unacceptable.[5]

After the publication of quotes from Rosenblum's 1969 interview, he got a call from Joe Stanton, a right-to-life physician. Stanton and

Herbert Ratner, an Illinois doctor known for championing breast-feeding, wanted to launch an organization for anti-abortion professionals and hoped that Rosenblum would join them. The organization, called Americans United for Life (AUL), became the home base for his anti-abortion activism over the next several decades. While Rosenblum never lost his faith in a muscular, liberal judiciary, AUL stressed that *Roe* was an anti-democratic decision rendered by activist justices.[6]

In the early 1980s, the Reagan administration and the conservative legal movement mounted a broad attack on what they described as an anti-democratic federal judiciary. Arguments about judicial activism were not new in the 1970s. In the 1930s, progressives like Felix Frankfurter had praised "judicial restraint" and chastised the Court for striking down laws protecting workers. In 1954, when the Supreme Court decided *Brown v. Board of Education* and invalidated school segregation laws, southern segregationists retooled attacks on judicial activism. In 1956, eighty-two members of the House and nineteen senators signed the Southern Manifesto, calling *Brown* an "abuse of judicial power."[7] By the late 1960s, when Richard Nixon attacked judges who did not practice "strict construction" of the Constitution, *Brown* was no longer the prime target of arguments about judicial overreach. Conservatives now had a growing list of "activist" decisions, including those on voting rights and protections for criminal defendants.[8]

In the 1980s, the Reagan administration and the New Right tapped into this growing conservative distrust of the courts. But making *Roe* the main symbol of a federal judiciary run amok exposed the contradictions inherent in debates about judicial activism. Some Reagan voters complained that the justices overrode the will of popularly elected legislatures, but others who opposed *Roe* saw the decision as activist because the Court ignored what they viewed as the unborn child's constitutional rights. Abortion rights supporters, meanwhile, sometimes labeled *Roe*'s critics proponents of judicial activism for attacking a constitutional right that the public seemed to support. This dialogue about *Roe* made clear that progressives and conservatives both wanted the courts to protect unwritten constitutional guarantees, even as they disagreed on what those guarantees were.

A New Litigation Strategy

In 1974, a year after the Supreme Court decided *Roe*, Dennis Horan, AUL's chairman, gave a speech that would change the organization's future. Horan was a lover of poetry and a Chicago trial lawyer with a fearsome reputation. His speech was supposed to focus on the conscientious objections of doctors, but he quickly turned to a subject he cared about even more: the creation of a public interest law firm that could advocate for the unborn child. Rosenblum thought that Horan had it exactly right: the anti-abortion movement needed a new litigation strategy to narrow and ultimately undo *Roe v. Wade*.[9]

Horan and Rosenblum seemed like an odd match. Rosenblum could be lots of fun and loved to spend hours debating everything from the nature of the administrative state to the rights of the poor. Horan seemed to work more than twenty-four hours a day, writing articles, suing the manufacturers of products, and strategizing about how to reverse *Roe*. While Horan made younger lawyers nervous, Rosenblum was what Clarke Forsythe, a junior colleague at AUL, called a "great encourager."[10]

To begin chipping away at the *Roe* decision, Horan and Rosenblum began by urging the Court to recognize the personhood of the unborn child.[11] Rosenblum's dream was that the Court would treat fetuses as rights-holding persons and thus make all abortions unconstitutional. But in the 1970s and 1980s, the Supreme Court had not come close to recognizing fetal personhood or a right to life. AUL had better luck in trying to change how Americans—and the Supreme Court justices—understood the Court's 1973 decision. The Court had already upheld a Missouri informed consent requirement in 1976 and rejected challenges to state laws limiting the use of public money or facilities for abortion, including in a 1977 case, *Poelker v. Doe*, in which the AUL successfully defended a ban on abortion in St. Louis's public hospitals. The message of these decisions was clear: it was easier to persuade the Court to reinterpret *Roe* than to reverse it. When AUL agreed to represent several conservative members of Congress, including Representative Hyde, as intervenors in the challenge to the Hyde Amendment, Rosenblum and his colleagues focused on a redefinition of *Roe* rather than a direct challenge to it. AUL lawyers also defended an Illinois Medicaid restriction in *Williams v. Zbaraz*. In *Zbaraz*, Rosenblum led the oral argument for the appellants against Bob Bennett, his close friend and colleague at Northwestern.[12]

Telling Taxpayers What to Do

Rosenblum was a strange choice to argue a case about Medicaid funding for abortion. A New Dealer to his core, he thought life should not be about money—and poor women should be able to have families without worrying about the government punishing them. He had advocated for welfare rights too: earlier in his career, he had submitted a brief on behalf of welfare recipients in New York who thought their payments had been cut off arbitrarily. As the oral argument in the Hyde Amendment case began to loom, however, he threw himself into arguing that there was no constitutional "obligation on the State to pay any of the medical expenses of indigents."[13] Poor women seeking a right to government assistance, AUL argued, would find "the entire tradition of American constitutional jurisprudence in their way."[14]

The 1980 presidential race made not only abortion but also the role of the federal judiciary a topic of dinner table conversation. Both

Barry Goldwater and Richard Nixon had denounced the liberal Supreme Court for ignoring the will of the people. Ronald Reagan, seeking to set himself apart from the primary field, tried to revive their arguments against judicial activism. At a Birmingham campaign stop, he noted that the High Court had blocked the Hyde Amendment from going into effect while deciding on its constitutionality. The *Harris v. McRae* case was not just about abortion, Reagan suggested. It was "a matter of whether the American people can hope to have any control whatsoever over their government's expenditures." *Roe* was the quintessential activist decision, Reagan suggested—a ruling that removed both abortion and government spending from the democratic process.[15] With his trademark dry humor, Hyde framed *Roe* the same way, noting that if the Court was hell-bent on usurping the power of Congress, the justices should take over the whole budget and send congressmen home to their families. Reagan and his allies suggested that *Roe* was antidemocratic because it put decisions about abortion in the hands of an unelected federal judiciary.[16]

Describing *Roe* as anti-democratic increasingly seemed to work for AUL. In June 1980, the Court upheld both the Hyde Amendment and the Illinois law disputed in *Zbaraz*. In *Harris v. McRae*, the Hyde Amendment case, the Court agreed that it made no difference if low-income patients had medical reasons for seeking abortion. The majority opinion echoed the reasoning of AUL's brief: nothing in *Roe* suggested that "a woman's freedom of choice carries with it a constitutional entitlement to the financial resources to avail herself of the full range of protected choices."[17]

When news came about *McRae* and *Zbaraz*, AUL lawyers spotted an opportunity. Republicans had begun describing *Roe* as a symbol of what was wrong with the liberal judiciary, and AUL could gain political leverage by doing the same. Describing *Roe* as an anti-democratic decision that prevented elected officials and the people from developing their own policies on abortion could unite right-to-lifers and other Reagan supporters, while obscuring the fact that some Reagan voters considered the Court activist because it ignored rights that conservatives supported, chiefly the rights of the unborn. Even Rosenblum, who found arguments about judicial activism distasteful and wrong, picked up on the idea that *Roe* was anti-democratic because it stopped states from developing their own laws on abortion. At a press conference after the *McRae* decision, a beaming Rosenblum described it as "a victory for the democratic process."[18]

The Battle over O'Connor

It remained to be seen whether Reagan's attack on the courts was more than a talking point. In the summer of 1981, less than a year into Reagan's first term in office, Justice Potter Stewart retired, giving the president his first chance to fill a Supreme Court vacancy.[19]

Many saw the nomination of the next justice as a bellwether for the rest of Reagan's presidency. Populist firebrand Pat Buchanan, who would become Reagan's communications director in his second term, wrote an editorial complaining that the Supreme Court that decided *Roe* had revealed itself to be a "tyrant" that gave First Amendment rights to strippers and followed the loathsome principle of "one person, one vote."[20] Reagan wanted to retain the support of Buchanan's followers, but he also wanted to be taken seriously by lawyers, judges, and the American Bar Association. It was one thing to win over Buchanan's fans; resembling him was another thing entirely.[21]

In filling the Stewart vacancy, Reagan fulfilled his promise to nominate a woman by selecting Sandra Day O'Connor, a former Arizona lawmaker and judge rumored to support abortion rights. He seemed unafraid of angering politicians on the far right of his party. "There will be a lot of sound and fury," said one Reagan aide, "but it will wind up signifying little or nothing when it's all over." But the

O'Connor confirmation battle exposed a real problem for Reagan's fragile new political coalition: right-wing voters meant different things when they denounced judicial overreaching—and had different ideas about how to change the federal judiciary.[22]

The brewing fight over desegregation through school busing proved as much. In 1954, *Brown* had held that laws racially segregating the public schools violated the Constitution, but the question of how to integrate them proved to be just as divisive. In the decades between 1954 and 1980, states become adept at preserving racial segregation, doing everything from closing schools to creating grant programs to offset the costs of education at all-white, private "segregation academies." By the mid-1970s, the United States Supreme Court had signed off on further-reaching remedial schemes to integrate schools, including the redrawing of school districts and the transportation of students within or between them. These practices sparked a violent backlash in cities from Boston to Detroit. Images of terrified Black students in buses confronted by angry mobs throwing rocks and bottles became a staple of national conversation (Boston, for a time, earned the dubious honor of being called the "the Little Rock of the North").[23]

By the 1980s, Ronald Reagan's Republican Party had helped to reframe conversations about integration. Rather than discussing the need to remedy segregation—or its consequences for students of color—the administration denounced "busing," a catchall for ambitious strategies to integrate schools. Republicans also increasingly contended that present-day segregation—which, they claimed, reflected innocent market forces and residential patterns—was far less concerning than the intentional discrimination addressed in *Brown*. This argument was problematic because intentional racism had shaped the neighborhoods of the 1980s—because of federal mortgage redlining, segregated housing projects and homeowners' associations, and discriminatory real estate practices. Although white resistance to busing had diminished substantially by the 1980s, denouncing it became a Republican priority—and conversations about busing soon shaped arguments about the role of the federal courts. John East, a North Carolina conservative who secured his Senate seat with the help of Jesse Helms's campaign finance machine, was pushing a bill that would strip the lower courts of jurisdiction in desegregation cases. While Reagan wanted it known that his administration opposed busing, almost every Reagan staffer feared that East's bill would appear extreme or be struck down by the courts. But court-stripping bills had gained currency on the right; other proposals, taking away jurisdiction on abortion or school prayer, were circulating in Congress.[24]

The scope of Congress's authority to strip the courts, and especially the Supreme Court, of jurisdiction had long been contested. On the one hand, the Constitution explicitly allowed Congress to take away the Supreme Court's jurisdiction in appeals from state or federal courts (court stripping was explicitly prohibited in cases in which the Court had original jurisdiction, such as disputes between states or between a state and the United States). In 1816, however, in a case called *Martin v. Hunter's Lessee*, Justice Joseph Story proposed that Congress could not concurrently strip the Supreme Court and lower federal courts of jurisdiction in the same case without violating the Constitution. Some prominent law professors rejected Story's reasoning, but others disputed Congress's power to strip the federal courts of jurisdiction. Given the uncertainty surrounding its constitutionality, conservatives angry at the Court were ready to give court stripping a try.[25]

Many within the Reagan administration feared the damage these bills could do. Court stripping struck many observers as radical. Leaders of the American Bar Association opposed to it ominously predicted a constitutional breakdown. Reagan wanted to remake the

Court but had little interest in the kind of backlash that seemed likely if a court-stripping bill passed. Besides, it was not clear that court stripping would please all of his constituents. While some conservatives wanted to weaken the federal judiciary, others simply wanted to make it more conservative. Nor would it clearly advance the president's agenda. O'Connor was not likely to be Reagan's last Supreme Court nominee. The president had little interest in undercutting the Court before he had the chance to remake it.

O'Connor's nomination proved that the Reagan administration had to achieve a difficult task: using the courts to mobilize right-wing voters without either splitting the various right-wing constituencies or veering to politically disqualifying extremes. Reagan staffers worried that doing nothing about the courts would alienate social conservatives—or lead them to stay home on Election Day. In September 1981, the Senate unanimously confirmed O'Connor, but Reagan's problems with the courts were getting worse. Thanks to Jesse Helms and John East, the court-stripping battle was heating up.

At War with the Court Strippers

By January 1982, Congress had twenty-four jurisdiction-stripping bills under consideration, and elite lawyers were panicking that one of them might pass. David Brink, the head of the American Bar Association, predicted that court-stripping would bring on the most serious constitutional crisis since the Civil War.[26]

Americans United for Life did not speak up for jurisdiction-stripping bills, even those purporting to protect fetal life. It was not that these bills seemed gratuitous: every anti-abortion amendment that Congress considered had failed badly in 1981. Rosenblum also joined the American Family Institute, a twenty-two-member, nonpartisan panel intended to advise the president on judicial selections that pledged to "work for the appointment of judges at all levels of the judiciary who respect traditional family values and the sanctity of human life." Court stripping, by contrast, struck him as foolish. To begin with, he believed that basic constitutional rights and the protection of the nation's most vulnerable citizens depended on an engaged, courageous federal judiciary. And as much as he made common cause with abortion foes in Congress, court stripping had a distinctly right-wing flavor that put him off (he disagreed with Jesse Helms on almost everything except abortion).[27]

Besides, court stripping seemed unnecessary. Rosenblum and Horan were convinced that the best way for the right-to-life movement to gain respect was to change the legal elite, not destroy it. Describing *Roe* as an anti-democratic decision could advance this change agenda. First, the argument appealed to Reagan voters who did not like what they viewed as a liberal Court but felt equally uncomfortable with the right-to-life movement. As important, framing *Roe* as anti-democratic reinforced the belief of many in AUL that Americans would oppose abortion if they understood what it meant for an unborn child. Rosenblum believed that at bottom, most Americans would agree with him on abortion if they truly understood the issue. Other AUL lawyers, who did not share Rosenblum's love of the Warren Court, saw arguments about judicial activism as crucial.[28]

Abortion rights supporters sometimes responded that a decision *reversing Roe* would be judicial activism. In the early 1980s, polls showed that most Americans supported the *Roe* decision while favoring a wide variety of abortion restrictions. Armed with this data, abortion rights supporters offered their own definition of judicial activism—it would be judicial overreaching to undo a constitutional right that the American people demanded. AUL leaders, in turn, zeroed in on how abortion rights had been created—by the federal judiciary, which was not elected or accountable to the people. At the same time, many right-to-lifers considered *Roe* activist for an entirely different reason: because the Court had ignored the protections for fetal rights written into the Constitution. While these debates produced a great deal of talk about judicial activism, there was no consensus on how to define it or when the judiciary should ignore the popular majority.[29]

In the early 1980s, Rosenblum was still fighting for a constitutional amendment banning abortion. In 1981, he took a key role in AUL's work on regulations protecting severely disabled newborns. The next year, an Indiana doctor advised the parents of a child born with Down syndrome and a birth defect requiring surgery to turn the procedure down because the child would never have a high quality of life. The parents refused the surgery as well as food and water for the infant, and Baby Doe died six days later. Rosenblum took a keen interest in regulations governing so-called Baby Doe cases, which reinforced his view that *Roe* authorized "the worst contemporary instances of discrimination."[30]

His work on the Baby Doe issues led him to see viability—the line drawn in *Roe* to determine when the state could ban abortion (and when its interest in protecting life became compelling)—as a weakness worth attacking. The Baby Doe cases, he believed, had triggered a backlash because Americans could see a living baby being harmed—and because they believed that with proper medical care, that baby could survive and thrive. Focusing on later abortions—and on the fluidity of the viability line—struck many in AUL as a logical next step.[31]

While AUL lawyers initially focused on viability, Edwin Meese III, the conservative lawyer who had been Reagan's enforcer since his California days, was more interested in presenting *Roe* as judicial activism. Reagan's attorney general, William French Smith, a former U.S. Navy lieutenant who planned to take a tough line on crime, pledged that the Reagan Justice Department would "diminish judicial activism" and used *Roe* as a prime example of the kind of decision the president wanted the courts to revisit.[32]

Beyond referencing *Roe* and a handful of other decisions, Smith offered little detail about what judicial activism meant. Various conservative constituencies defined it in very different ways. Gun rights enthusiasts eagerly hoped that the Court would recognize an individual right to bear arms under the Second Amendment and criticized the Court as activist for ignoring what they saw as an obvious constitutional commitment. Right-to-lifers derided the Court for failing to recognize fetal personhood. While some conservatives wanted the Court's power reduced, others wanted a more conservative Court to recognize other implicit rights. The conservative consensus on *Roe* as "activism" concealed deep disagreements about what judicial overreaching was.[33]

The Reagan administration saw no need to wade into these philosophical questions. What the president wanted was far simpler—to identify *Roe* with judicial activism while saying nothing that would expose him to charges of extremism. Reagan staffers laid out plans for achieving this balance. In August 1982, Reagan staffers Mike Uhlmann and Stephen Galebach penned a memo urging the president to push for a statute that would permanently ban abortion funding and encourage the Supreme Court to overrule *Roe v. Wade*.[34]

One advantage of such a bill, Galebach and Uhlmann wrote, was that it would "not involve jurisdiction stripping." The administration did not need to spark a constitutional crisis or undermine the power of the federal judiciary if the president had a chance to transform it. Reagan could instead propose a vague definition of overreaching that satisfied most conservatives, while strategizing to change the composition of the Supreme Court. Framing *Roe* as a symbol of judicial activism made sense as part of this agenda. "Supreme Court reversal of *Roe*," Uhlmann and Galebach wrote, "is the easiest way to end this tragic episode of judicial overreaching."[35]

Defining Judicial Activism

By 1984, AUL lawyers were talking about *Roe* in the same way. In 1983, Rosenblum waited for the Supreme Court's decision in *City of Akron v. Akron Reproductive Health Services.* Its ruling in the case would make clear whether laws imposing heavy restrictions on abortion (while still recognizing the basic right) could stand—and would offer a first glimpse of the kind of justice Sandra Day O'Connor would be.[36]

When the decision came down in late June, the justices voted 6–3 to invalidate the ordinance and struck down an informed consent provision on which right-to-lifers had pinned their hopes. But Rosenblum was more interested in O'Connor's dissent. Joined by two of her colleagues, she wrote that the Akron ordinance raised no major constitutional problems. "Neither sound constitutional theory nor our need to decide cases based on the application of neutral principles," she stated, "can accommodate an analytical framework that varies according to the 'stages' of pregnancy." In that dissent, AUL attorneys saw something they could work with.[37]

By 1983, the right-to-life movement had given up on a constitutional amendment—the last chance to pass one, a measure cosponsored by Senators Orrin Hatch and Thomas Eagleton, had gone down in flames the previous year. Americans United for Life rolled out a new strategy centered on the argument that *Roe* was an activist decision. On the last day of March 1984, AUL introduced its plan at a major national conference, "Reversing *Roe* Through the Courts." Some five hundred people attended, including representatives from the 2.6-million-member Lutheran Church–Missouri Synod and staffers from the White House.[38]

AUL's leaders planned to "unite the movement around a relatively uncontroversial proposition, that the Court should reverse itself." Pitching *Roe* as undemocratic, a necessary step in this strategy, would "augment existing scholarly critiques of *Roe*" and "lend greater intellectual respectability to the pro-life position." Rosenblum also argued that Americans were already pro-life but had been misled about what *Roe* held, how poorly it was reasoned, and why people had abortions. Complaining that most statistics were supplied by "abortion advocates," he called for "new legitimate sources of abortion data." Many at the AUL conference also positioned *Roe* as an activist decision. Fighting *Roe*, wrote AUL's Steven Baer, meant awakening "the slumbering national majority to rise and defeat the devastating national policy of abortion on demand."[39]

At first it seemed that AUL's strategy would not get off the ground. Senator Orrin Hatch had proposed a permanent ban on Medicaid reimbursement for abortion (the Hyde Amendment, a rider to an appropriations bill, had to be renewed every year). Rosenblum testified in favor of Hatch's bill, but Congress did not pass it. Then in 1985, AUL got in financial trouble. The American Civil Liberties Union had challenged a 1979 Illinois abortion restriction and won in district court. When Illinois dropped its appeal, AUL stepped in to defend the state restriction; Dr. Eugene Diamond, an Illinois pediatrician, agreed to act as the named appellant with AUL providing his legal services. In 1986, the Supreme Court took up AUL's appeal in that case, *Diamond v. Charles*, as well as an ACLU challenge to Pennsylvania's abortion regulations, *Thornburgh v. American College of Obstetricians and Gynecologists.*[40]

In May 1986, the Supreme Court voted unanimously that Dr. Diamond did not have standing to appeal the district court's decision. It then struck down all of Pennsylvania's abortion regulations and batted down requests to reverse *Roe*. The loss in *Diamond* left Diamond—and thus AUL—with a bill for more than $200,000 for the other side's attorney's fees (AUL had to borrow from another pro-life group, the National Right to Life Committee, to cover the costs).

But *Thornburgh* had a silver lining. Four of the justices had agreed that Pennsylvania's law was constitutional—and questioned whether the Court in *Roe* got it right.[41]

Equating *Roe* with judicial activism suited the Reagan administration too. Reagan staffers continued to caution the president against siding with the Court's most vitriolic critics on the right; in 1985, John G. Roberts, the associate counsel to the president (and future chief justice of the Supreme Court), warned the president that "unalloyed jurisprudential iconoclasm . . . could be a disaster." Besides, several of the justices were old enough to be mulling retirement, and it would suit neither Reagan nor conservative voters if the president stripped the Court of power just when new justices could help advance conservative aims. White House Counsel Fred Fielding laid out the "key points" of a politically palatable position on *Roe* and judicial activism: that "the Constitution prescribes a limited role for the judiciary, one that does not infringe on the popularly elected and politically accountable branches." This approach, Reagan would emphasize, was not "an attack on the courts" but an effort to keep the judiciary "free from partisan politics by leaving politics to the political branches."[42] But the more Americans talked about *Roe* as a symbol of judicial activism, the more the contradictions in that position became visible.

From Scalia to Bork

The battle over the Supreme Court nomination of Robert Bork proved to be something of a coming-out party for the Federalist Society and the conservative legal movement. Before the 1980s, Republican presidents had considerable success in nominating Supreme Court justices, but once on the bench, many of their picks turned out to be moderate or even liberal. The problem, some believed, was that most elite lawyers and law schools leaned left. This began to shift after 1982, when three law students, Steven Calabresi, Lee Liberman, and

David McIntosh, decided to develop an alternative to what they perceived as liberal orthodoxy on law school campuses. That April, two hundred guests gathered in New Haven for an event hosted by the law students' new group, the Federalist Society. The mood was heady. Two of the headliners at the event, Antonin Scalia and Robert Bork, would be nominated for the Supreme Court in the next five years.[43]

Rosenblum had known Scalia since the early 1980s when they were members of the Administrative Conference of the United States, an independent body that recommended reforms of administrative agencies. Scalia had a large family of his own, a razor-sharp intellect, and an acerbic sense of humor. It was no secret that he was very conservative; his colleagues on the DC Circuit Court of Appeals called him Ninopath (a play on "sociopath") because he was so ideologically unwavering. But Scalia was replacing Warren Burger, the former chief justice, another irascible conservative who had called for the overruling of *Roe* and who often found himself in dissent. Liberals did not see the point of torpedoing his confirmation when it seemed unlikely to change the Court's ideological balance.[44]

The Bork nomination was different. Bork would replace Lewis Powell, the justice who often cast the swing vote in abortion cases. And Bork was even more outspoken than Scalia; he was the leading proponent of a new theory of anti-trust law, had ridiculed the Court's decision recognizing marital couples' right to use birth control, and had described *Roe* as indefensible.

Bork's 1987 confirmation hearings exposed how conflicted Americans often were when they made *Roe* shorthand for judicial activism. The White House planned to defend Bork as a champion of judicial restraint, a jurist who would resist the activism that *Roe* represented. But Bork's opponents—a group that included one hundred progressive interest groups and most of the Senate's Democrats—exploited many Americans' fundamental ambivalence about the federal judiciary. In

September 1987, Delaware senator Joseph Biden, the architect of the Senate campaign against Bork, issued a report calling him "a conservative activist and not a practitioner of judicial restraint." As evidence, Biden pointed to Bork's frequent willingness to break with popular opinion. While Americans favored legal abortion and contraception, Bork "opposed the decision upholding the right of married couples to use contraception" and viewed the right to abortion as unconstitutional. Groups like AUL were arguing that *Roe* was anti-democratic because it took abortion out of popular politics, but Biden countered that it would be more anti-democratic to overrule the decision, because the American people backed a right to choose. In Biden's telling, Bork was an activist with no respect for majority opinion. Both Biden and Reagan denounced judicial activism, but there was no agreement on what the phrase meant—or what role the federal judiciary should play.[45]

By the end of 1987, the Reagan administration had to wave the white flag on Bork. The Senate voted against his confirmation by a vote of 58–42. Reagan nominated Anthony Kennedy, a much less controversial California judge, who was quickly confirmed. Then, in May 1988, Dennis Horan died of a massive heart attack at fifty-six years of age. Rosenblum stepped up to serve as the chairman of Americans United for Life, a position he would hold until 1995.[46]

Rosenblum liked to remind his colleagues in the right-to-life movement that he had never voted for Ronald Reagan. A few years earlier, he had given a major lecture arguing that Edwin Meese's views on originalism (and judicial activism) were hard to credit—and that the attorney general's response to specific Supreme Court decisions had nothing to do with the principles of strict construction he claimed to defend. Rosenblum still advocated for a liberal federal judiciary that would recognize the rights of those least able to protect themselves. But as AUL chairman, he helped to shape a strategy centered on the claim that *Roe* should be overruled as both wrong and anti-democratic.[47]

Activism and Popular Opinion

Inconsistency did not make the arguments about judicial activism any less politically potent. George H. W. Bush, Reagan's gentlemanly vice president, had once seemed allergic to hardball campaigning, but he had a change of heart when it came to equating *Roe* and judicial activism. For the 1988 Republican presidential nomination, Bush faced several primary challengers on his right, including Pat Robertson, a televangelist heading a multi-million-dollar television empire, and New York representative Jack Kemp, who had spent years endearing himself to the right-to-life movement. Even Donald Trump, a gaffe-prone New York real estate impresario, dropped hints that he might run because Bush was not a real conservative. At the end of the Iowa caucuses, Bush finished third to Robertson and Senator Bob Dole of Kansas and seemed to be in trouble. To regain his footing, he lurched to the right; that and his vastly superior fundraising machine got him the nomination and the opportunity to take on Michael Dukakis, the Democratic governor of Massachusetts, in the general election. At a campaign stop in South Bend, Indiana, Bush warned that Dukakis would nominate "doctrinaire liberals" to the Supreme Court like the ones responsible for *Roe* and "the excessive judicial activism of the 1960s and 1970s."[48]

In 1989, it seemed that AUL might get the chance to use arguments about judicial activism to take down *Roe*. The justices that year agreed to hear an abortion case called *Webster v. Reproductive Health Services*. With Anthony Kennedy now on the Court, there seemed to be a majority ready to undo abortion rights.[49]

Webster was a challenge to a series of Missouri abortion restrictions, including a preamble declaring that life began at conception, viability testing at twenty weeks, and a ban on the use of federal money, facilities, or employees for abortion. AUL held a meeting to strategize about how its allies should frame the case. Those present planned to praise specific dimensions of the Missouri law, but they hoped for something bigger. In asking the Court to reverse *Roe*, AUL and its allies would focus on arguments about the role of the judiciary in American democracy. Missouri stressed that *Roe* was an activist decision that took regulation of abortion away from "the people and . . . the political processes the people have devised to govern their affairs." AUL's brief urged the Court to turn away from activism and "return the issue to the people by overruling *Roe v. Wade*." The organization elaborated on these arguments in its newsletter, telling readers that "*Roe* usurped the judicial function on abortion, and exacerbated the judicial social turmoil over abortion." Rosenblum, in a draft op-ed that was never published, wrote that the "Supreme Could would honor the democratic process simply by upholding the Missouri regulations." *Roe*, he suggested, "failed to mesh with either the tenets of democratic governance or of the Judeo-Christian tradition's reverence for life." The draft teased out some of the tensions in conservatives' arguments about judicial overreaching. Right-to-lifers denounced the Court as activist both for taking the abortion issue away from the people and for ignoring what Rosenblum referred to as reverence for life, a tradition that many abortion opponents believed had persuaded the authors of the Fourteenth Amendment to recognize fetal personhood.[50]

Abortion rights advocates replied that the reason some saw *Roe* as an activist decision—that nothing in the text or history of the Constitution clearly mentioned a right to abortion—applied with equal force to the right to use birth control, to marry, or to raise one's children. Reversing *Roe*, in this analysis, would be undemocratic not only because it would anger most Americans but because it would open the door to the elimination of rights that enjoyed even more popular support. Missouri tried to distinguish among these cases by arguing that only abortion involved the taking of a human life (and that states criminalized abortion when the Fourteenth Amendment was ratified), but abortion rights activists seemed to have landed a blow. Opposing judicial activism was much easier than defining it.[51]

When *Webster* came down, Rosenblum was pleased: the Court upheld the Missouri statute and called into question *Roe*'s trimester framework. The hardest issue was Missouri's effort to set the limit of fetal viability at twenty weeks. The Court acknowledged that this requirement might conflict with *Roe* by defining viability in a way that could not be second-guessed by individual physicians. But the majority suggested that the real problem was *Roe*, not any choice made by Missouri legislators. The Court ultimately did not reverse *Roe*, but AUL leaders nevertheless believed that *Webster* "invited states to pass laws that more aggressively challenged *Roe*." AUL had equated *Roe* with judicial activism, and the Court seemed to agree.[52]

Close to a Saint

Rosenblum helped to craft the right-to-life movement's strategy in the biggest abortion case decided since 1973, *Planned Parenthood of Southeastern Pennsylvania v. Casey*. Less than a week before the decision was handed down, he gave an interview in his office, clearing room for reporters to squeeze in between stacks of books. The anti-abortion movement, he said, had added so many exceptions to the liberty recognized in *Roe* that they had reached "the point where you can argue that [*Roe*] never made sense in the first place."[53]

The Court did not reverse *Roe* in 1992, and three years later, Rosenblum stepped down as chairman of Americans United for Life. He kept his seat on the board and continued working with AUL, first promoting informed consent laws that might discourage some from having abortions, then battling to make medication abortion less easily available. He also spoke out in favor of affirmative action programs for racial minorities and welfare programs. As he entered his late seventies, his health declined. His kidneys began to fail; he required dialysis and eventually lost some mobility, but he still made time for his students, meeting them at home with the assistance of home health aides and his son Jon, a labor lawyer who helped care for his father in his final years. When Rosenblum died in 2006 his allies in the anti-abortion movement were heartbroken. Steve Calabresi, the co-founder of the Federalist Society and a Northwestern Law School colleague, remarked that Victor Rosenblum might be a saint.[54]

In truth, Rosenblum was a complicated man: a defender of welfare rights who stood up in court to save the Hyde Amendment, a person with profound liberal convictions who helped to forge an anti-abortion strategy that strengthened right-wing politicians for whom he would never vote. Similar contradictions ran through debates about judicial activism and *Roe*. Denouncing *Roe* as an activist decision united a fractured group of conservatives angry at the Court. Some believed *Roe* was activist because it took power away from elected officials; others took issue with the Court's failure to recognize fetal personhood. Abortion rights supporters and their political allies sometimes claimed to despise activism too, arguing that activist judges were those who would undo rights, like the one recognized in *Roe*, that enjoyed popular support. These competing ideas exposed how little agreement there was about the role that the Court should play in the nation's democracy.

Nor was Rosenblum's position on the Court easy to explain. What everyone knew was that he went to his grave revering Earl Warren, who had done more than anyone else to cement the Supreme Court's role as a guardian of rights. And the year before Rosenblum's death, he still had the energy to help his Northwestern Law School colleague Stephen Presser and Clarke Forsythe, an AUL attorney he had mentored, with an article on why *Roe* and its companion case, *Doe v. Bolton*, were "unconstitutional usurpations of self-government."[55]

4

Women Who Have It All

In early 1992, when the Supreme Court looked ready to reverse *Roe v. Wade*, everyone was talking about equality for women. More women were enrolling in college than ever before; more were becoming engineers, doctors, and lawyers. Bill Clinton, the soft-voiced former Arkansas governor running for the White House, often drew less media attention than his wife, Hillary, whom reporters embraced as "the sartorial symbol of the new feminist."[1] *Murphy Brown*, the blockbuster sitcom, featured a tough-as-nails feminist who shattered glass ceilings while single parenting. Those on opposing sides of the issue battled about what overruling *Roe* would mean for women who wanted a college education, a career, and parenthood.[2]

Two feminists with opposing views of abortion, Linda Wharton and Myrna Gutiérrez, helped to make *Roe* a symbol of the kind of equality many working women were debating in those years. The Nipper Building in Camden, New Jersey, loomed large in Wharton's childhood. An imposing brick tower crowned with the image of a stained-glass trumpet, it was home to the Radio Corporation of America (RCA), the world's largest seller of music. Wharton's parents met while working at RCA churning out television sets. They married and fled with other white families to Cherry Hill, a New Jersey suburb where all the houses looked the same and every afternoon, the children could disappear on their bikes until dinnertime. Wharton's mother was the kind of woman people called vivacious, a natural entertainer who loved to cook and bake and host parties.[3]

But to Linda, something was not right. Her mother often had to take part-time jobs so her children could have nice things; first she managed the candy shop at a local department store, then she was a bookkeeper for a local restaurant. When it was clear her daughter was headed to college, she took a grueling job at Melitta, a local factory, packing coffee into bags on the graveyard shift. Yet when Linda's parents got home from work, her mother was a whirlwind, cooking, serving, cleaning, not pausing until after nine o'clock at night. Her father simply sat and read the newspaper.[4]

The older Linda got, the more she learned that the inequality she saw at home was the norm everywhere. Playing sports in high school, she went to all the boys' games but noticed that no one came to hers. She went to college thinking she might be a journalist, landed in law school instead, and met her future husband in line at the bookstore. By the time the Supreme Court was ready to hear *Planned Parenthood of Southeastern Pennsylvania v. Casey*, she had become the kind of woman Murphy Brown might have befriended: a mother of two with a supportive husband, experience at a big law firm, and a new gig in public interest law defending equality for women. Wharton helped to make *Roe* a symbol of the equality women had just begun to enjoy.[5]

Myrna Gutiérrez was also the kind of woman the media showcased in the 1990s. She grew up in East Los Angeles in the largest Latino enclave in the United States. Her mother, a seamstress at a garment factory, loved to host parties in the mild California winters. She was not passionate about her work and felt a job was simply something you had to do. Myrna always thought her mother was regal (she wore Chanel perfume to her factory job), but it was her father who sparked her interest in social justice. He was constantly talking about civil rights, helping someone find a job, or navigating an immigration issue. Her first memory was of sitting with him watching John F. Kennedy on television. She loved to hear him tell his story. His mother died when he was about ten years old, and his father, an alcoholic, disappeared; he had to beg his cousins for food, but he made his way to the United States and opened a business, a battery shop.[6]

Myrna decided that rather than just make a living, she would pursue a career she loved. She was one of the few Latinas to attend the University of Southern California in the 1980s, working eighteen hours a week to pay the tuition that her scholarship would not cover. When she took a position at the university public relations office as part of her work-study program, it struck her that being right got you only so far without effective messaging.[7]

After graduation, she took a public relations job at El Centro Community Mental Health Center in East Los Angeles, then handled philanthropic donations for the 7Up/RC Cola Bottling Company. Next it was a public relations position at Westinghouse Electric, then a job at the largest Black-owned ad agency in the United States. But after her father died suddenly, everything changed. Gutiérrez, who grew up Catholic, had always opposed abortion, but the issue had not played an important role in her life. In grieving for her father, however, she reached a stage where his loss sparked profound anger. She went to a pro-life rally, where she expected everyone to share her rage, but it turned out to be one of the most peaceful events she had ever seen. There she met Jeannie French, who connected Gutiérrez with others in the Professional Women's Network, a group of left-leaning, pro-life female professionals. French also recommended Gutiérrez to Americans United for Life, which was looking for someone to lobby the telecommunications giant AT&T to stop donating to Planned Parenthood. Gutiérrez said yes and began a long relationship with the right-to-life movement. While Wharton worked to make *Roe* a symbol of equality for women, Gutiérrez presented *Roe* as a threat to women who were promised the world and then were left sick and without support.[8]

Gutiérrez and Wharton were part of a broader conversation in the 1990s about *Roe* as a symbol of equality for women. The anti-abortion movement, which had focused heavily on fetal rights in the 1970s and 1980s, increasingly began promoting claims that abortion damaged women's health. Abortion rights supporters had made equality arguments as far back as the late 1960s, but in the late 1980s and early 1990s, these claims were not always central to the movement's political advocacy. In the courts, however, feminists like Wharton stressed a signature argument about equality, one focused not on the sex stereotypes said to motivate anti-abortion legislators but on the connection between career, education, and access to abortion.

Wharton and Gutiérrez also spotlighted what was missing in broader debates about whether *Roe* furthered or undermined equality for women. Wharton began to stress that the rights guaranteed by *Roe* were not available equally, and that abortion access alone was not enough to allow women with fewer resources to catch up. Gutiérrez argued that communities of color were offered access to abortion rather than a true chance at the American dream. Both women raised complex issues about what it meant to make *Roe* a symbol of equality for women when so many obstacles unrelated to abortion stood in their way.

The dialogue about *Roe* and equality took a sharp turn in the late 1980s when Operation Rescue catapulted itself onto the national stage. Randall Terry had dropped out of high school to pursue a career in rock and roll, seemingly dooming himself to a life of low-wage jobs. But after he said that God spoke to him on the side of a road in Rochester, New York, he found a way to be a star. Terry planned to bring thousands to protests, force the closure of clinics across the country, and rack up record numbers of arrests. That, he thought, would make news.[9]

Operation Rescue mounted its first clinic blockade in 1987 in Linda Wharton's hometown of Cherry Hill. The organization grew quickly, hosting blockades from Los Angeles and Philadelphia to Atlanta and Tacoma. The nation's best-known televangelists came to speak at rescues; the Republican Study Committee, a coalition of conservatives in the House of Representatives, pledged its support. Operation Rescue even offered a customized spring break experience for college students.[10]

Randall Terry certainly did not praise the new opportunities available for women. Juli Loesch, a left-leaning pro-life feminist, worked as a spokesperson for Operation Rescue in its early days because she believed Terry could mobilize anti-abortion activists whom others had failed to reach (a handful of other women also made headlines for the organization). But Operation Rescue's leaders resisted demands to put women in prominent positions, and the mostly white male evangelical ministers who dominated the organization had no interest in Loesch's vision of feminism. Ridiculing the idea of a woman's right to choose, Terry wrote that *Roe* instead stood for the idea that "child-killing is a protected right."[11]

Feminists and civil libertarians, making *Roe* a symbol of the equality that women sought, pointed to Operation Rescue as the polar opposite of that ideal. Linda Wharton was one of the feminist attorneys who crafted this strategy. She had stayed in Philadelphia after law school, and in the late 1980s she was working at Dechert, a corporate law firm, while taking pro bono jobs on the side. The Women's Law Project, a prominent feminist public interest firm in town, called her to help stop an upcoming abortion blockade, and Wharton agreed to seek a court injunction.[12]

Wharton argued under a federal civil rights statute that blockaders targeted women not because they engaged in a specific activity (abortion) but because they were women. In her view, defending *Roe* had everything to do with ensuring that women could get an education, pursue a career, and close the wage gap with men. Gutting *Roe* and denying women access to abortion, by extension, both reflected and reinforced sex discrimination. Similar arguments had persuaded district courts around the country to stop blockades from getting underway.[13]

Abortion rights leaders used the media circus surrounding Operation Rescue to link *Roe* to the opportunities then becoming available to women. As the 1990s began, women had started marrying later and attending college in much higher numbers. Rates of workforce participation increased substantially from the 1960s to the 1990s for women of every race, with greater numbers joining traditionally male professions, from law and engineering to medicine. The average ratio of women's to men's pay, which had hovered around 60 percent since the 1950s, hit 75.2 percent in 1990. At the end of August 1990, President George H. W. Bush declared the first Women's Equality Day to "celebrate the continued social and economic advancement of women." Abortion rights supporters in the 1990s increasingly connected *Roe* to that kind of equality.[14]

In May 1989, at its New York City headquarters, Planned Parenthood hosted a strategy summit to respond to Operation Rescue and reframe its messaging around *Roe*. After some discussion, those present settled on a plan to link *Roe* to women's equality (and describe blockades as anti-woman). Those speaking to the press were advised to stress that women were heckled and harassed by blockaders who wanted to take away *Roe*'s guarantee of equal treatment. The key, the strategists explained, was to describe Operation Rescue as a project led by men who wanted to deny women their rights.[15]

Abortion rights groups again equated *Roe* and equality for women when a growing number of states began passing laws mandating parental involvement in abortion (thirty-seven states out of fifty would eventually do so). It was hard for abortion rights groups to oppose these laws, explained NARAL pollster Harrison Hickman, when

Americans thought of mandating parental consultation as a sensible step to protect children.[16]

At first, attorneys for groups like NARAL and the American Civil Liberties Union argued that such laws would endanger minors who were victims of parental abuse.[17] In the political arena, the movement generally stressed arguments about choice, believing these claims would resonate with a larger group of voters, including those who found abortion distasteful. But in the context of parental involvement, especially in court, groups like NARAL tried directly connecting *Roe* to equality for women.[18]

In 1990, the Supreme Court was set to decide two cases on parental involvement: *Ohio v. Akron Center for Reproductive Health* (referred to *Akron II*) and *Hodgson v. Minnesota*. The Minnesota law challenged in *Hodgson* required minors to wait at least forty-eight hours after notifying both their parents (the only exceptions covered threats to a patient's life as well as victims of abuse or neglect who had informed the authorities). A separate part of the statute created a judicial bypass option that allowed a court to block the law's more rigid provisions. Under the bypass procedure, a minor could get an abortion if she convinced a court that she was mature enough to decide for herself or if the procedure was in her best interest. The attorneys challenging the Minnesota law stressed that it would create consequential delays for minors. The ACLU also argued that a right to abortion was necessary to ensure a young woman's future prospects: "Pregnancy continuation poses not only greater physical risks for teenagers, but greater psychological, economic and educational consequences as well. Teenage motherhood eliminates life choices, not only for the teenage mother, but for her children."[19]

While *Hodgson* was pending, anti-abortion leaders began to worry that Operation Rescue was convincing Americans that *Roe* really was a symbol of women's equality. The leaders of Americans

United for Life thought that the solution was to paint abortion providers and pro-choice lobbyists as women's real enemies. Clarke Forsythe, who helped pioneer this strategy, might have been the scrappiest of the young lawyers in AUL's office; most had come from Northwestern (often directly from Victor Rosenblum's constitutional law class), but Forsythe, a convert to the Republican Party who had graduated from Valparaiso, had volunteered his time for free before being offered a paid job. Between 1989 and 1991, he worked to promote model laws outlawing sex-selection abortion and urged his colleagues to highlight the state's "important interest in preventing sex discrimination, whether against unborn boys or unborn girls."[20]

AUL had some success with this strategy in Pennsylvania, which introduced a sex-selection ban (among other restrictions) in 1989.[21] In January 1990, Wharton and a colleague at the Women's Law Project, Kathryn Kolbert, challenged the constitutionality of every part of the Pennsylvania law except for the sex-selection provision and a twenty-four-hour waiting period. Believing it was likely unconstitutional, a district court blocked the law from going into effect. Then in June, the Supreme Court handed down decisions in *Hodgson* and *Akron II*, upholding both restrictions.[22]

After *Hodgson*, the justices got involved in a case that more directly described *Roe* as a symbol of equality for women, *Bray v. Alexandria Women's Health Clinic*. The case began in metropolitan Washington, DC, when nine abortion clinics sued to prevent a blockade. Jayne Bray, a leader of Operation Rescue, was named as a defendant; her husband, Michael, a pastor from Bowie, Maryland, had recently served four years in prison for a string of clinic bombings. At his trial in 1985, Jayne had testified that she was "tickled pink" by the bombings.[23]

In September 1990, the Court of Appeals for the Fourth Circuit in *Bray* affirmed the judgment of the district court granting an in-

junction preventing blockades. The following month, the Senate confirmed David Souter, George H. W. Bush's choice to replace Supreme
Court justice William J. Brennan, a liberal stalwart. Souter had little
track record on abortion (or anything else), having just joined the
First Circuit Court of Appeals, but most court watchers assumed he
would share Bush's skepticism about a constitutional right to choose
abortion. In February 1991, with Souter on the bench, the Supreme
Court agreed to hear Jayne Bray's appeal.[24]

It seemed to Guy Condon that *Bray* was just the start of redefining the relationship between *Roe* and women's equality. As the new
president of AUL, Condon argued that the right-to-life movement
had made little progress because the movement's rhetoric made it
"seem against women, against the democratic process if [it defies] traditional religious principles, and even against one another."[25] Condon
wanted his colleagues to respond by arguing that *Roe* had undermined
equality for women by damaging their health, and that those with the
"most to gain from abortion—the abortionists—are mostly male and
sleazy."[26]

As Condon worked to retool AUL's strategy, Thurgood Marshall,
a liberal justice and former head of the NAACP Legal Defense and
Education Fund, announced that he would retire in June 1991. George
H. W. Bush selected Clarence Thomas, a Black conservative critic of
affirmative action and abortion, as his replacement. In September,
when Thomas was facing public questioning from the Senate, Anita
Hill, the first Black woman to be a tenured law professor at the University of Oklahoma, reported that Thomas had sexually harassed her
while he was her boss at the Equal Employment Opportunity Commission. Thomas's confirmation hearing exposed questions about *Roe*
as a symbol of equality that were not always addressed in either pro-
choice or pro-life arguments. While pro-choice leaders suggested that
access to abortion had allowed many more women to get ahead in

their careers, pro-lifers suggested that abortion traumatized women and made new opportunities harder to seize. Neither side discussed how unattainable those opportunities remained for many, especially those with the fewest resources or those, like Hill, confronting the most discrimination.[27]

By the 1990s, courts had begun to take sexual harassment more seriously. The response to Hill's testimony, however, showed that the politics had not changed much. A 1991 CBS/*New York Times* survey showed that four in ten women had experienced sexual harassment at work, but many still found it hard to believe women like Anita Hill. Republicans lobbied to vote on Thomas's confirmation despite her allegations, insinuating that Hill's account could not be trusted because she had waited nine years to accuse Thomas of harassment. Several other witnesses came forward to back Hill's account, but after pausing for a week, the Senate proceeded to a vote without hearing from any of them. He was confirmed, 52–48. With Thomas on the Court, there seemed to be more than enough votes to reverse *Roe*. As important, Hill's story—and the Senate's willingness to dismiss it— complicated the narratives of opportunity for working women advocated by both sides of the abortion debate. While fighting about whether *Roe* embodied new options for career women, neither side fully considered what working women had to sacrifice to seize those options.[28]

And the opportunities were not equally available. In the 1990s, upward mobility was still far more likely for white women than for women of color. The generational transfer of wealth harmed women of color, whose families often began with fewer resources; lower rates of marriage for people of color—marriage often meant more than one family income and was correlated with economic mobility for women—also made it harder for some to take advantage of new opportunities. Even career women like Wharton and Gutiérrez often lacked support from the government, their employers, and their communities; in 1990, a Pennsylvania study found that working married women performed more than 80 percent of the childcare. Women were taking on more professional jobs, but female CEOs, law partners, and senior government officials were unusual. While pro-choice and pro-life advocates contested the relationship between abortion and equality for women, abortion access was only one factor shaping whether women had opportunities for advancement.[29]

When Thomas joined the Court, Linda Wharton and Kathryn Kolbert were strategizing about the possibility that their Pennsylvania case, *Planned Parenthood v. Casey*, would land before the justices. The Third Circuit Court of Appeals had just upheld most of Pennsylvania's law; the majority opinion authored by Judge Walter K. Stapleton invalidated only a measure requiring women to notify their husbands before getting an abortion. It seemed unlikely that the Supreme Court would save abortion rights, but Wharton and Kolbert thought their best chance was to make *Roe* a symbol of what women needed to get ahead.[30]

At first, Wharton and Kolbert focused on the basic principle that *Roe* advanced equality for women, even if they did not think a win in the Pennsylvania case was realistic.[31] Most likely, they thought, the Court would hold that abortion was not a fundamental right—and might even hold that abortion bans had a rational basis so long as they made an exception for the life of the patient. Their pessimism aside, the lawyers wanted to make the best case—and making *Roe* a symbol of equality for women, they felt, would do that. "By affording women greater control over their childbearing," they argued in their brief, "*Roe* has permitted American women to participate more fully and equally in every societal undertaking." Wharton and Kolbert reasoned that control over one's childbearing was a necessary ingredient for women seeking to "continue their education, enter the workforce, and otherwise make meaningful decisions consistent with their own moral choices."[32] Few of the anti-abortion briefs in *Casey* said much about equality for women. When anti-abortion lawyers raised the subject of discrimination, it was to argue that the Supreme Court was biased against the unborn child, or against men who were denied decision-making power about a partner's abortion.[33]

When *Casey* came down in June 1992, the Court surprised observers who had expected *Roe* to be gone. Harry Blackmun and John Paul Stevens joined an opinion written by Sandra Day O'Connor, Anthony Kennedy, and David Souter preserving what the Court called the "essential holding" of *Roe:* the "right of the woman to choose to have an abortion before viability and to obtain it without undue interference from the State."[34]

Wharton and Kolbert's argument made its most significant impact in the Court's discussion of precedent. In theory, the justices hesitated to reverse past decisions, but they did not view adherence to established doctrine as "an inexorable command." In evaluating whether to preserve a precedent, the Court considered whether a past rule was unworkable, whether people relied on the existing rules in ordering their business, and whether changes in the law or the broader society had undermined a decision's effectiveness. The Court wove Wharton and Kolbert's argument into its reasoning about reliance.[35]

The *Casey* opinion concluded that women had relied on *Roe* to take advantage of the very opportunities that Wharton and Kolbert described. "The ability of women to participate equally in the economic and social life of the Nation," *Casey* said of *Roe*, "has been facilitated by their ability to control their reproductive lives."[36]

But the plurality (Justices Blackmun and Stevens did not join this part of the opinion) got rid of *Roe*'s trimester framework, which the opinion described as "rigid" and "unnecessary," and replaced it with a new test. After *Casey*, abortion regulations would be unconstitutional only if they had the purpose or effect of creating a "substantial obstacle" for people seeking abortion. In applying this test, the Court upheld an informed consent law much like the ones right-to-lifers had advocated since the early 1980s. "In attempting to ensure that a woman apprehend the full consequences of her decision," the opinion explained, "the State furthers the legitimate purpose of reducing the risk that a woman may elect an abortion, only to discover later, with devastating psychological consequences, that her decision was not fully informed."[37]

In the aftermath of *Casey*, Condon recruited Myrna Gutiérrez to help his organization fight Americans' image of *Roe* as a symbol of equality for women. To carry out AUL's plan, Gutiérrez began giving talks to corporations and grassroots groups as well as reaching out to Spanish-language media. She pursued a two-pronged strategy: to use the mass media to reach Americans and policymakers who were undecided on abortion, and to train other right-to-lifers to do the same. She wrote op-eds, created and distributed talking points, and trained activists, lawmakers, and the crisis pregnancy center staff on how to approach the media. Groups like AUL insisted that *Roe* had not made women equal but had only damaged their psyches and bodies. Later in the 1990s, a growing body of research found no evidence that abortion increased the risk of trauma disorders, infertility, or breast cancer, but early in the decade, AUL insisted that the safety of abortion was far from clear. The group's leaders also insisted that there was no proof that access to abortion had actually helped anyone. In official talking points, for example, AUL argued that there was "no evidence that *Roe v. Wade* advanced women's rights outside the area of abortion."[38] Gutiérrez echoed those arguments, but she also picked up on issues left out of mainstream conversations. In her view, equality was not just a matter of giving women access to abortion or protecting them from it. Defending legal abortion, she argued, allowed the government to behave as if women were already equal to men and racism was a thing of the past. In her view, *Roe* was an excuse not to address the discrimination and poverty that affected communities like the one where she grew up.[39]

Casey cast a black cloud over Gutiérrez's early months at AUL. Before June 1992, money had been rolling in, with the organization drafting legislation and fielding advisors for state legislators. After the *Casey* decision was announced, when Gutiérrez was only three months into the job, she had to lay off AUL's entire public relations department except for her assistant. Guy Condon was ready to call it quits in law and politics—he took a position at Care Net, a network of crisis pregnancy centers.[40]

When the smoke had cleared after the 1992 presidential election, it looked like Condon was on to something. Bill Clinton defeated the incumbent, George H. W. Bush, carrying thirty-two states and the District of Columbia. Political commentators argued that the abortion issue had hurt Bush, who had tacked sharply to the right on the issue to win over supporters of his primary opponent, Pat Buchanan. In office, Clinton was more strongly pro-choice than any of his predecessors, including Democrat Jimmy Carter; he immediately eliminated limits on abortion counseling at federally funded clinics, lifted the Mexico City policy, which prohibited U.S. international family planning funds from being used for counseling or information on abortion, and opened the door to federally sponsored research on fetal tissue. Gutiérrez was crestfallen about Clinton's win but felt she might be the best spokesperson for her movement at a time when Democrats controlled the White House and both houses of Congress.[41]

The Court's decision in *Bray v. Alexandria Women's Health Clinic* allowed right-to-lifers like Gutiérrez to hope that the justices did not really see *Roe* as a symbol of opportunity for women. The National Organization for Women's brief in *Bray* detailed the hardships that blockades created for women; some could not return on a different day because of limited resources for childcare and transportation; others had come back to have a dilation device removed, began bleeding, and suffered medical complications when they could not enter a clinic for care. "Women literally fall in the door crying," one witness testified.[42]

A federal civil rights statute, part of the Ku Klux Klan Act of 1871, required a conspiracy to deprive a vulnerable group of civil rights, and NOW claimed it could show one. *Roe*, the group argued, served as a shield for women's civil rights. When blockaders took away a woman's right to abortion, she was "denied equality of treatment in respect of constitutional liberty."[43]

In *Bray*, NOW faced off against anti-abortion activists quite unlike Myrna Gutiérrez. Jay Sekulow had gained fame as the attorney for Operation Rescue. The son of a Jewish clothing buyer for a department store, Sekulow had moved to Atlanta with his family, attended Atlanta Bible College, and become a member of Jews for Jesus, a group of Jewish converts to evangelical Protestantism who claimed to have harmonized Jewish religious traditions and born-again Christianity. After law school, he, his brother, and several classmates had started a business flipping historic properties, but the venture imploded. Sekulow, buried in unpaid bills, reinvented himself as a lawyer for the Christian right.[44]

In *Bray*, he argued that Randall Terry was not targeting women as a class but abortion as an activity. Moreover, he suggested that identifying *Roe* with equal treatment was "an affront to the sincerity of countless women and men—including judges, legislators, scholars, and a multitude of others—who regard human abortion as the killing of innocent persons."[45]

The Supreme Court bought this argument. In January 1993, six justices held that feminists could not use federal civil rights law to stop clinic blockades. The majority saw no conspiracy to stop women from coming from out of town. Nor could feminists allege a plot to deny women the right to choose or equal treatment under the law because the Constitution protected these rights only against interference by the government, not by private citizens. The majority was unconvinced that opposition to abortion could be equated with misogyny.[46]

Bray encouraged those who thought it was possible to redefine the relationship between *Roe* and equal opportunity. Gutiérrez found a willing partner in AUL's new president, Paige Comstock Cunningham, a self-described feminist mother of three who had attended Condon's alma mater, Wheaton College, Illinois, and expressed concern about ongoing sex discrimination.[47]

After *Casey*, Cunningham planned to prioritize informed consent laws. The organization called these "women's right to know" laws, a play on *Roe's* "right to choose." Making *Roe* a symbol of what women did not know, rather than the new opportunities they had won, was an important move. If voters thought *Roe* denied women opportunities to parent or remain healthy, it would be easier to elect Republicans and confirm sympathetic judges. And if abortion had nothing to do with equal opportunity, the foundation of the *Casey* opinion (and of *Roe's* right to choose) would be gone.[48]

Cunningham laid out this new strategy at an April 1993 meeting of the organization's board of directors. A month earlier, in Pensacola, Florida, Michael F. Griffin had waited for Dr. David Gunn outside his abortion clinic and shot him dead. Gunn left behind a wife and two children.[49]

The escalation of anti-abortion violence made Cunningham's strategy seem even more important. She urged her colleagues to "shift the rhetoric from 'abortion is murder' and the 'unborn are precious' to place more emphasis on the women." While Gutiérrez agreed with the plan to argue that *Roe* was not a symbol of equality for women, she sometimes saw the need for an even broader shift. The opportunities for women heralded in *Casey*, after all, were far more available to women who were white and relatively well-to-do. Gutiérrez wanted to argue that the government used the availability of abortion as an excuse to ignore the discrimination and obstacles facing low-income women of color.[50]

Wharton, meanwhile, was also moved by *Casey* to push beyond abstract arguments identifying *Roe* with sex equality. Her personal experience reinforced her conviction that access to abortion notwithstanding, even the most privileged career women could not easily balance work and parenting; they lacked the support. Wharton had been forced to step in as acting managing attorney after only six months at the Women's Law Project. The path to *Casey* had been a blur: parenting a three-year-old and a kindergartener, flying to New York for brief-writing sessions that could run late into the night, talking to the press.[51]

While they still focused partly on arguments identifying *Roe* with equality after the *Casey* decision came down, Wharton and Kolbert increasingly argued that the opportunities they had stressed in *Casey* were not available to all women, and neither was access to abortion. To the extent *Roe* protected equality for women, that guarantee required "a contextualized, fact-intensive analysis that acknowledges the current real-life challenges women face in accessing reproductive health care services and gives careful consideration to the ways in which the challenged restrictions exploit and exacerbate those realities."[52]

The two planned to gather evidence of how seemingly neutral restrictions could make it impossible for women to access abortion (a strategy that had paid dividends in the challenge of Pennsylvania's spousal notification law). Perhaps the undue burden test would allow abortion rights lawyers to show that many women, especially women of color, were not well positioned to take advantage of new opportunities—and that abortion restrictions affected some patients far more gravely than others.[53]

In the spring of 1993, Wharton and Kolbert returned to court to give more meaning to the newly minted undue burden test. In *Casey*, the Court had created a new constitutional rule: abortion regulations could not be unduly burdensome. Wharton and Kolbert, however, insisted that the Court had not reached a final decision about whether any part of Pennsylvania's law created an undue burden. They asked for the opportunity to reopen the record, gather new evidence, and prove that the law was far more oppressive than it seemed. In May 1993, a district court granted their request, but the Third Circuit Court of Appeals turned away their pleas to reopen the record. Wharton and Kolbert asked the Supreme Court to stay the decision, but Justice Souter, one of the architects of the *Casey* opinion, refused, concluding that Kolbert and Wharton had already had their chance to develop evidence at trial.[54]

Even as groups like AUL emphasized protecting women from abortion, Gutiérrez also worried that the abortion debate ignored the fact that women like her mother had never had the same opportunities as their white counterparts, and legal abortion had done nothing to change that. "When poor pregnant women face financial crisis, unemployment, or abusive homes, shrill voices cry abortion," she argued in a 1994 letter to the editor. "After abortion, when problems remain, society blames poor women for contributing to the welfare rolls."[55]

In the mid-1990s, however, such ideas seemed to have no place in politics. Political commentators had spent much of 1993 obsessing over Clinton's health care bill. The administration kept its precise contents under seal; in the Beltway, lobbyists for big tobacco, big medicine, and big pharma jockeyed to make sure the reform did not damage their interests. Everyone seemed to support some form of universal health care, but the details remained up in the air.[56]

By 1994, the bill was in deep trouble. Republicans smelled blood following an investigation into the Clintons' involvement in White-water, a failed Arkansas real estate scheme that led to criminal convictions of the Clintons' partners. With the president wounded, Bob Dole, the Senate majority leader, denounced universal health care as "a massive overdose of government control."[57] The demise of health care reform came amid a broader loss of support for programs to aid the poor. Desperate for a policy win, Clinton vowed to end "welfare as we know it" by imposing work requirements and time limits for welfare programs. Republicans, in turn, demanded time limits on payments, proposed bans on support for legal non-citizen immigrants and unmarried adolescent mothers, and argued that welfare benefits should be administered as a block grant program.[58]

For Gutiérrez, things came to a head after the 1994 midterm election. Most pro-lifers were elated by the result: Republicans took control of the House of Representatives for the first time since 1952. Led by Newt Gingrich, a former professor with a short fuse, the GOP ran on a "Contract with America" that promised to reduce government waste, balance the budget, and cut taxes, Social Security, and welfare. The Contract with America took a particularly hard stand against programs for the poor. Gutiérrez had stressed that *Roe* could not offer women equality in part because people of color and low-income Americans needed significant help, rather than access to abortion. The 1994 election suggested that neither the Republican nor Democratic Party was interested in helping them.[59]

By 1995, Gutiérrez was convinced that the abortion debate had moved past her. She decided to leave Chicago and move back to California to be closer to her mother and sister. But even there, she could not put enough distance between herself and the increasingly toxic politics in Washington; she produced shows for affiliates of the Public Broadcasting System and worked as a public relations consultant for everyone from NASA to the *Los Angeles Times*. She did some work on the side for the right-to-life movement but more often focused on other social justice issues, from youth obesity at the Centers for Disease Control to literacy at the *Los Angeles Times* Festival of Books.[60]

In 1996, Wharton left the Women's Law Project for academia. The demands of litigation and family had worn her down. At Stockton University in New Jersey, she taught a course on women in the law, wrote on sex discrimination, and worked toward the ratification of an Equal Rights Amendment to the Constitution.[61]

Wharton and Gutiérrez, both of whom identified as feminists, shaped a broader debate about whether *Roe* facilitated or destroyed equality for women. In seeking to challenge restrictions on abortion for minors and save *Roe*, major pro-choice organizations identified it with equal opportunity, suggesting that access to abortion allowed women to pursue better educations, more fulfilling careers, and richer lives. Pro-life organizations responded that *Roe* had made women physically and mentally ill.

Both women strained against the limits of this dialogue. Wharton stressed that making abortion a right had not given many women access to it or helped them control when they became parents. It had not provided better defenses against racism or sexism. Gutiérrez thought the government used *Roe* as an excuse to ignore discrimination and poverty. Conversations about *Roe* and equality sometimes suggested that better opportunities were available to women who seized them, but as Wharton and Gutiérrez both recognized, Anita Hill's story implied the opposite.

In 1993 and 1994, dueling books questioned the veracity of Hill's statements; one, by Senator John Danforth of Missouri, insinuated that her claims stemmed from "erotomania, a rare delusion of some women that particular men in positions of power, such as supervisors or political figures, have romantic interests in them."[62] Writing for the

Washington Post, columnist Richard Cohen saw Hill as a casualty of Beltway power politics. Thomas might have lied, Cohen wrote, but any man would have done the same. After all, Thomas was fighting "for his very essence—his reputation, his career, his carefully constructed conservative persona." As for Hill's career, Cohen ended the piece without saying anything at all.[63]

5

Simply a Scientific Question

Becoming an abortion provider never seemed to be Martin Haskell's destiny. His parents came from the most storied families in Birmingham, Alabama: the Mudds, on one side of the family, had helped to found the city, served as judges, established banks, built hotels, and, in antebellum times, owned slaves. Haskell was born into a deeply segregated city. His mother always worried about her neighbors' good opinion; his father, who ran a division at U.S. Steel, moved the family to affluent Mountain Brook, an enclave that locals called "the tiny kingdom." Haskell felt especially warmly toward the family's maid, Kate, a Black woman who lived with her two sons and daughter east of Center Street, which defined the city's color line.[1]

After school, he and Kate watched zany skits and musical numbers on the *Kate Smith Hour*; both joked that Martin's Kate should have a variety show of her own. Haskell got the idea of being a doctor from television too; he saw a special on the humanitarian, theologian, and 1952 Nobel Peace Prize winner Albert Schweitzer and decided to follow a similar path. Kate, who called him Master Martin, certainly believed he could be a physician. She told him that one of her sons was going to college. Martin wanted to deliver her children's Christmas presents in person, but his mother forbade it. There was no way, she said, that Martin could cross the color line.[2]

When Kate died, Martin felt he had failed her. His parents did not let him go to her funeral. The experience haunted him—Kate had not been healthy, but no one had done anything to help her. A physician like Dr. Schweitzer, he thought, might have made a difference.[3]

Haskell's father accepted the idea of his son's being a doctor as long as he got out of the South and stayed away from California, a place he considered too wild for a sheltered southern boy. Martin went to college in Ohio, then returned to Alabama for medical school. He headed to Cincinnati in January 1974 for his residency with plans to become an emergency room physician. Saturday mornings, he drove to Columbus and learned how to perform abortions from Dr. Harley Blank, who had opened the Founder's Women's Health Center, the first abortion facility in Ohio. After finishing his residency, Haskell worked in an emergency room but kept performing abortions at the Women's Center in Cincinnati. When the clinic owner had a nervous breakdown, Haskell stepped in, and abortion became his full-time job.[4]

He found it incredibly rewarding to help his patients, many of whom desperately needed a competent doctor, and he wanted to learn from the most experienced physicians in his field and master the most complex techniques. He met his wife, a New Jersey girl with royal Russian ancestors, at a horse show in Akron in 1978; they got engaged on Thanksgiving three years later, married that New Year's Eve, had two children, opened another abortion clinic, and purchased others in subsequent years.[5]

Nothing seemed to faze Martin Haskell. He endured sit-ins and pickets and people screaming terrible things. In 1985, John Allen Brockhoeft, a former mail carrier who had joined the anti-abortion terrorist group Army of God, firebombed Haskell's Cincinnati center, forcing it to close for two months because of fire and smoke damage. There was scorn from other doctors, including the head of the medical society in one of the towns in which he operated. But Haskell generally saw these issues simply as problems to be solved.[6]

Haskell got pulled into a debate about *Roe* as a symbol of scientific expertise. Right-to-lifers suggested that the *Roe* Court had twisted the facts to reach a result the justices found palatable. Over time, they broadened this attack to suggest that *Roe* was the work of a scientific establishment poisoned by political correctness. Abortion rights supporters replied that it was anti-abortion activists who ignored science, creating parallel institutions and identifying their own experts when leading authorities rejected their conclusions. Pro-choice leaders made *Roe* a symbol of physicians' freedom to rely on sound evidence and make the best decisions for their patients. Neither side's argument was static: right-to-lifers at one point began presenting *Roe* as an example of the flaws in how elite institutions studied science and how the media covered it, while abortion rights leaders began framing it as a decision that balanced difficult moral questions with hard science. The debate as a whole revealed the nuanced issues around the politics of science. Many people struggled to balance the need for ethical guidelines with the desire not to slant the conclusions of scientific research.

These conversations about *Roe* and science also reflected broader battles in the 1990s and 2000s. Debates about the causes and extent of climate change and the safety of common childhood vaccines divided Americans about the reliability of elite scientific institutions and media coverage of scientific topics. The concern about blind deference to scientific experts was already decades old. In 1978, political scientist Peter Skerry chastised the *Roe* Court for its "naïve view of science as capable of not only transcending, but also deciding, moral and ethical matters."[7] The *Roe* opinion, he thought, only dressed up elite preferences as scientific facts. In the 1960s and 1970s, neoconservatives saw this as a widespread issue in the Court's use of science.[8]

Unthinking deference to experts had been costly in the past. Reporters and others detailed dark episodes of abuse by scientists and doctors: the forced sterilization of people of color from the 1950s to the 1970s, nonconsensual Cold War experiments involving radiation exposure, and the Tuskegee Study, in which Black test subjects who were often unaware they had syphilis were left untreated so that researchers could study the disease's long-term effects. These scientific horror stories yielded contradictory lessons. It was dangerous to collect or interpret even the best evidence without ethical guardrails. But the abusive practices exposed in the 1970s also seemed to reflect a blurring of the line between politics and science. Those debating the relationship between *Roe* and science struggled to reconcile these opposing conclusions.[9]

Haskell found himself at the center of these struggles after he gave a paper on a specific abortion procedure, intact dilation and extraction. In the second trimester, doctors generally relied on dilation and evacuation, in which a doctor dilated the cervix and then used forceps to remove fetal tissue. Haskell's colleague, California-based physician Jim McMahon, argued that some patients would benefit from an alternative that removed a fetus intact rather than piece by piece. A syllabus of Haskell's paper on this method leaked after he gave his presentation. In Minnesota, anti-abortion activists began circulating a line drawing of the procedure, and national anti-abortion groups soon called for a ban on the procedure.[10]

When Republicans took control of Congress in 1994, Charles Canady, a Republican who represented a conservative chunk of Florida north of Tampa, sat down with Doug Johnson of the National Right to Life Committee and Keri Folmar, a conservative Christian lawyer, to discuss how to ban the procedure described in Haskell's paper. Claiming he could not find a label for the procedure in medical textbooks, the congressman dubbed it "partial-birth abortion" because it looked to him like infanticide. "The bill creates a legal definition of 'partial-birth abortion,' " Johnson later explained to members of National Right to Life Committee, "and would ban any variation of that method—no matter what new idiosyncratic name any abortionist may invent to refer to it—so long as it is 'an abortion in which the person performing the abortion partially vaginally delivers a living fetus before killing the fetus and completing the delivery.'"[11]

In seeking to ban partial-birth abortion, groups like NRLC framed *Roe* as a symbol of the politicization of science. While *Roe* suggested that scientists did not agree when human life began, anti-abortion leaders had no doubt: life began at conception, and ultrasound images, genetic research, and fetology proved as much. *Roe*'s holdings, they charged, reflected political preferences, not hard science. And NRLC leaders suggested that abortion rights supporters continued to bend the facts. At congressional hearings on a federal partial-birth abortion ban, Dr. Nancy Romer, an obstetrician-gynecologist who practiced near Haskell's Dayton clinic, said that the procedure Haskell described actually damaged women's health.[12]

In October 1995, when Haskell's home state banned partial-birth abortion, he challenged the ban's constitutionality with the help of Kathryn Kolbert and the Center for Reproductive Law and Policy. While he contended that the bill was unconstitutionally vague and impermissibly swept in the far more common dilation and evacuation technique, he mostly emphasized that it lacked an exception for patients' health. Haskell equated *Roe* with respect for science and argued that "women's health must be of paramount concern." Under *Roe*'s standard, he contended, the bill unconstitutionally denied women access to "the safest, most available late-term abortion procedure."[13]

Charles Canady, who followed the proceedings in Ohio, wanted to counter arguments about the lack of a health exception in such bills. Haskell's suit assumed that *Roe* protected women's health and gave doctors the power to rely on the best scientific evidence. Canady thought *Roe* reflected a mix of liberal politics and feminism that had no place in medicine. "As to the mother's health," he wrote, "leading physicians have stated that partial-birth abortion is unnecessary and may actually pose risks to maternal health, such as uterine rupture and cervical incompetence." While Haskell's suit was pending, Congress passed a federal ban on what it called partial-birth abortion, which was vetoed by President Clinton. It seemed the battle lines had been drawn: the fight to criminalize dilation and extraction would depend on how Americans understood the relationship between *Roe* and scientific evidence.[14]

As Congress fought over partial-birth abortion, Martin Haskell debated going into hiding. When Representative Henry Hyde invited him to Washington to testify, he refused because his wife was worried about his safety. But public scrutiny did not persuade him to stop performing abortions; in 1994, he purchased a medical center in Akron, the third he would operate. In 1996, Akron Right to Life held a literal exorcism at the clinic.[15]

During the protests and threats, Haskell's friend George Tiller was never far from his mind. Tiller, like Haskell, was one of the few doctors in the country who performed abortions relatively late in pregnancy. While most people who knew Haskell saw him as a charmer, Tiller could be abrupt. The son of a family doctor from Wichita, he went to college on a swimming scholarship, became a U.S. Navy flight surgeon, and then took over his father's practice after his family died in a plane crash. When he started receiving visits from women seeking abortions, he realized that his father had performed illegal abortions—and more than a few. By 1985, Tiller decided to focus on providing abortions.[16]

There was a tight-knit group of abortion providers who treated one another like family; Haskell and his wife visited Tiller's Colorado vacation home for skiing trips. For Haskell, the friendship was easy to explain. Both men were shaken by the 1994 murder of Dr. John

Britton and his security guard outside a Pensacola clinic by extremist Paul Hill. Like Britton, Haskell and Tiller had regular protestors at their clinics who might do the same thing. George Tiller was one of the few people in the world who understood what it was like to be Martin Haskell.[17]

In challenging abortion restrictions, including in the litigation over Ohio's ban on partial-birth abortion, Haskell and Tiller made *Roe* a symbol of commitment to science. Haskell's lawyers stressed that *Roe* not only relied on sound medical evidence but allowed doctors to do the same. In December 1995, in *Women's Medical Professional Corporation v. Voinovich*, a district court blocked enforcement of Ohio's law but, like Clinton's spring 1996 veto of a federal ban, the decision only catalyzed the anger of right-to-life activists, who had long believed that *Roe* buried the scientific truth about fetal life. Doug Johnson began describing opposition to the partial-birth abortion ban as reflecting not only the federal judiciary's bias but also that of the mainstream media, which he described as unfair, "misleading," and full of "one-sided medical information."[18] A group of physicians opposed to abortion, including Dayton's Nancy Romer, founded Physicians Ad Hoc Coalition for Truth, known as PHACT, to counter what they saw as the bias of the media and the governing class. "We, as physicians, can no longer stand by," the group explained in a fall 1996 press release, "while abortion advocates, the President of the United States, and newspapers and television shows continue to repeat false medical claims to members of Congress and to the public."[19]

In the late 1990s, as PHACT pledged to "defeat the 'science fiction' of partial birth abortion advocates with 'science fact,'" right-to-lifers also began to frame *Roe* as representing the politicization of the public health establishment itself.[20] NRLC leaders contended that elite medical organizations whitewashed the facts to preserve abortion rights, making abortion seem far safer than it really was. With Bill

Clinton in office and violence against abortion clinics in the news, feminists pushed the Food and Drug Administration to approve mifepristone, or RU 486, a drug that was part of a two-drug abortion protocol in use in Europe since the 1980s. After the FDA began clinical trials of the drug, right-to-lifers again equated *Roe* with doctors' willingness to put political correctness before patient health (prochoice groups responded that because RU 486 had been safely used by more than a quarter million women in Europe, there was no medical question about its safety). Anti-abortion groups also claimed that abortion was related to an increased risk of breast cancer. Dr. Joel Brind, a former Democrat who taught endocrinology at Baruch College, got hold of some early studies connecting abortion to breast cancer risk. Even after the *New England Journal of Medicine* published a definitive 1997 study finding no such connection, Brind did not change his mind. Americans United for Life continued pushing for informed consent laws mandating that patients hear that abortion would increase their risk of breast cancer even after the *New England Journal* study came out.[21]

These conflicts over *Roe* and science hit home for Haskell. In the summer of 1997, his Dayton clinic was the site of Operation Rescue's largest blockade of the year. Haskell felt optimistic because Bill Clinton had cruised to reelection the year before; his opponent, Kansas senator Bob Dole, carried only nineteen states. Just the same, working at the Dayton clinic that summer was not easy. Protests spilled into the streets from dawn well into the night.[22] Operation Rescue called the event "The Return to Truth," a reference not only to biblical teachings but to what blockaders saw as the scientific truth justifying their opposition to abortion. Similar arguments seemed to play well in popular politics. "Partial-birth abortion," NRLC explained in a 1997 fundraising letter, "dramatically proves everything we have always said—and that is that abortion deliberately kills a precious child." Unresolved questions about dilation and extraction further energized NRLC. In 1997, the executive committees of both the American Medical Association (AMA) and the American College of Obstetricians and Gynecologists (ACOG) issued statements that they could find no case in which dilation and extraction was the only procedure that could protect a patient's life or health. At the same time, both organizations insisted that physicians needed to have the option of performing any procedure, including dilation and extraction, that would be best for an individual patient. Statements like those made by the AMA and ACOG energized NRLC leaders who wanted to focus on partial-birth abortion.[23]

While dismissing a strategy centered on partial-birth abortion, Harold Cassidy also stressed arguments about *Roe* and science. A New Jersey attorney and former Democrat, Cassidy had made a name himself representing genetic parents in surrogacy and adoption cases. This work convinced him that mothers have a fundamental right to a relationship with their children before and after birth, and that conviction moved him to join the pro-life movement. In the mid-1990s, he launched a new litigation effort called the Global Project, centered on a plaintiff whom Cassidy called Donna Santa Marie. According to Cassidy, Santa Marie had not wanted an abortion and said so at a clinic, which then turned her away, but her parents kept pressuring her. A second clinic, she said, had terminated her pregnancy after asking no questions. Cassidy planned to use her case to show that *Roe* ran contrary to established scientific evidence—and that the Court had substituted political preferences for hard data. "The Santa Marie case," he wrote, "has assembled a team of scientists and doctors who have established that new recombinant DNA technology establishes that life begins at conception."[24] Scientific evidence did not tell a story as neat as Cassidy would have suggested—pro-choice groups responded that while an individual's DNA did not change after conception, when life began remained more contested as both a philosophical and religious matter. Nevertheless, Cassidy's argument had a clear appeal to many in the anti-abortion movement, especially those looking for an alternative to Operation Rescue. The murders of Drs. David Gunn and John Britton in 1993 and 1994 intensified demands for protections of abortion clinic employees and damaged the reputation of clinic blockaders. By 1994, Congress had passed the Freedom of Access to Clinic Entrances Act (FACE Act), which made it a federal crime to use force against, threaten force against, or physically obstruct those entering clinics. The tough new penalties put in place by the FACE Act deterred all but the most dedicated blockaders. In any case, the blockade movement had been divided by the issue of violence against abortion providers, with some members of Operation Rescue debating when the killings of abortion doctors might be justified. Weakened, smaller, and radicalized, Operation Rescue could no longer challenge organizations like the National Right to Life Committee for dominance, but many right-to-lifers were still looking for an alternative plan of attack, and Harold Cassidy appeared to have identified one.[25]

The effort immediately attracted the support of major players in the right-to-life movement. Robert George, a leading pro-life scholar, worked with Cassidy on the project, and Paul Weyrich, the founding father of the New Right, allowed Cassidy to hold the project's first meetings in the offices of the Committee for the Survival of a Free Congress. Cassidy planned to expose the political rot he saw at the heart of *Roe*'s scientific conclusions and "establish . . . that there is a separate, complete, unique human being throughout the gestational period." While NRLC and Cassidy agreed that *Roe* stood in tension with science, Cassidy suggested that better research could lead to the elimination of abortion rights.[26]

Bans on partial-birth abortion began to make their way through the courts. In July 1998, a district court ruled that a Nebraska law prohibiting a procedure whereby a doctor "partially delivers vaginally a living unborn child before killing the unborn child and completing the delivery" was unconstitutional as applied to Dr. LeRoy Carhart and his patients. After an appellate court upheld that ruling, the Supreme Court agreed to hear the case.[27]

Anti-abortion briefs in *Stenberg v. Carhart* stressed that *Roe*'s supporters ignored science whenever it suited them. PHACT argued that dilation and extraction was never medically necessary, even though "abortion rights orientated experts were clearly willing to go into federal court and testify as to the efficacy of the D&X."[28] Abortion rights supporters fired back that dilation and extraction had undeniable medical benefits for some patients—and that if there was genuine scientific uncertainty, the High Court should break the tie in favor of preserving women's health. "Especially for women with particular health conditions," the American College of Obstetricians and Gynecologists and other amici argued, "there is medical evidence that D&X may be safer than available alternatives."[29]

In a 5–4 decision issued in June 2000, the Court in *Stenberg v. Carhart* struck down Nebraska's law. The majority reasoned that the law was unconstitutionally vague because it did not clearly define the procedure that was prohibited—and potentially swept in dilation and evacuation, the safest and most common second-trimester procedure. The Court acknowledged disputes about the need for a health exception but suggested that *Roe* and *Casey* rightly relied on individual physicians to use "appropriate medical judgment for the preservation of the life or health of the mother." The *Stenberg* opinion suggested that *Roe* resolved scientific disputes by deferring to doctors with the most expertise on abortion and the best information about their patients' needs. The uncertainty about the need for dilation and extraction, wrote Justice Stephen Breyer for the majority, meant that there was "a significant likelihood that those who believe that D&X is a safer abortion method in certain circumstances may turn out to be right. . . . If so, then the absence of a health exception will place women at an unnecessary risk of tragic health consequences."[30]

Writing in dissent, Justice Anthony Kennedy suggested that the government had an important interest in preventing the medical profession or the broader society from becoming "insensitive, even disdainful, to life." As for scientific uncertainty, lawmakers had the right to "take sides in a medical debate, even when fundamental liberty interests are at stake and even when leading members of the profession disagree with the conclusions drawn by the legislature." When scientific evidence was disputed, Kennedy suggested, *Roe*'s deference to physicians did not make sense. The more uncertainty there was, the freer legislators should be to make their own judgments—and take into account their moral objections to abortion.[31]

Kennedy's dissent energized right-to-lifers who wanted to tie *Roe* to the politicization of science. Doug Johnson and other NRLC leaders believed that the partial-birth abortion ban had raised questions about the science underlying *Roe* and "turned many Americans away from support for abortion in general."[32] Harold Cassidy, who did not see the partial-birth abortion strategy as particularly effective, still favored what he described as a science-centered alternative. "The unstated premise of the Global Project," he explained, "is that the Justices of the United States Supreme Court do not understand the nature of abortion and that if they are only given the necessary scientific and medical data, they will recognize the error of their ways and overrule *Roe*." In 2000, he received a query from Norma McCorvey, the Roe in *Roe v. Wade*, who said she now regretted her involvement in the case. McCorvey had become pro-life in 1995 and wanted to see if she could get the decision reversed.[33]

Cassidy forwarded her request to Allan Parker, a San Antonio attorney whose Justice Foundation, a nonprofit founded in 1993, specialized in fighting for school choice for conservative parents. Parker began representing both McCorvey and Sandra Cano, the Doe in *Doe v. Bolton*, who also felt guilty about her involvement in the creation of abortion rights (neither woman had actually had an abortion). Parker and Cassidy believed that if they could make *Roe* a symbol of the politicization of science (and present evidence of the damage done by abortion), the Supreme Court might be persuaded to reverse it. At a 2001 anti-abortion rally at Savannah Rapids Pavilion, Parker introduced an initiative he called Operation Outcry, a plan to collect five thousand affidavits from women who regretted their abortions. *Roe* had put politics before evidence, Parker claimed; Operation Outcry would "establish a tidal wave of truth to sweep across America."[34]

But while right-to-lifers and supporters of abortion rights both claimed to have science on their side, both sides stressed that moral and constitutional norms should guide debate. While it accused the opposition of playing politics with medical evidence, NRLC primarily viewed partial-birth abortion as an ethical rather than medical issue. "As Americans have come to understand that partial-birth abortion is a terrible evil," NRLC leaders explained to their members, "they are also realizing that any abortion is wrong."[35] NARAL and Planned Parenthood identified *Roe* with respect for scientific evidence but thought that science alone could not resolve conflicts about partial-birth abortion. The issue, NARAL's leaders suggested, came down to "women's moral capacity to make complex reproductive decisions."[36]

The rise of the conservative media fueled the right's growing distrust of the scientific establishment. In the mid-1990s, Rush Limbaugh helped to make conservative talk radio a national phenomenon. Later in the decade, he and other conservative hosts took on several scientific topics, chief among them climate change. Researchers had been sounding the alarm about the damaging effects of man-made global warming for over a decade, and in 1997, as part of the Kyoto Protocol, industrialized nations agreed to cut their CO_2 emissions. In 2001, however, George W. Bush, the new Republican president, backed out of that commitment. Limbaugh and other conservative commentators cheered Bush's decision and argued that fears of climate change were left-wing scaremongering, not hard science (despite mounting evidence of climate change, Limbaugh often proclaimed that the "environmentalist wackos are going wacko").[37]

The conservative media's coverage of autism and its alleged connection to common childhood vaccines reinforced its audience's distrust of elite science. After the Centers for Disease Control and Prevention reported an increase in autism in the late 1990s, physician Andrew Wakefield published a 1998 article linking the disorder to vaccines for measles, mumps, and rubella. Researchers debunked Wakefield's conclusions, criticized his research methods, and revealed that he had received money from plaintiffs suing vaccine manufacturers. Nevertheless, an anti-vaccine movement flourished in the United States. In 2000, Republican representative Dan Burton of Indiana held hearings on the connection between vaccines and autism. Parent groups formed to advocate against vaccines, suggesting that doctors were ignoring inconvenient truths.[38]

Distrust of the legacy media deepened the growing suspicion of elite scientific organizations, including those that weighed in on the abortion debate. Limbaugh often made the media part of the story. He noted that with all the coverage devoted to global warming, only Fox News, a right-leaning twenty-four-hour news channel founded in 1996, frequently brought on climate change skeptics. Conservatives burnished their credentials by arguing that the science was unsettled, and the legacy media refused to say so. Distrust of medical authority and the legacy media shaped the conversation about *Roe* too. Right-to-life leaders sometimes drew support from medical organizations in the fight against partial-birth abortion, but when the experts failed to support right-to-lifers' claims, groups like NRLC insisted that the process had never been fair, because organizations like the American College of Obstetricians and Gynecologists had a pro-abortion bias that slanted their analysis. *Roe*, they suggested, was the ultimate symbol of the media and medical elites' willingness to ignore scientific evidence that did not suit their agenda.[39]

In Martin Haskell's view, there was no bona fide medical disagreement about the benefits of dilation and extraction. He served as an expert witness in several constitutional challenges to bans on the procedure, and through the late 1990s and early 2000s, he continued performing abortions in his clinics. Public debate around partial-birth abortion had made him even more of a target. In Dayton, a local medical association mulled taking action against him for performing what members viewed as an advanced surgical procedure outside a hospital without being board certified. William Stalter, the head of the county medical association, told the press that Haskell was "performing a terrible, hellacious procedure—he's sucking the brains out of babies."[40]

If Haskell tried to keep a low profile, George Tiller was defiant. In 2001, Operation Rescue returned to Wichita, and John Ashcroft, a staunch opponent of abortion who was then the U.S. attorney general, assigned U.S. marshals to protect Tiller, who seemed to almost enjoy the fight. In 2002, Tiller had offered free abortions to celebrate the twenty-ninth anniversary of the *Roe* decision—something that became an annual tradition until his death. In 2003, when George W. Bush signed the federal Partial-Birth Abortion Ban Act into law, Operation Rescue put out a press release calling Tiller "the most experienced partial-birth abortionist in the world" even though he rarely performed any dilation and extraction procedures.[41]

Haskell, meanwhile, had more legal troubles. In 2003, inspectors with Ohio's state health department accused him of illegally running an outpatient surgical center without a license or transfer privileges at a local hospital. After he was unable to reach an agreement for his Dayton center, he asked for a waiver, was refused, and had to close the facility. He went to court and argued that the licensure requirement was unconstitutional. Again, he identified *Roe* not only with respect for medical evidence but with deference to the doctors who best understood their patients. These arguments had mixed results in the lower courts: a district court blocked enforcement of the transfer requirement in 2003, but not much later, the Sixth Circuit Court of Appeals upheld a revamped version of the state's partial-birth-abortion ban, reasoning that the law's health exception was broad enough to protect patients.[42]

The focus on partial-birth abortion suited what was left of Operation Rescue, which positioned *Roe* as a symbol of the elites' willingness to ignore the biblical and scientific truth about life in the womb. In 2002, Troy Newman, a former engineer who had quit his job to work for Operation Rescue, moved his splinter group (formerly Operation Rescue West) to Wichita to torment Tiller full time. Newman's group launched the Truth Truck, a white Isuzu plastered with gruesome images of abortion, that drove around the country proclaiming that *Roe* was built on lies.[43]

By 2005, constitutional challenges to the federal Partial-Birth Abortion Ban Act were making their way to the Supreme Court. That year, however, Sandra Day O'Connor announced she was retiring to take care of her husband, who had Alzheimer's disease. Then Chief Justice William Rehnquist passed away after a battle with cancer, giving President Bush the chance to put two new justices on the Supreme Court. John Roberts, the boyish circuit judge whom Bush made chief justice, had worked on anti-abortion briefs in the president's father's administration. Samuel Alito, a judge on the Third Circuit Court of Appeals, also had a track record of anti-abortion work while serving in the Reagan administration and had been the only judge in the *Casey* litigation to hold that spousal involvement requirements were constitutional.[44]

When the Court agreed to hear *Gonzales v. Carhart*, the case challenging the federal partial-birth abortion law, arguments about *Roe* and the politicization of science set the terms of debate. The Center for Reproductive Rights (formerly the Center for Reproductive Law and Policy), which took the lead in challenging the statute, contended that there was more research than ever backing the need for dilation and extraction. In the center's brief, *Roe* stood for patients' ability to get the best care, backed by the strongest scientific evidence. Relying on data suggesting that dilation and extraction was the safest procedure for certain patients, doctors' amicus briefs argued that "physicians' ethical commitments to their patients require that they maximize patient safety within the parameters of learned professional judgment."[45] Stressing that *Roe* gave physicians the ability to rely on the most current data (more of which by the mid-2000s backed the idea that dilation and extraction was the most suitable choice for some patients), ACOG asserted that there was a clear-cut "medical consensus" that "dilation and extraction offers health benefits."[46]

Congress responded that the apparent consensus cited by ACOG was a result of the "disparate treatment" of doctors who opposed abortion.[47] *Roe*, they suggested, was the work of a politicized judiciary and medical establishment. The American Center for Law and Justice argued that scientific conclusions about the safety of *any* abortion had been hopelessly compromised. "This Court should take with a very large grain of salt any assertion that abortion is healthy for women, much less some sort of panacea," the group argued in its brief.[48] The Thomas More Law Center linked *Roe* to "propaganda," not science, and charged that "partial-birth abortion supporters have no problem deceiving the public in order to advance their agenda."[49]

Allan Parker's Operation Outcry also weighed in on *Roe*'s relationship to science. The brief stressed "extensive evidence" gathered by state and federal lawmakers on the safety of abortion. Medical researchers, the brief suggested, had not always acknowledged the harm done to women because they did not want to admit to anything that would damage abortion rights. The same was true of the *Roe* opinion, in which the justices had manipulated the facts to reach their desired result. "The evidence from post-abortive women," the brief argued, "now shows that abortion is merely a short-term 'solution' with long-term negative physical and psychological consequences."[50]

In *Gonzales v. Carhart*, the Court offered a quite different view of the relationship between *Roe* and science than the one set out in *Stenberg* just seven years before. The justices ultimately voted 5–4 to uphold the federal Partial-Birth Abortion Ban, with Justice Anthony Kennedy, the most notable dissenter in *Stenberg*, writing the majority opinion. Rather than suggest that *Roe* rightly let physicians resolve uncertain medical questions, Kennedy's opinion implied that legislators were better suited to resolve ambiguous scientific matters, using moral as well as medical judgment. The line between politics and science was not always clear in the abortion debate, he implied, and politicians sometimes could do just as well as abortion providers in telling the two apart. He opened the opinion with two competing descriptions of dilation and extraction, one offered by Haskell and one from Haskell's former nurse, Brenda Shafer, who had joined the anti-abortion movement. Kennedy repeated Haskell's description of steps in the procedure involving the placement of "scissors into the base of the skull" and use of a suction catheter to "evacuate the skull contents." He then repeated Shafer's description of the "baby's arms jerking out" before the doctor "sucked the brains out." When thus placed side by side, the two accounts suggested that there might be no single, objective way to view dilation and extraction, and that disgust with the procedure—and moral objections to it—had just as much validity as a dispassionate medical description.[51]

Kennedy next considered whether the government had an adequate justification for passing its law. There were, he said, new governmental interests supporting the bill, such as a desire to ensure that people respected fetal life or a wish to preserve the reputation of the medical profession. He also relied on Allan Parker's brief to suggest that scientists had discounted the experiences of women who had regretted their decision to end a pregnancy. There were, he acknowledged, no "reliable data to measure the phenomenon," but he took Cano's brief, together with common sense, as proof that many women agonized over their abortions and suffered "severe depression and loss of esteem." *Roe* had equated scientific knowledge with the conclusions of organizations like the American Medical Association and ACOG, but Kennedy's opinion in *Gonzales* suggested that *Roe* was wrong to give the medical establishment a monopoly on scientific truth.[52]

Kennedy reached a similar conclusion on the need for a health exception. He opened his opinion by stressing that "the evidence presented in the trial courts and before Congress demonstrates both sides have medical support for their position." The quality of that evidence—and who found it convincing—did not change the Court's reasoning. The mere fact of "documented medical disagreement" was enough to give Congress freedom to act.[53]

Allan Parker saw the *Gonzales* decision as the beginning of an effort to use science to dismantle *Roe*. David Reardon, an engineer, launched the Elliot Institute, which funded studies suggesting that abortion caused post-traumatic stress (or that most women who had abortions were coerced into the procedure). Harold Cassidy promoted similar arguments as part of a sweeping informed consent law introduced in South Dakota, which required doctors to tell patients that a fetus or unborn child was a "whole, separate, unique, living human being" and that abortion increased the risk of certain health conditions, including suicidal ideation. Parker compared his movement's work "to the long struggle to inform Americans about the risks of smoking." *Roe*, he suggested, had buried the scientific truth, but anti-abortion activists would bring it to light.[54]

As devastating as *Gonzales* was to Martin Haskell, he was relieved the following year when the Ohio Department of Health dropped its efforts to close his Dayton clinic, the only one operating in the area. In 2008, Haskell finally found three physicians at Miami Valley Hospital willing to sign a transfer agreement. The hospital also agreed to take those who suffered complications if none of the three physicians were available.[55]

National Right to Life Committee leaders were happy to equate Haskell with *Roe* itself. Building on arguments about fetal pain forged during the conflict over partial-birth abortion, the organization began sponsoring laws that banned abortion at twenty weeks, the point at which a handful of physicians said a fetus could experience pain. Most researchers believed fetal pain was not possible until some point in the third trimester, but Doug Johnson and his colleagues at the National Right to Life Committee questioned those scientists' integrity. As a matter of legal doctrine, National Right to Life could encourage state and federal lawmakers to pass "pain-capable" laws because the Supreme Court might uphold any provision involving a matter the justices considered scientifically uncertain. Politically, these laws offered a platform for arguments that *Roe* had ignored the science to advance a pro-abortion agenda.[56]

In 2009, supporters of pain-capable bills tapped into a broader distrust of leading scientific organizations. Conservative media, together with social media platforms like Facebook, stoked doubt about everything from the safety of vaccines to the plausibility of global warming. In 2002, the National Vaccine Injury Compensation Program had set up its Omnibus Autism Proceeding to aggregate autism-based lawsuits against the federal government. Congress assigned initial management of cases to eight special masters, subordinate officials appointed by the U.S. Court of Federal Claims. The first major case, *Cedillo v. Department of Health and Human Services,* had begun two years earlier when the parents of a girl with autism and other disabilities argued that her condition was caused by two government-mandated vaccines. The Cedillos suggested that thimerosal, a vaccine ingredient, had degraded their daughter's immune system, and that a vaccine for measles, mumps, and rubella had given her a persistent infection that led to the development of autism. In 2009, three special masters concluded that there was inadequate proof that any vaccine or vaccine ingredient caused Cedillo's autism, a ruling that only seemed to energize the anti-vaccine movement. Rebecca Estepp, a leading anti-vaccine activist, dismissed the outcome as typical of a biased justice system. "The deck is stacked against families in vaccine court," she said. "Government attorneys defend a government program, using government-funded science, before government judges."[57]

The same distrust of scientific elites fueled conservative hostility to policies on climate change. Following his 2008 election, President Barack Obama pushed what politicians called a cap-and-trade bill, which would set progressively tighter limits on the total emissions of greenhouse gases and allow companies to buy and sell permits to emit those gases. The House narrowly passed the bill in June 2009, but Republicans rallied against it, and the Senate never brought it to a vote. "We all know it's a scam," one climate skeptic said of cap and trade.[58]

These conflicts, like clashing interpretations of *Roe,* reflected the unsettled debate over the proper role of science in setting public policy.

While fights about the dilation and extraction procedure raged on, pro-life groups identified *Roe* with a pervasive political correctness that had compromised the scientific establishment. Abortion rights groups responded that *Roe* had freed doctors from politics and allowed them to focus on what their patients needed. But at times, both abortion foes and abortion rights supporters insisted that science alone should not determine abortion policy; moral and ethical questions should inform and sometimes override scientific conclusions. The more Americans talked about *Roe* and science, the more contradictions emerged.

The politics of science took a more personal toll on Martin Haskell. In May 2009, his wife told him that Scott Roeder, an anti-abortion extremist, had murdered his friend George Tiller at a time when his luck finally seemed to have turned. Kansas had an unusual procedure whereby citizens could demand a grand jury proceeding by collecting a requisite number of signatures. In 2008, anti-abortion activists had mustered enough support to convene a grand jury, and for six months, citizens in Sedgwick County, Kansas, met to investigate Tiller's practice. At the end, no indictments were issued, but he was back in court a few months later, this time facing nineteen misdemeanor charges for performing an abortion without seeking a second opinion, as required by state law (Kansas prosecutors alleged that the doctor with whom Tiller conferred worked for him and thus could not, under state law, give a second opinion). A jury acquitted him in March 2009. Less than three months later, he was dead.[59]

Tiller had been serving as an usher at church when Roeder murdered him. Roeder, it turned out, had attended Tiller's trial and tried to glue shut the doors to his clinic; he wrote on an Operation Rescue message board that Tiller ran "a concentration camp" and needed "to be stopped before he and those who protect him bring judgment upon our nation." As always, Tiller was wearing body armor, but it did not matter. Roeder shot him in the head at point-blank range.[60]

Tiller was fond of catchphrases, "Tillerisms," as his friends called them, and he liked to tell Martin Haskell that nothing could stop a determined assassin. Like Tiller, Haskell was on a top ten list of possible targets of anti-abortion violence. He too had taken precautions; he drove to work in an armored vehicle and had an armed security guard to accompany him. And like Tiller, he found some solace in his faith.[61]

Even after Tiller's murder, Haskell often felt some empathy for the people who hated him so much. Right-to-lifers described him as a monster, someone shielded by the bogus science at the heart of the *Roe* opinion. Abortion rights supporters sometimes treated him as a hero, a doctor willing to sacrifice everything to speak the truth about *Roe* and the science of abortion. Haskell himself mostly felt sadness for anti-abortion activists, who seemed to him misguided and unable to understand the pain of others while still calling themselves Christian. He did not stop performing abortions after George Tiller's murder. The thing that haunted him most was that decades after missing the funeral of his beloved Kate, his wife kept him from attending his friend's memorial service because she feared for his safety. More likely than not, he would have been next.[62]

6

Roe and Race

Questions of race had always shaped what Americans meant when they talked about *Roe*, but by the start of the twenty-first century, something felt different. Catherine Davis, one of those who transformed the conversation about *Roe* and race, grew up the second of three daughters in Southfield Village, a brick public housing complex in Stamford, Connecticut. It was a world away from where her parents' people came from, Halifax County, a green corner of southern Virginia where winter meant rain rather than ice. Catherine's father was a carpenter who struggled to get work because he was Black; the carpenters' unions in Stamford did their best to ensure that jobs went to white workers. Her mother worked as a maid for wealthy families in Greenwich.[1]

In Connecticut, Catherine could sometimes almost forget about her race, but in the summer, the Davises took their girls to the family homestead in Virginia. Once, Catherine went into the white part of a department store there and was grabbed by a manager. The only reason she was forgiven was that she was from Connecticut and had not known any better.[2]

Before long, Catherine Davis could not help but know. She got admitted to Tufts, moved to Medford, Massachusetts, and began studying the human mind. But she hated the dirty snow and the white neighborhoods where it was not safe for her to go. She worked through the summer to graduate a year early, and when she got pregnant, she had an abortion. She did not want a child, even though she knew her mother would have helped raise one. For that reason, Catherine could not bring herself to tell her. Abortions, her mother always said, were white women's nonsense.[3]

Davis graduated from college with a dual degree in psychiatry and education. A few years later, she got pregnant again; she was seeing an engineer, but she was not looking for marriage, and he was not asking. She had her son, began working on education at the Urban League, and started graduate school. She was living in her sister's basement and working on her degree while her son went to elementary school, but then she got pregnant again. After a second abortion, she swore never to repeat the experience.[4]

She found Jesus in 1984, moved to Virginia the following year, and began working for the state government. She struck up a relationship with a musician but eventually swore off sex outside of marriage. For her musician, that made her a challenge. She gave in to temptation one last time, but when she got pregnant, she kept her word and decided to carry the pregnancy to term. During her pregnancy, in 1987, abortion came up as a topic in church Bible study. Catherine had never discussed her abortion experience with anyone, but now she decided to face it. Her pastor prayed for her, conveyed the Lord's forgiveness, and gave her a book, *Grand Illusions: The Legacy of Planned Parenthood.* Davis devoured the book, which argued that Planned Parenthood had been founded by racists trying to destroy the Black community. She had always thought she could recognize bigots: she had seen the face of the man at the department store in Virginia, the kids screaming at her from car windows in Medford. But after the 1980s, as a working mother of two, she primarily came to associate racism with Planned Parenthood and its connection to *Roe v. Wade.*[5]

Kierra Johnson was a child when Catherine Davis first volunteered to be a speaker for Virginia Right to Life. Johnson was born in

Valdosta, Georgia, a flat country that produced pulpwood and lumber and turpentine. Her father was twenty years older than her mother and worked as a police officer near the Florida-Georgia line. Her mother, a military brat, had learned to adjust on the fly. She worked full-time for the Department of Justice, sometimes took extra jobs to make ends meet, and made time to help her two daughters with their homework.[6]

Kierra's younger sister, Amber, was three years younger but had the same birthday. Kierra was painfully shy, a super nerd who loved to make people laugh. Amber was dynamic, charismatic—the kind of person who had no trouble making new friends in a new school. That was a needed skill because the family was constantly on the move: first to Atlanta, then Aurora, Colorado. In Colorado, everyone they met asked them how they had overcome racism in the South. The truth was that things were worse in Aurora. One morning, when Amber got to middle school, she found a racial epithet spray-painted on her locker with a message telling her to "go home." Kierra, the only Black student in many of her high-school classes, felt alone calling out the racism she saw in the books she was assigned to read and the comments her teachers made. Once, her classmates performed in blackface at a school talent show.[7]

Kierra stayed in Colorado for college, but when she was a freshman, her parents and sister moved again, to Ft. Lauderdale, Florida. Over the next year, her parents separated and her father became ill. In her sophomore year, Amber called one night when Kierra was getting ready to go out with friends and told Kierra she was pregnant. Amber was sixteen years old.[8]

Kierra, who was part of student government in college, took a passionate interest in the abortion issue. When she saw her sister in Florida, her feelings were even clearer. Amber had made what everyone said was the right choice: decided against abortion, had her baby, and married the boy's father when she was nineteen. And yet when Amber went out with her son, everyone gave her judgmental looks. With another child on the way and little support from school, she struggled and eventually dropped out. Kierra supported a right to choose, but for Black women like her sister, it seemed that any choice they made was the wrong one, and people would scorn them for making it.[9]

Feeling helpless in the face of her father's illness, her parents' separation, and her sister's struggle to balance school and parenting, Kierra dropped out of college and headed for a new city, accepting a fellowship at Choice USA, a group founded in 1992 by Gloria Steinem, one of the nation's most famous feminists. Something else had changed as well: in 1999, on the way home to Colorado from the Gloria Steinem Leadership Institute, she met a woman who would later become her first girlfriend. Kierra believed passionately that choice requires not only the ability to decide whether to have a child but also the means to raise the children one wanted. In her early years at Choice USA, Kierra found that no one asked what reproductive justice actually meant. And as a queer person of color, she saw that Choice framed the issue in a way that made sense mostly to straight, white people. Reproductive justice, she thought, had to include talking about *Roe* in a way that made sense to people like her.[10]

The March for Women's Lives, a major pro-choice rally in April 2004, proved to be a turning point for young activists of color who wanted to revolutionize how people talked about *Roe*. The campaign to ban partial-birth abortion, championed by groups like NRLC, had brought a significant drop in support for legal abortion. In 1992, 67 percent of college-age women favored keeping abortion legal in all or most circumstances; by 2003, that number had fallen to 55 percent. Established pro-choice organizations like NARAL and Planned Parenthood responded by announcing a major protest in the nation's capital to build support for legal abortion among younger women.

Choice USA collaborated with a variety of organizations committed to reproductive rights and justice, including the National Latina Institute for Reproductive Health, the Pro-Choice Public Education Project, the Third Wave Fund, and the Civil Liberties and Public Policy Program at Hampshire College, to bring a bigger and more diverse group of advocates to the event. The leaders of these organizations, almost all women of color under thirty, demanded both decision-making power in organizing the march and time on the stage during the event.[11]

Among this new generation of leaders were Crystal Plati, the executive director of Choice USA, the daughter of immigrant parents from Cyprus; Silvia Henriquez, the head of the National Latina Institute for Reproductive Health and an immigrant from El Salvador; and Kalpana Krishnamurthy, the head of the feminist Third Wave Foundation, who saw *Roe* through the lens of debates in South Asia, where abortion was tied to issues ranging from economic independence to domestic violence. Like these advocates, the young people working at Choice USA had a different vision for the future of reproductive justice organizing. By 2001, nine years after its founding, Choice USA had chapters on forty college campuses, advocating for "the right of each person to decide when or if they will have sex, when or if they will be pregnant, and when or if they will have a child."[12] Steinem worried about the apathy of younger women and urged Plati and her colleagues to "nurture and develop the next generation of reproductive rights activists."[13]

But the young people and people of color working on the ground for Choice USA had broader ambitions—and a different perspective on how to redefine *Roe*. Rejecting the narrative that young people and people of color took abortion rights for granted, Kierra Johnson insisted that "real reproductive freedom is something that many young people have never known, whether it's because they can't afford the health care they need or because they haven't been informed of all their options." Getting younger people of color active was not about overcoming apathy but about "giving people the tools, networks, support, and opportunities they need to define the movement and be effective leaders."[14]

The March for Women's Lives crystallized the concerns of many people of color who were frustrated with messaging around *Roe*. In October 2003, Loretta Ross, a Black reproductive justice activist, warned that people of color felt so marginalized by the event's organizers that they were "prepared en masse to reject the March, particularly at grassroots level."[15] But rather than reject the march, Johnson believed that people of color had "enough clout not to be marginalized" and could change the way the event was structured.[16] She was right: after an extensive push, activists of color successfully demanded that the march focus not on arguments about choice but on claims about the lives of pregnant people and "political and social justice for women and girls regardless of their race, economic, religious, ethnic or cultural circumstances." As important, organizations that advocated for reproductive justice for people of color, including SisterSong, joined the event's steering committee (Ross eventually became the march's co-director).[17]

Activists of color who met to plan the march, including Ross, described how pro-choice messaging should change. "We've made it legal, but we haven't made it safe," one advocate explained. "We've made it medically safe, but not socially safe."[18] "When we define choice," Plati said, "it's about a woman's right to decide if and when she will have sex, if and when she will get pregnant, if and when she will carry a pregnancy to term, and if and when she will raise a child."[19]

After 2007, questions of race took on additional importance in the abortion debate. The election of a Black, pro-choice president encouraged those on both sides to use *Roe* to talk about the relationship between reproductive and racial justice. Anti-abortion activists, tracing a direct line from the eugenics movement of the early twentieth century to the contemporary pro-choice movement, blamed high abortion rates in communities of color on the racism of abortion providers and of those who defended *Roe*. The racist eugenics movement was still decimating communities of color, they argued, and *Roe* was part of it. Pro-choice groups often responded that the decision pointed toward a more comprehensive program of reproductive justice that people of color badly needed. It had given many people of color access to safe, legal care for the first time, giving them more of a say about when they became parents and helping them seek better lives in the face of ongoing discrimination.

These contradictory positions reflected complicated questions about reproduction and race. While zeroing in on real disparities in access to services, pro-choice groups had just begun to grapple with the very real history of racism in the family planning movement, and how that history limited the available choices in the present day. The mainstream pro-choice movement still sometimes praised the founders of the family planning movement as heroes and played down issues, like the ban on Medicaid funding of abortions, that most affected people of color. Right-to-life groups, by contrast, often conflated the movements for eugenics, population control, and legal abortion, framing racism as intentional rather than structural. These arguments, too, oversimplified the nature of the discrimination that drove people of color to have abortions at disparately high rates—and denied the responsibility of the government in creating conditions that made it hard for people of color to raise children. These difficult conversations—about the costs of and constraints on reproductive choice for people of color—surfaced in the contradictory ways that people like Catherine Davis and Kierra Johnson described *Roe v. Wade*.

The stakes in the debate over *Roe* and race grew alongside public awareness of racial disparities in abortion rates. In 2008, the *Washington Post* and other media outlets reported on a major study by the Guttmacher Institute, the research arm of Planned Parenthood, showing that the racial demographics of abortion had changed dramatically since 1973. While abortion rates had fallen in all racial groups between 1974 and 2004, they fell more slowly for people of color, who made up a growing percentage of the total number of procedures performed. By 2004, Latina women were ending their pregnancies at a rate more than twice that of white women; the rate for Black women was nearly five times higher. The more attention focused on racial disparities in abortion rates, the more forcefully antiabortion leaders connected *Roe* to racism. "The primary agenda," wrote Randall K. O'Bannon in the *National Right to Life News*, "has never been women's health or their liberation, but control of their fertility for eugenic purposes."[20]

Catherine Davis had always seen these arguments as central. She had left Virginia in 1995 when her pastor moved to Georgia. At the time, the state legislature was considering a bill that would downsize the state workforce and provide terminated employees with some severance pay. Unsure about whether to follow her pastor to Georgia, Davis decided that if the bill passed, it meant God wanted her to move. It did, and she resettled her two kids in Gwinnett County, Georgia, in 1995. At a bus stop one winter day after she moved, another child shot her daughter with a BB gun, but because Davis's child was wearing a puffy winter coat, she was not seriously injured. Furious about how law enforcement handled the matter, Davis contacted her representative but was not given the help she wanted. She decided to run for office herself.[21]

As a Republican congressional candidate in a deeply Democratic district, she had no staff, less than $15,000 in the bank, and a full-time job as the regional manager for Sprint's Human Resources in the Southeast. Her platform denounced same-sex marriage and abortion, called for the abolition of the Internal Revenue Service, and promoted charter schools and voucher programs. To no one's surprise, she lost in 2002, 2004, and again in 2006. But she had found a community of likeminded Black Republicans. Davis had a finger on the pulse of how people like her thought about abortion. More and more, she thought, everyone was paying attention to the connection between *Roe* and race.[22]

Kierra Johnson had realized the same thing. But it seemed that mainstream pro-choice organizations like NARAL and Planned Parenthood continued to address their programming to white, straight, relatively well-to-do women—those the least likely to be affected by new restrictions on abortion or contraception. Donors, like the leaders of the wealthier pro-choice organizations, feared that changing messages might damage their cause. In 2005, for example, the Packard Foundation, a major donor to pro-choice organizations, ran a study on the pluses and minuses of different public relations campaigns around *Roe*. While acknowledging that connecting *Roe* to reproductive and racial justice would "reflect experience of women & families of color," the study suggested that reproductive justice messaging was insufficiently focused on abortion. By contrast, the study proposed that arguments about a right to choose were preferable because they reflected a "new willingness to acknowledge that abortion [was] undesirable" and made sense at a time when there was more "emphasis on birth control and prevention."[23] Other pro-choice focus group studies proposed similar strategies centered on "personal responsibility," calculated to appeal to voters unsure about abortion.[24]

In the latter half of the 2000s, however, groups like the National Organization for Women and NARAL did at times emphasize arguments about reproductive justice. But arguments about a right to choose or even the importance of personal responsibility remained prominent. "Our vigorous defense of the right to choose," wrote Kate Michelman of NARAL and Frances Kissling, the former head of Catholics for Free Choice and a fellow at Harvard's Radcliffe Institute, "needs to be accompanied by greater openness regarding the real conflict between life and choice, between rights and responsibility." Emphasizing questions of race still sometimes struck the leaders of groups like NARAL as unnecessary or unwise.[25] Frustrated that people of color continued to be marginalized, Johnson argued that the fate of *Roe v. Wade* meant the most to people of color, and people of color were the least likely to have real reproductive autonomy. "Those who are the most threatened are the most likely to fight," she said in 2007. "It's absurd to leave them on the sidelines."[26]

Barack Obama's election made the relationship between *Roe* and racial politics even more salient. In one of the more surprising moments of the 2008 primary season, NARAL Pro-Choice America endorsed Obama over Hillary Clinton, one of the pro-choice movement's most vocal supporters over the past decade and a half. Historically, Blacks had tended to be more opposed to abortion than other racial groups (by 2009, this was no longer the case), but Obama's rise challenged this narrative. As Nancy Keenan of NARAL Pro-Choice America explained in 2008, the nation's first Black president would be the one to "decide *Roe*'s fate."[27]

Obama's ascendancy tied abortion rights to civil rights, making Black right-to-lifers even more committed to exposing what they saw as a history of racism shaping abortion law. Catherine Davis and her colleagues seized on the 2009 arrest of Walter Hoye, a Black Baptist minister from Berkeley, California, who routinely protested outside a clinic in Oakland's Alameda County, and engaged people entering the facility in what he called a "friendly conversation" to dissuade them from having abortions. A judge found that Hoye's activities violated

Oakland's 2008 bubble-zone ordinance, which created a one-hundred-foot protected area around reproductive health clinics. Within this area, the law prohibited anyone from approaching closer than eight feet of another individual for the purpose of counseling or protest. Jackie Barbic, the executive director of a clinic in West Oakland, argued that the law was necessary to protect patients from harassment and to prevent potential acts of violence against clinic staff (James Kopp, an anti-abortion activist who had once chained himself inside the Oakland clinic, had gone on to murder Dr. Barnett Slepian in Amherst, New York, in 1998). When Hoye continued approaching people outside the clinic, the judge convicted him of violating the ordinance, and Hoye argued that it violated his freedom of speech. Davis, in denouncing the judge's action, called *Roe* "government sponsored eugenics." The Supreme Court had sided "with those who want to exterminate Blacks."[28]

Kierra Johnson also wanted race to be more central to the way Americans talked about *Roe*, especially with Congress debating the Affordable Care Act (ACA), Obama's signature reform proposal. The ACA prohibited insurers from denying coverage for preexisting conditions, extended insurance options for parents of college-age children, created an individual mandate that required everyone to have insurance coverage or pay a penalty, and introduced health insurance exchanges in each state. In 2009, the bill seemed likely to pass because Democrats controlled both houses of Congress, but Representative Bart Stupak, a pro-life Democrat from Michigan, worried that the bill would lead to a massive outlay of federal money for abortion. Together with Republican Joe Pitts of Pennsylvania, Stupak proposed an amendment prohibiting the use of federal funds "to pay for any abortion or to cover any part of the costs of any health plan that includes coverage of abortion" except in cases of rape, incest, or a threat to the patient's life. Pro-choice groups, including Planned Parenthood, launched a Stop Stupak campaign to preserve the ACA's abortion coverage. Reproductive justice organizations joined the coalition as well, but they described their efforts in different terms. Johnson framed *Roe* as part of the struggle for justice not only for those seeking abortion but also for people of color, immigrants, and LGBTIQ Americans. "The same young people who are fighting to keep anti-abortion language out of the health care bills," she wrote, "are also fighting to ensure that lesbian, gay, bisexual, transgender people fit in to broader health care reform, making sure that immigrant women don't fall through the cracks."[29]

Behind the scenes, Obama negotiated with Stupak, promising an executive order barring the use of federal funds for abortion or for insurance plans covering it. Then, in the fall of 2009, Catherine Davis, Georgia Right to Life, and the Radiance Foundation, an Atlanta-based pro-life organization, paid to put up eighty billboards in metropolitan Atlanta denouncing *Roe* and proclaiming, "Black children are an endangered species." The billboards directed viewers to toomanyaborted.com, a website featuring claims that one of Margaret Sanger's goals in founding Planned Parenthood was to reduce the Black population.[30]

The Atlanta billboards galvanized a broader effort by anti-abortion groups to link *Roe* to racism, much of it led by white anti-abortion leaders with little history of focusing on racial issues. Davis's billboards brought new attention to *Maafa 21*, a film produced by Texas activist Mark Crutcher. Crutcher had made a name for himself in the 1990s by encouraging anti-abortion attorneys to bring medical malpractice lawsuits against abortion providers. In *Maafa 21*, Crutcher argued that *Roe* had led to "Black genocide in the twenty-first century." The film traced what he described as the origins and present-day influence of the eugenics movement on abortion and suggested that *Roe* made it possible for racists to decimate the Black community.

Critics responded that Margaret Sanger was not racist (or not especially so for her time) and that Black women *demanded* access to birth control and abortion, regardless of what Sanger had thought. Beyond the specifics of Crutcher's film, supporters of reproductive justice argued that relatively high rates of abortion in the Black and Latinx communities reflected a lack of access to resources and services, not any intentional racism by abortion providers.[31]

By 2010, arguments about race defined some of the most cutting-edge approaches to restricting abortion. Lila Rose, an undergraduate at the University of California, Los Angeles, founded a group called Live Action, which became known for slick viral videos claiming to expose the truth about Planned Parenthood. One high-profile video depicted a Planned Parenthood employee agreeing to a donation meant to pay for Black women's abortions. James O'Keefe, the pro-life activist masquerading as a donor, could be heard on tape saying, "The less black kids out there, the better." Rose's video, together with the Atlanta billboards and *Maafa 21*, energized the legislative effort to defund Planned Parenthood. Since the passage of the Hyde Amendment in 1976, Congress and many states had prohibited the use of Medicaid dollars for abortion, but right-to-life activists wanted to shut down all government sources of funding for Planned Parenthood, including state and federal family planning grants. Pro-life groups like Americans United for Life argued that because money is fungible, support for Planned Parenthood's family planning services would free up cash for abortions. In 2010, a handful of states proposed laws blocking Planned Parenthood and other entities that performed abortions from receiving Medicaid or family planning money of any kind, even to cover other services such as contraception or testing for sexually transmitted infections.[32]

Other states picked up on Catherine Davis's claims that women of color were being coerced into having abortions. In Georgia, Chip

Pearson, a Republican state senator from an affluent Atlanta suburb, championed a bill that created criminal punishments for encouraging a woman to have an abortion, prohibited doctors from targeting people of color, and banned the use of abortion for race or sex selection. "If there is one thing that we can do as legislators to protect the next generation," Pearson said, "it would be to make sure abortions are rare, uncoerced and not done to promote some . . . agenda related to the gender or race of the child."[33]

Such bills became easier to pass after the 2010 midterm election, which was a coming-out for the right-wing Tea Party. The Tea Party first emerged in 2009 after CNBC commentator Rick Santelli launched into a diatribe against President Obama's foreclosure relief plan, calling for a "tea party" of responsible Americans to fight the government's willingness to coddle irresponsible Americans at taxpayers' expense. Soon, self-proclaimed Tea Party groups spread across the country, with local chapters founded by mostly white, middle-class Americans angry about what they saw as policies privileging the interests of immigrants, young people, and people of color. Major conservative donors fueled the Tea Party's rise. FreedomWorks, launched in 2004 with the aid of conservative megadonors David and Charles Koch, spent $10 million in 2010 to put Tea Party candidates in office. Its sister organization, Americans for Prosperity (the two groups had emerged after an internal rift divided the Koch-founded Citizens for a Sound Economy in 2004), spent over $30 million to sink Obama's proposed health care reform. This largesse was well spent: Republicans, who had held only thirty-three of ninety-nine state legislative chambers before 2010, gained control of fifty-three total chambers by the end of the election.[34]

Tea Partiers presented their cause as a fight for smaller government —the movement's "Contract from America" would have banned caps on carbon emissions, lowered taxes, balanced the budget, and repealed the Affordable Care Act. Neither abortion, immigration, nor racial justice made the list of priorities. But a string of racially charged incidents changed the narrative. In 2009 and early 2010, Tea Party rallies featured Confederate flags, racist jokes about President Obama, and claims that Obama was neither Christian nor an American citizen. Studies showed that Tea Party members were 25 percent more likely to be racially resentful than other respondents; other research found that nearly three-quarters of Tea Partiers thought Black Americans would "be as well off as whites if they just tried harder." To polish his movement's image, Matt Kibbe of FreedomWorks launched DiverseTea, a group designed to mobilize Tea Partiers of color, in September 2010. A month later, the NAACP issued a report that raised concerns about racism within the Tea Party, and polls continued to show that people of color were underrepresented in Tea Party organizations.[35]

On abortion, Tea Party Republicans in office began by using the playbook created by established anti-abortion groups like Americans United for Life, limiting the coverage of abortion on health insurance exchanges and requiring patients to view an ultrasound. By 2011, however, they were introducing new restrictions based on arguments about race and *Roe*. Lawmakers in Indiana, Wisconsin, and North Carolina proposed bills to defund Planned Parenthood; Arizona Republicans proposed a ban on abortions based on the fetus's race, sex, or disability. Tea Partiers responded to accusations of racism by turning them against Planned Parenthood.[36]

By 2013, Kierra and Amber Johnson found themselves in very different places. Kierra was married, proudly queer, and raising children while holding one of the most prominent jobs in the pro-choice movement. Amber was on a much harder path. She had taken years to finish her GED and struggled financially. She was twenty-four years old and divorced, with three children that her mother had to help her raise. She encountered more legal troubles, moved to Dallas, then had another son. Kierra, who believed wholeheartedly that her sister had the right to make her own reproductive decisions, saw at close hand what the liberty provided by *Roe* meant, not just for Amber but for her children and their grandmother. People of color might have a right to choose, Kierra thought, but they received no support for the decisions they made.[37]

The newly Republican state legislatures passed a record number of abortion restrictions in 2011—135 compared to just 89 the previous year. These legislators soon turned their attention to the arrest of a Black abortion doctor, Kermit Gosnell, in Philadelphia for murder. Gosnell grew up in the city, the only son of a gas station operator and a government clerk. As a young man, he had won acclaim for starting teen aid and drug rehabilitation programs in impoverished West Philadelphia. An early supporter of abortion rights, he opened his first clinic in 1972; by 2010, he was operating facilities in Philadelphia, Delaware, and Louisiana. But complaints piled up over the years, and in 2010, the Drug Enforcement Agency raided the Philadelphia clinic after an investigation turned up illegal drug use at the facility. The raid revealed that clinic staff had killed a patient, Karnamaya Mongar, a refugee from Myanmar, by giving her an accidental overdose of a powerful painkiller. Gosnell was charged with involuntary manslaughter in Mongar's death; he faced seven additional counts of first-degree murder and a slew of lesser charges for killing children born alive after abortions by "snipping" their spinal cords. Reports described horrific conditions inside Gosnell's clinic, with blood on the floors and furniture, and unsterile medical equipment.[38]

Gosnell became a symbol of the intersection of *Roe* and racial politics. In Congress, Mike Pence, the third-highest-ranking House Republican (and future vice president), invoked *Roe* and Gosnell in his efforts to deny federal funding to Planned Parenthood. Billboards about racism and abortion appeared in New York City, Chicago, and

California. Right-to-lifers, many of them white, presented Gosnell as the real face of the abortion rights movement. "Margaret Sanger, founder of Planned Parenthood once said, 'more children from the fit, less from the unfit,' " said Black pro-life activist Reverend Clenard Childress Jr. "That's the ideology at work here."[39]

Abortion rights supporters presented *Roe* as a ruling that spared people of color from having to undergo dangerous abortions like the ones offered at Gosnell's clinic. *Roe*, they argued, alleviated some of the painful effects of racial discrimination by allowing people of color access to safe and legal abortion.[40]

While Black right-to-lifers like Catherine Davis wanted to situate *Roe* in a broader conversation about racism, groups like AUL often found it inconvenient to talk about the race of Gosnell's patients, or of those who worked at the clinic. Marjorie Dannenfelser, the head of the Susan B. Anthony List, a well-funded nonprofit that worked to elect pro-life candidates, described Gosnell's case as a reminder that "exploitation of women and complete disregard for their health and well-being are problems endemic to the entire abortion industry."[41] Charmaine Yoest of Americans United for Life used the trial as evidence of "an unimpeachable case for better regulation of the abortion industry."[42]

By 2012, Americans United for Life and the National Right to Life Committee were using the case to promote their existing agendas. AUL championed legislation designed to protect children born alive after an abortion. George W. Bush had signed the federal Born-Alive Infants Protection Act in 2002, extending legal protections to infants born after an attempted abortion, but Yoest thought the law did not spell out the standard of care required of doctors should an infant survive an abortion. NLRC used the case to draw attention to its legislative priority since 2009, the Pain-Capable Unborn Child Protection Act, which would ban abortion at twenty weeks, the point at which NRLC said fetal pain was possible.[43]

In May 2013, a jury convicted Gosnell of three counts of murder, one count of involuntary manslaughter, and over two hundred lesser charges. He agreed not to appeal his conviction to avoid a possible death sentence. Response to his trial reflected the contradictory ways that people discussed abortion and race. At first, right-to-lifers presented Gosnell as a product of the world *Roe* had created—one in which people of color and their unborn children were the targets of a particularly pernicious form of racism. Abortion rights supporters responded that Gosnell was the exception who proved the rule. People of color had the most to gain from safe, legal abortion, and they had benefited most from its legalization under *Roe*. Kermit Gosnell, a Black man who had once helped the community he later victimized, complicated both narratives. So did Gosnell's patients.[44]

The story of racism in Mantua, the West Philadelphia neighborhood where Gosnell operated, little resembled the black-and-white narrative set out in films like *Maafa 21*. Mantua came into existence because of redlining, a policy introduced in 1933 by the Home Owners' Loan Corporation, a program intended to expand home ownership. Corporation staff flagged majority Black neighborhoods as risky zones for investment and disqualified people in those neighborhoods from receiving home loans. In Mantua, redlining led to disinvestment in infrastructure and schools, residential segregation, poverty (more than half of Mantua's residents lived below the poverty line in 2018), and poor health outcomes, including higher rates of cancer, mental illness, preterm births, and tuberculosis. Anti-abortion leaders seeking to make *Roe* a symbol of intentional racism neglected these messier questions about the legacy of racism and how it shaped the choices of Gosnell's patients.[45]

But dismissing Gosnell as an outlier while defending *Roe* as a guarantor of safe health care for people of color also glossed over important complexities. Gosnell was exceptionally indifferent to the safety of his patients and to the line between infanticide and abortion.

But the fact that people in communities like Mantua had abortions at higher rates suggested that the broader society was failing poor people of color in ways that pro-choice leaders did not always know how to overcome or even discuss. The more complex questions of race became, the easier it was to drop the subject altogether.

By the summer of 2013, Americans United for Life had done just that. Denise Burke, the legislative director of AUL's biggest post-Gosnell initiative, the Women's Protection Project, did not even mention race when promoting a mandate that abortion clinics have admitting privileges at a hospital within thirty miles. AUL also promoted legislation requiring clinics to comply with the rules governing ambulatory surgical centers. Texas passed this package of restrictions in 2013 after a fierce legislative debate in which Kermit Gosnell's name came up frequently; racial issues, much less so. "Texas' common-sense regulation of Big Abortion has broad public support for good reason," explained Charmaine Yoest.[46]

On the pro-choice side, meanwhile, the movement for reproductive justice was gaining influence. Groups like NARAL and Planned Parenthood had for decades played down policies that disproportionately affected people of color, partly because those programs seemed less inspiring to major donors and Democratic Party bigwigs. Rarely, for example, did these organizations focus on eliminating the Hyde Amendment, the ban on Medicaid funding for abortion that Congress had passed (and still passes) every year since 1978. When reproductive justice organizers called for a broader agenda, groups like Planned Parenthood sometimes demurred. In Mississippi in 2011, for instance, the organization fought a "personhood amendment" that would have criminalized all abortions in the state, while ignoring a voter identification law that some reproductive justice activists in the state opposed.[47]

If larger pro-choice organizations did not initially broaden their focus, by the mid-2010s there was a flourishing parallel reproductive

justice movement. In 2014, Kierra Johnson's Choice USA renamed itself
Unite for Reproductive and Gender Equity (URGE) to reflect its
broader reform platform. The same approach energized students across
college campuses, who reframed what it meant to defend *Roe v. Wade*.
On the Amherst campus of the University of Massachusetts, for example, a student organization celebrated the anniversary of *Roe* by commit-
ting to address "diverse issues like poverty, immigration reform, queer
rights and racial justice that are all deeply connected to the fight for reproductive justice."[48] Reproductive justice organizations like the Sister-
Song Reproductive Justice Collective (founded in 1997) and the Black
Women's Health Imperative (formed in 1984) not only addressed other
issues, from immigration to sex education to voting rights, but also pow-
erfully explained how abortion restrictions affected people of color.[49]

After 2014, the larger, older pro-choice groups increasingly began
to grapple with intersectionality and the need to connect abortion
rights to a broader reproductive justice analysis. In part, Planned Parenthood and NARAL were responding to criticism from groups like
SisterSong; when the *New York Times* published a story on the move
away from arguments tying *Roe* to a right to choose, Monica Simpson
of SisterSong wrote a letter to Planned Parenthood asking why it had
not credited people of color for organizing the reproductive justice
movement in the first place. Connecting their cause to reproductive
justice also made sense for NARAL and Planned Parenthood because
both were struggling to reach younger Americans put off by the single-issue, choice-based messaging most associated with *Roe*. To reach
that audience, Planned Parenthood launched Generation Action, an
initiative to mobilize college-age Americans with a message that
linked *Roe* to federal civil rights law, "racial justice, poverty, LGBTIQ
rights, and reproductive justice."[50]

Anti-abortion organizations replied that *Roe* symbolized racism,
not reproductive justice. Representative Trent Franks, a Republican

from Arizona, revived efforts in Congress to ban sex-selection abortions, and North Dakota became the first state to ban abortions both for reasons of sex and for genetic abnormalities like Down syndrome. In 2015, Catherine Davis, who had founded a new nonprofit called the Restoration Project, announced a march across the Pettus Bridge in Selma, Alabama, echoing Dr. Martin Luther King's 1965 five-day march from Selma to Montgomery. Davis argued that an area abortion provider performed more than ten abortions a month without being properly licensed and was thus violating the law. The march, she said, would show that "Black women matter."[51]

Meanwhile, the law known as HB2, Texas's version of the Women's Health Protection Act, was headed for the U.S. Supreme Court.[52] The litigation of *Whole Woman's Health v. Hellerstedt* again brought to the surface conflicting ideas about the racial politics of abortion. The National Advocates for Pregnant Women (NAPW) and other amici described Texas's HB2 as a symptom of a broader problem with moving away from the protections provided by *Roe.* "The same rationales invoked by States to make abortion procedures in safe medical settings 'illegal,' " NAPW explained, "are being relied upon to turn women who become pregnant and are unable to navigate the thicket of abortion restrictions into *criminals*"—particularly the "low-income women and women of color . . . disproportionately targeted for arrest and punishment."[53] The National Women's Law Center described *Roe* as a decision protecting "equal dignity for women," especially for "women of color and women in the poorest areas of Texas."[54] A coalition of groups, including URGE, argued that *Roe* helped women of color overcome the "devastating history of pervasive inequality across nearly all aspects of reproductive healthcare."[55]

Anti-abortion lawyers argued that after *Gonzales v. Carhart,* the Supreme Court required deference to state legislators, especially where there was scientific uncertainty. When looking for evidence of that uncertainty, right-to-life lawyers pointed to the Gosnell case as evidence that bills like HB2 were needed to protect women. "Because of [a] poor safety record in Texas and reports of abominable danger-ous practices at abortion facilities elsewhere in the country," argued the American Association of Pro-Life Obstetricians and Gynecolo-gists in its brief, "the legislature passed HB2 with the overarching pur-pose of 'increas[ing] the health and safety' of abortion patients and providing them with 'the highest standard of health care.' "⁵⁶ Allan Parker and Operation Outcry made a similar point in their own brief, featuring not the stories of people of color like Gosnell's patients but those of white women who regretted abortions, like Molly White, who was then serving in the Texas legislature.⁵⁷

While *Whole Woman's Health* was pending at the Supreme Court, a presidential campaign was underway. The 2016 election pitted Hillary Clinton, a mainstay in U.S. Democratic politics, against Donald Trump, a self-proclaimed billionaire. Trump kicked off his campaign at Trump Tower by suggesting that Mexico sent rapists and drug pushers into the United States, promising a "Muslim ban" that would prevent Muslim migrants from entering the United States, and pledging to build a wall on the nation's southern border. He also courted the anti-abortion movement. Earlier in his career, Trump had been pro-choice and against a ban on partial-birth abortion, and he had donated to pro-choice candidates, including Clinton. To reassure socially conservative voters, he pledged to nominate "pro-life" Supreme Court justices and even called for punishing people who had abortions (the latter comment, which contradicted anti-abortion talking points, did Trump no favors with some pro-life voters). Clin-ton, by contrast, called *Roe* and abortion not just "women's issues" but "family issues," "economic issues," and "justice issues."⁵⁸

When the Supreme Court decided *Whole Women's Health* that June, the justices struck down both provisions of HB2 by a vote of 5–3

(Antonin Scalia, who had passed away in 2015, had not yet been replaced). The majority also revamped the undue burden test applied to abortion restrictions, requiring lower courts to "consider the burdens a law imposes on abortion access together with the benefits those laws confer." It also stressed that in applying the "undue burden" test from *Planned Parenthood v. Casey,* trial judges should not blindly defer to legislators but should instead conduct an independent review of the evidence in the case. The majority acknowledged the relevance of Gosnell's case, describing his behavior as "terribly wrong," but treated it as an aberration.[59]

The *Whole Woman's Health* opinion recognized the constitutional significance of burdens such as increased travel times and crowded facilities, which more often affected people of color. But the majority opinion, like the briefs submitted by most anti-abortion organizations, deleted race from the story of HB2's effects.[60]

Whole Woman's Health reflected the contradictory ways that Americans talked about *Roe* and race. Race played a large role in determining who sought out abortion, and who was affected by restrictive laws. Yet the conversations about race and abortion too often tended to be narrow and strategic. Anti-abortion activists often stressed the history of racial bias in the family planning movement without grappling with either the nuances of that history or the structural obstacles facing people of color in the present. Abortion rights supporters increasingly tied *Roe* to reproductive justice, but by avoiding the sometimes-ugly history of debates about abortion and family planning, they made it harder to talk about high abortion rates in communities the government had often left behind.

In 2016, Donald Trump shocked most Americans when he won the race for the White House, carrying thirty states while losing the popular vote. Catherine Davis was not surprised. She thought Trump was nothing but good news.[61]

The newly elected president already had the chance to nominate one Supreme Court justice to replace conservative stalwart Antonin Scalia. Davis had approved when Mitch McConnell, the Senate majority leader, prevented Obama's choice to replace Scalia, Merrick Garland, from even receiving a hearing. But she was sure *Roe* would be gone soon no matter who sat on the Supreme Court. She believed the Court would come to understand that a pregnant woman was carrying an unborn child. That, after all, was what she had realized all those years before.[62]

She felt even more certain of *Roe*'s fate in 2019, after she read Clarence Thomas's concurring opinion in *Box v. Planned Parenthood of Indiana and Kentucky.* The Court had rejected a challenge to an Indiana state law dictating the disposition of fetal remains, but it declined to address the constitutionality of a separate provision that banned abortion based on fetal race, sex, or disability. Thomas wrote a long solo concurrence suggesting that Indiana had every right to ban what he called "eugenic abortions." He described at length the racism that he said had infected the family planning movement, the pro-choice cause, and *Roe* itself. "Enshrining a constitutional right to an abortion based solely on the race, sex, or disability of an unborn child," Thomas wrote, "would constitutionalize the views of the 20th-century eugenics movement."[63]

For Catherine Davis, Thomas's concurrence was close to perfect. She was retired then; her son, who lived in Connecticut, was raising three boys of his own, and her daughter was a manager in a Home Depot warehouse. Davis was more than ready for the day when the Supreme Court got rid of *Roe.* But sometimes, late at night, the prospect worried her a little. She thought of all the women who had grown to expect access to abortion, many of them women of color, who might order abortion pills on the internet. What should happen to people like that? At times, they reminded her too much of the person she used to be.[64]

Kierra Johnson was sure that any Supreme Court decision on abortion would be at most a temporary setback. People would continue to demand access to abortion no matter what the Court said. Her father had passed away in Texas the year before Donald Trump was elected, and in 2016, Amber's oldest son, Christian, age twenty, took his own life. Kierra Johnson dedicated much of her life to the fight for reproductive justice, and she strongly supported the right to choose. But for women of color like Johnson, her mother, and her sister, nothing about reproductive choice was easy—because of racism, because of struggles with mental health or money. Nothing about the freedom to choose was simple for Amber's mother, who had to help raise her grandsons and granddaughter. Nor was it simple for Kierra, who chose to marry and raise children with another woman. Nothing was simple for Amber, who was met with challenges at every turn and lost her firstborn—a movie-loving, football-worshipping, beautiful boy who would never see the age of twenty-one. *Roe* might stand for a right to choose, but reproductive justice for people of color seemed impossibly far away, and no freedom was free.[65]

7

Religious Liberty and Equal Treatment

Janet Folger Porter saw herself at the forefront of two wars, one waged against innocent children, the other against Christianity. Porter grew up in a Cleveland suburb, the only daughter in a family of four, and she learned at an early age how to hold her own in an argument. At age nine, when her family attended one of Billy Graham's crusades, Janet stepped forward to declare that God was real. She believed that everyone was a sinner, and the wages of sin were death. When it came to who would pay the price, she explained, there were two options: (A) Janet Folger Porter; or (B) Jesus. She chose option B.[1]

She did not think much about abortion until high school, when her teacher brought in guest speakers to present opposing views on the issue. The pro-life speaker showed a slide of babies in garbage bags, and Porter recoiled, but she did not find an outlet for pro-life work until she went to college and co-founded a chapter of Students for Life at Cleveland State University. She had a flair for the dramatic: to depict the lives lost to abortion, she created a display that reached three stories high, supported by helium balloons. Some of her college classmates did not approve of her, but Porter did not mind being hated. Enraging the right people meant she was doing something right.[2]

Porter quickly became a rising star in Ohio Right to Life. She worked under Mark Lally, a meticulous lawyer who had taught for a time at the St. Thomas Aquinas School in nearby Zanesville. In the late 1980s, while attending a major right-to-life legislative conference with Lally, Folger proposed an idea: laws banning abortion when doctors could detect brain waves or a fetal heartbeat.[3] The judges and lawmakers she addressed dismissed her idea, but they did not know how she reacted to being patronized.[4]

As the chief lobbyist for Ohio State Right to Life, she was instrumental in the passage of the nation's first ban on partial-birth abortion, in 1995. Two years later, she moved to South Florida to work for D. James Kennedy, a prominent televangelist and former tango instructor known for his intellectual approach to ministry. She took charge of Kennedy's fledgling Center for Reclaiming America, where she argued that the nation had declared war on Christians, especially when it came to gay rights and legal abortion. The common denominator, she believed, was that leftists claimed to champion freedom of conscience while "forcing people to embrace their behavior." In 2003, she left the center to found her own group, Faith2Action.[5]

Right-to-lifers like Porter saw abortion as an act of unjustified killing—one that ignored scientific evidence of the personhood of the fetus. After 2008, abortion foes also believed that religious liberty and abortion had become increasingly intertwined. To begin with, some abortion foes suggested, *Roe* created a single national standard and did not let those with different religious beliefs follow their own faith traditions, even when they comprised a majority of a state's voters. After the passage of the Affordable Care Act, right-to-lifers suggested that supporters of *Roe* were so intent on protecting legal abortion that they would force Christian employers to subsidize it and would censor Christians who spoke out against it. Preserving *Roe*, in this analysis, came at a steep cost to religious liberty. Abortion rights supporters responded that *Roe* safeguarded freedom of conscience by allowing Americans to follow the dictates of their own faith. The right to choose, they argued, protected different religious views.

As conversations around *Roe* and conscience changed, the idea of religious liberty, which had once commanded support across the political spectrum, had gotten caught up in the culture wars. Religious liberty came to mean partisan politics rather than authentic pluralism.

The tension over *Roe* and religious liberty began to heat up in 2009, after President Obama introduced a contraceptive mandate into the federal Affordable Care Act. Employer insurance plans were required to cover all contraceptives approved by the Food and Drug Administration; employers could either abide by the mandate or face a penalty. The Department of Health and Human Services accommodated religious employers and nonprofits but not for-profit businesses, which the department concluded could not hold religious beliefs.[6]

With the implementation of this mandate, conservative Christian arguments about religious liberty gained a broader audience. Arguments about a war on Christianity had taken off in the 1990s, when the Supreme Court rejected attempts to dismantle abortion rights—and when same-sex couples began campaigning for the right to marry. Conservative Christian groups often framed legal abortion and LGBTIQ rights as forcing Christians to forsake their own beliefs. The Alliance Defense Fund (later Alliance Defending Freedom, ADF), founded in 1993 by a prominent group of televangelists, funded training, litigation, and strategy sessions for Christian attorneys defending restrictions on abortion or same-sex marriage. Porter's former boss, D. James Kennedy, was one of the founders. ADF president Alan Sears insisted that the real agenda of pro-choice or LGBTIQ rights groups was not to protect their own freedom but "to attack *your* right as a Christian to oppose their legal agenda."[7] "It is the Democratic Congress, the liberal-biased media and the homosexuals who want to destroy all Christians," argued televangelist Pat Robertson in 1994.[8]

By 2000, ADF had been involved in nineteen Supreme Court cases and won 110 favorable outcomes in the lower courts. The group described challenging *Roe* as part of a program to ensure that "Christians retain their right to proclaim the Gospel."[9] Janet Porter's Center for Reclaiming America also fought for religious liberty while stressing that *Roe* authorized child killing. Some of Porter's allies believed that supporters of abortion were willing to limit the religious freedom and free speech of Christians in their efforts to save *Roe*. Sometimes conservative Christians spoke of a war on Christians; other times they spoke of religious liberty. Equating the two had strategic benefits. The language of religious liberty invoked the free exercise clause of the Constitution; it also suggested that Christians were exceptionally devoted to their faith—and in danger of having their liberties stamped out. Progressive as well as conservative leaders had long played an important role in advocating and defending religious liberty. But in the 2000s, an increasingly prominent idea of religious liberty—with a strong partisan valence—framed opposition to abortion as a matter of religious faith, while presenting support for abortion rights as purely secular.[10]

The contraceptive mandate gave these arguments even more prominence among conservative Christians. In November 2009, a group of 145 evangelical, Catholic, and Orthodox Christian leaders released the "Manhattan Declaration: A Call of Christian Conscience," a forty-seven-hundred-word manifesto detailing threats to religious liberty. Drafted by Princeton professor Robert George, evangelical leader and repentant Nixon advisor Chuck Colson, and Timothy Beebe, the dean of an evangelical school in Alabama, the declaration asserted that the *Roe* decision and the contraceptive mandate were major threats to religious freedom. It was not simply the case that defenders of religious liberty tended to oppose *Roe* and legal abortion (though that was certainly true). The declaration suggested that progressives' desire to save *Roe* was itself a threat. The signatories vowed not to "comply with any edict that purports to compel our institutions to participate in abortions." Within weeks of its unveiling, over 280,000 people had signed the declaration. Richard Land, the president of the Southern Baptist Convention's Ethics and Religious Liberty Commission, argued that this widespread support showed that Christians who dared to challenge *Roe* felt they were under "sustained assault by various elements of this society."[11]

The signers of the declaration took issue with the contraceptive mandate largely because they saw it as an extension of *Roe*. Some conservative Christians believed that certain FDA-approved contraceptives, including common intrauterine devices and emergency contraceptives, were abortifacients because they prevented the implantation of a fertilized egg. (The American College of Obstetricians and Gynecologists argued that IUDs and emergency contraceptives worked by preventing fertilization or delaying or preventing ovulation.) Conservative Christians filed lawsuits challenging the mandate under the federal Religious Freedom Restoration Act (RFRA), a federal law setting exacting requirements for any government action that burdens religious exercise.[12]

Supporters of abortion rights, together with other progressives, argued that the signers of the declaration had no respect for the freedom of conscience of anyone who disagreed with them, not least when it came to reproductive rights. What motivated challenges to *Roe* and calls for religious liberty, they argued, was not a desire to protect Christianity from attack but a wish to impose one faith on the nation, including those with faith-based commitments to *ensuring* contraceptive access. Barry Lynn, executive director of Americans United for the Separation of Church and State, charged that "these religious leaders want to see their doctrines imposed by force of law."[13]

Some right-to-lifers maintained that the defense of Christianity demanded more than just making space in the public square for those who disagreed. It required laws reflecting the will of God. This view influenced some in the personhood movement, which called for state constitutional amendments recognizing the personhood of the unborn child and immediately banning abortion. Starting in 2008, personhood proponents tried and failed several times to amend Colorado's constitution, and Personhood USA, a national group championing similar measures, formed to mount a more sustained nationwide campaign. Janet Porter developed an alternative. In late 2010, she attended the wake of her former boss, Mark Lally, full of frustration that her mentor had never seen a day when abortion was illegal throughout America. Nor would she, Porter believed, unless right-to-lifers changed tactics. Since she first formulated it in the late 1980s, her idea of banning abortion when a doctor could detect a sign of life had struck her as wise, and she revisited it after Lally's death. Porter, who had written Christian self-help books about her single years, had finally married an accountant who shared her love of worship music. Just after moving back to Ohio, the Porters were throwing a housewarming party when Janet's husband quipped that she should undo *Roe* while she was in town. Porter agreed.[14]

The next morning, she prepared breakfast for friends who had spent the night and wrote the words "heartbeat bill" on a whiteboard. She assembled a team of lawyers to help her write the bill. The statute that emerged would make it a felony to perform an abortion after a doctor identified a "detectable heartbeat"—roughly six weeks after a person's last menstrual period. (Critics of the bill stressed that because no heart had formed by then, the term "heartbeat bill" was misleading.) Under *Roe* and *Casey*, the right to abortion applied until viability, the point at which survival was possible outside the womb—at the time, judged to be somewhere between twenty-one and twenty-four weeks. A heartbeat, Porter argued, was a universal sign of life: more emotionally resonant and scientifically reliable than viability, which "changes with the year and hospital in which a child is born."[15]

By the end of 2011, Porter had traveled to ten states to encourage them to adopt the bill. Professor David Forte, one of the lawyers who had helped draft it, argued that "fetal heart rate is an indicator of . . . survivability."[16] For this reason, he said, a heartbeat bill replaced the line drawn by *Roe* with something that made more sense and protected far more unborn babies. "All will see," he wrote, "that a fetus with a beating heart is a person destined to be born, not because pro-lifers say so, but because nature has decreed it."[17]

Some right-to-lifers kept their distance from Porter. They did not like that she energetically promoted the claim that President Obama had been born abroad, was not a U.S. citizen, and so could not legally be president. Some right-to-life leaders dismissed her heartbeat bill as unrealistic, and her arguments that Christianity was being criminalized as counterproductive. Porter ignored the condescension of those she saw as begging for crumbs. If her colleagues in the anti-abortion movement told her that passage of a heartbeat bill was impossible, she said, she would introduce them to the God of the impossible.[18]

Battles about *Roe* and religious liberty heated up in 2014 after the Supreme Court issued its decision in *Burwell v. Hobby Lobby Stores, Inc.*, holding that the ACA's contraceptive mandate violated the federal Religious Freedom Restoration Act. Some right-to-lifers suggested that progressives were so intent on saving *Roe* that they did not respect the freedom of choice of those with religious objections to abortion-inducing drugs. "The pro-abortionists are not content with establishing a legal right for pregnant mothers to use these drugs," wrote conservative columnist David Limbaugh. "They're using the coercive power of the state to compel people to pay for a procedure they find morally repugnant."[19] Others saw *Roe* as preserving the same pluralism reflected in the contraceptive mandate: a guarantee that individuals could make their own choice about reproduction, including those in faith traditions that treated contraceptive use as a religious imperative. "The real threat to religious liberty," explained the *New*

York Times editorial board in March 2014, "comes from the owners trying to impose their religious beliefs on thousands of employees."[20]

Hobby Lobby, the crafts store leading the litigation in the Supreme Court case, was a closely held for-profit corporation owned by a religious family, the Greens, who believed that the contraceptive mandate forced them to make an impossible choice in their employee health coverage: cover contraceptives that they felt were abortifacients or face penalties. Right-to-lifers supporting the Greens argued that the mandate reflected a troubling reinterpretation of *Roe*. "If the Mandate is allowed to survive this Court's review," argued the pro-life Thomas More Law Center, "then the right to abortion and contraception that the Court has previously recognized is no longer based on a right to privacy" but on "a dramatically unjust use of government power."[21] The conservative Life, Liberty, and Law Foundation similarly argued that under *Roe*, women had a right to abortion but had "no accompanying right to draft their employers as unwilling accomplices who must pay for it."[22]

Those supporting the mandate argued that it strengthened freedom of conscience. "Contraception," the National Women's Law Center and others argued in an amicus brief, "puts women in control of their fertility, allowing them to decide whether, and when, to bear children."[23] Lambda Legal, a public interest litigator focused on LGBTIQ rights, contended that women seeking to use contraception could point to decisions that protected "the most intimate and personal choices a person may make in a lifetime."[24]

The Supreme Court's 5–4 opinion in *Hobby Lobby* left less room for a balance between competing conscience-based views about contraception. The Court held that closely held, for-profit businesses could be rights-holding people under RFRA, and it had no trouble concluding that the mandate seriously burdened the Greens' religious exercise. Pro-choice groups had argued that pluralism required placing certain burdens on religious employers—in part because employees might *use* contraception for reasons of conscience. To balance these competing ideas of religious liberty, the government proposed that only those most directly involved could raise an objection. The Greens were several steps removed from any employee's decision to use contraception, the government argued, and so did not face a substantial burden.[25]

The Supreme Court instead held that what mattered was that the Greens had an "honest conviction" that they were taking the lives of unborn babies. Justice Alito, writing for the majority, refused to conclude that the Greens' religious beliefs were "mistaken or insubstantial." Even assuming, he wrote, that the government had a compelling interest in expanding contraceptive access, it had still violated RFRA by not exhausting less restrictive alternatives, such as directly funding contraception, or offering businesses like Hobby Lobby the exemption available to nonprofits and certain religious employers.[26]

The *Hobby Lobby* decision moved the relationship between *Roe* and religious liberty to the center of the nation's political agenda. And when the Supreme Court agreed to hear *Obergefell v. Hodges*, a major case on same-sex marriage, the litigants on both sides presented themselves as champions of freedom of conscience. When the fight to legalize marriage for same-sex couples began in earnest, in the mid-1990s, it at first produced a backlash, with states and the federal government passing "defense-of-marriage" acts that defined marriage as a relationship between one man and one woman. But in 2003, the Massachusetts Supreme Judicial Court recognized a state constitutional right to same-sex marriage. Other state courts issued similar rulings, but the results in state courts were mixed. Advocates of same-sex marriage turned to the federal courts, scoring an important win in *United States v. Windsor,* which struck down the federal Defense of Marriage Act in 2013.[27]

Christian conservatives suggested that a decision allowing same-sex couples to marry would be another *Roe*. Defending his state's marriage limit, Michigan solicitor general John Bursch argued that *Roe* stood for the principle that "government cannot interfere in . . . private choice" but had no duty "to recognize and give benefits to anyone."[28] Others went farther. Amici opposed to same-sex marriage described *Roe* as having trampled on many Americans' religious liberty, with what the conservative National Organization for Marriage called "democracy-destructive consequences."[29] The United States Conference of Catholic Bishops also described *Roe* as a decision that ignored religious liberty. A similar decision on same-sex marriage, the bishops suggested, "would generate a panoply of church-state litigation" and a backlash "even greater than [the conflict about] abortion."[30]

These arguments failed to carry the day in *Obergefell*. Justice Kennedy's majority opinion concluded that the due process and equal protection clauses of the Fourteenth Amendment required recognition of a "personal right to choice regarding marriage." Kennedy went to considerable trouble to reassure conservative Christians that the opinion did not require any religious believers to set aside their deeply held convictions, but some of the dissenters did not buy it. Justice Alito's dissent warned that the decision would be used "to vilify Americans who are unwilling to assent to the new orthodoxy."[31]

Obergefell heightened conservative Christians' anxieties about religious liberty. So did a 2015 study released by the Pew Research Center suggesting that the number of respondents identifying as Christian had plummeted nearly 8 percentage points in just seven years, while those identifying with no religion in particular had risen by more than 6 points. Right-to-lifers argued that supporters of *Roe* tried to silence Christians in no small part because of their positions on abortion. Many, like Janet Porter, worked on both abortion and religious liberty. The year *Obergefell* came down, she directed a film, *Light Wins*, that told Christians to defend their faith before it was too late. In promoting the film, Porter described *Obergefell* as "the *Roe v. Wade* of marriage" and "a definitive ruling that could make Christian believers a target."[32]

She spent much of 2015 pushing Ohio lawmakers to adopt a heartbeat bill. The right-to-life movement was hardly united behind her. Arguing that her strategy would backfire, NRLC refused to back the bill, and James Bopp, the organization's general counsel, flew down to Columbus to testify against it. The Ohio legislature passed Porter's heartbeat bill only to see John Kasich, the state's Republican governor, veto it and sign a twenty-week abortion ban instead.[33]

The election of Donald Trump, whose campaign fused concerns about religious liberty and opposition to abortion, changed the heartbeat bill's prospects. In 2017, when Trump nominated Neil Gorsuch to replace Antonin Scalia, Russell Moore, the president of the Southern Baptist Convention's Ethics and Religious Liberty Commission, wrote that Gorsuch would be a "stalwart advocate for religious liberty and human dignity at all its stages."[34] In May, in what it described as a bid to protect religious liberty, the Trump administration announced that it would draft regulations to roll back the contraceptive mandate and eliminate discrimination protections for transgender federal employees. By early 2018, Trump had placed conservative Christians in prominent positions in his administration and created a new division within the Department of Health and Human Services to protect employees with objections to abortion or certain treatments for LGBTIQ patients.[35]

That year, Janet Porter had her hands full with a new role. She was the spokesperson for Roy Moore, the Republican nominee for the Alabama Senate seat vacated by Jeff Sessions, who had resigned to become Trump's new attorney general. Moore, who had recently stepped down from the Alabama Supreme Court, beat establishment candidates in the primary only to face allegations of sexual misconduct with teenage girls while he was in his thirties. Porter argued that the "Democratic Party, the pro-abortion lobby, and Democratic donor George Soros" were conspiring to destroy him.[36]

The sexual misconduct accusation ultimately sank Roy Moore, but Porter had no time to pause before Anthony Kennedy, the Court's longtime swing vote on abortion, announced his retirement in the summer of 2018. Trump chose Brett Kavanaugh, regarded as one of the most conservative judges on the DC Circuit Court of Appeals, to replace Kennedy. Controversy engulfed Kavanaugh's confirmation after Christine Blasey Ford, a psychology professor from California, accused the nominee of sexually assaulting her at a high school party in the early 1980s. But Republicans controlled the Senate and wanted to push Kavanaugh's nomination through. Following heated debate and a brief FBI investigation, he was confirmed by a vote of 50–48.[37]

Before Kavanaugh joined the Court, federal courts had declared heartbeat bills unconstitutional and blocked them from going into effect. To make matters worse, a federal statute, the Civil Rights Attorney's Fees Award Act of 1976, allowed the prevailing party in certain civil rights cases to recover their attorneys' fees; after losing a challenge to its heartbeat law, North Dakota had to pay the Center for Reproductive Rights almost a quarter of a million dollars. When Kennedy was the Court's swing vote, it hardly seemed worth the trouble to pass a law the Supreme Court would invalidate, but after Kavanaugh's confirmation, state lawmakers believed the Court had five votes to gut abortion rights or reverse *Roe* outright.[38]

Kentucky and Mississippi passed heartbeat bans in March 2019, followed by Ohio in April. In May, Georgia not only passed a six-week ban but recognized fetal personhood when a doctor could detect fetal cardiac activity. Alabama passed a law criminalizing abortion at fertilization, with no exception for rape and incest, with violators subject to ninety-nine years in prison.[39]

To Mark Lee Dickson the heartbeat campaign signaled new political opportunities. He was born into the equivalent of pro-life royalty in Gregg County in northeastern Texas. His grandfather, Glenn Canfield, was a northern implant who had worked for Lone Star Steel, started successful metallurgy businesses of his own, and run the county's Republican Party. As a child, Dickson would always study the fetal models at the booth his grandfather set up at the county fair for Right to Life of East Texas (Mark was sometimes allowed to take the model of a twelve-week-old fetus home). Despite Canfield's success, Dickson grew up poor. His father was a mechanic who severely injured his back and was limited in the jobs he was physically able to do; after Mark started school, his mother began working at the school cafeteria to keep the same hours as her two boys, then worked at local dollar stores. When Dickson was in the eighth grade, his parents took him to a church presentation called "Heaven's Gates and Hell's Flames," and he committed his life to Jesus Christ.[40]

But even after he began regularly attending church, Dickson struggled with depression and suicidal thoughts. The more he thought about suicide, the more he came to despise the idea, especially after several friends and classmates ended their lives over broken relationships. He began to connect the conversations he had with his grandfather about abortion with his struggles over suicide; both, he thought, involved another human being determining the value of a person's life. Suicide became central to Dickson's sense of what it meant to oppose *Roe*.[41]

After his grandfather died in 2006, Dickson joined the pro-life movement as a way to stay connected to a man he had so admired. He became a director of Right to Life of East Texas, and then, at twenty-six, founded a church in Longview, a social media–friendly ministry that attracted college students and millennials who sometimes met for breakfast at the local Chick-fil-A. Some in Dickson's circle considered themselves abortion abolitionists. They rejected the pro-life label, ridiculed incremental attacks on *Roe*, called for the punishment of women and pregnant people in addition to doctors, and proclaimed a willingness to defy laws that treated abortion as a legal medical procedure. Dickson, who sympathized with these abolitionists, found it hard to believe that no abortion ban had survived since the *Roe* decision. He also became active on end-of-life issues after hearing the story of two parents trying to keep their thirty-nine-year-old son, Jonathan, from being taken off life support. Dickson, Texas Right to Life, and Dickson's state senator, Bryan Hughes, later teamed up on the case of Carolyn Jones, a woman about to be removed from life support because of Texas's Advance Directives Act, which allowed hospitals to withdraw life-sustaining care that both the attending physician and a hospital ethics committee deemed to be "medically inappropriate."[42]

Dickson became more anxious about abortion after the Supreme Court agreed to hear a Louisiana abortion case, *June Medical Services v. Russo*. Louisiana had passed an admitting privileges law identical to the Texas law, HB2, struck down by the Supreme Court just four years earlier. Dickson had run into a news story from the 1990s describing a pro-choice philanthropist willing to donate land and a building for an abortion clinic just across the Louisiana state line. Concerned that if Louisiana closed its clinics after *June Medical*, one might open in Waskom, Texas, he approached the mayor about making the town a "sanctuary city for the unborn" by banning abortion. In June 2019, the city was poised to act, but Dickson was convinced that it would not be loving one's neighbor to give the city leaders an ordinance that could result in their being sued into oblivion. He texted Senator Hughes for advice.[43]

Dickson showed Hughes the ordinance he had drafted for Waskom. Hughes had recently worked with Jonathan Mitchell, the former Texas solicitor general, on a religious liberty bill that gave him an idea on how to solve Waskom's problem. Chick-fil-A, which served as Dickson's de facto office, had come to Hughes and Mitchell's attention after the San Antonio airport excluded the restaurant chain from its list of prospective vendors because it had made donations to organizations opposed to same-sex marriage. The Atlanta-based Cathy family, who owned Chick-fil-A, often spoke of their commitment to the "biblical definition of the family unit."[44]

In 2019, he and Mitchell proposed what Texans would come to call the Save Chick-fil-A bill, which prohibited any government entity from taking any "adverse action" based on "the person's membership in, affiliation with, or contribution, donation, or other support provided to a religious organization." The government would not enforce the prohibition; instead, anyone whose rights had been (or could be) violated could bring a lawsuit and win attorneys' fees. Hughes did not want to use criminal penalties because progressive prosecutors nationwide had vowed not to enforce a heartbeat ban if such a law went into effect. Civil enforcement allowed Christians to defend themselves.[45]

Mitchell and Hughes later expanded on the civil enforcement idea written into the Save Chick-fil-A bill: the city could ban abortion and the possession of abortion pills but could outsource enforcement to private citizens. According to Mitchell and Hughes, this meant that abortion providers would not have standing to sue the city or its agents in federal court. Generally, federal standing doctrine required not only that someone suffer a real injury at the hands of the defendant but also that a favorable judicial decision could provide some form of redress. When it came to redress, Mitchell and Hughes relied on a 2001 case called *Okpalobi v. Foster*. In 1999, Louisiana had passed a law allowing women to sue abortion providers for injuries to themselves and their unborn children. When abortion providers challenged the constitutionality of the law, the Fifth Circuit Court of

Appeals concluded that they lacked standing to sue the state because the government and its agents could neither stop private citizens from suing nor block state courts from entertaining suits. Hughes and Mitchell thought the same argument could apply to Waskom: because the sanctuary city ordinance assigned enforcement to private citizens, the city would have no authority to stop private citizens from suing, and courts would hold that any abortion provider hauling the city into court lacked standing to do so.[46]

In June 2020, the Supreme Court's decision in *June Medical Services v. Russo* made Hughes and Mitchell's plan seemed far-fetched. In a 5–4 ruling, the Court struck down Louisiana's admitting privileges law. Chief Justice John Roberts, who had voted to uphold a similar law just four years earlier in *Whole Woman's Health v. Hellerstedt*, agreed with his more liberal colleagues that Louisiana's law violated the Constitution, but he did not join the majority's opinion. Instead, he stressed the importance of stare decisis, a doctrine requiring respect for the Court's precedents. He seemed unlikely to reverse *Roe* in the short term.[47]

An adverse outcome in the Supreme Court was hardly enough to discourage Dickson. The premise of his sanctuary city movement was that *Roe* had silenced Christians for too long—and that it was "not good enough to say we value the lives of our unborn neighbors if there are no actions to back those words up." By allowing "anyone, including any relative of the unborn child, to sue the abortionist or anyone who aids and abets the abortionist for the death of the unborn child," Dickson argued, the law would create an "important deterrent to the abortion industry from moving into their jurisdiction."[48]

Dickson's efforts got a boost in the fall of 2020 when Justice Ruth Bader Ginsburg passed away after a long battle with cancer. Ginsburg, who had helped launch the ACLU's Reproductive Freedom Project in the 1970s, had been the Court's most eloquent defender of abortion rights.[49]

To replace Ginsburg, Trump moved quickly to nominate Amy Coney Barrett, a young judge and former professor of law at Notre Dame. Barrett excited right-to-lifers because she was a brilliant lawyer, a devout Catholic, strongly pro-life, and a member of People of Praise, a small Christian group founded in Indiana. During her confirmation hearings for the Seventh Circuit Court of Appeals, California senator Dianne Feinstein had proclaimed that "the dogma lives loudly within" Barrett and that, as a judge, she would rule according to her religious beliefs. Barrett's testy exchange with Feinstein teed up a softball question from Republican senator Ben Sasse of Nebraska, who asked what it would mean if "people with certain religious views were excluded from public life." Barrett replied that considerable harm would result, including "infringements on religious freedom." To some observers, the exchange made Barrett a symbol of the war on Christianity. Planned Parenthood, together with other critics of her nomination, responded that Barrett would strike a blow against religious liberty— both by voting to reverse *Roe* and by concluding that "judges shouldn't follow the law if it clashes with their religious beliefs."[50]

After the Senate confirmed Barrett by a vote of 52–48, right-to-lifers felt even more confident, but the 2020 presidential election soon dashed some of the movement's hopes. Major news networks called the election for Democrat Joe Biden, who won 306 votes in the Electoral College and just over 51 percent of the popular vote. Trump claimed he was the victim of a massive election fraud. He filed sixty-two legal challenges, urged state officials to find additional votes, promoted audits of the results in contested states, and asked Republican state legislators to send alternative slates of delegates to Congress. Janet Porter eagerly backed him; a video detailing what she described as proof that Trump won made the rounds on social media.[51]

Mark Lee Dickson's biggest win to date came after Trump left office. In Lubbock, Texas, a city of over 250,000, Planned Parenthood of

Greater Texas opened a clinic, and anti-abortion residents collected enough signatures to put a sanctuary city proposal before the city council. When the council unanimously voted down the proposal, Dickson then got enough signatures to put the ordinance to a popular vote, and the town approved it, with 62.5 percent of voters in favor. Planned Parenthood of Greater Texas filed a lawsuit in federal court, arguing that the Lubbock law violated the right to choose recognized by *Roe*. District judge James Wesley Hendrix, whom Donald Trump had nominated in 2019, agreed with Lubbock that federal courts had no jurisdiction to hear the case because abortion providers lacked standing to sue. "Like the defendants in *Okpalobi*," Judge Hendrix wrote, "the city and its officials have no authority to prevent a private plaintiff from invoking the ordinance or to tell the state courts what cases they may hear."[52]

The Court had the opportunity to take an abortion case not long after Dickson's Lubbock win. *Dobbs v. Jackson Women's Health Organization* involved a Mississippi law banning abortion at fifteen weeks, the point at which the state said fetal pain was possible. Both *Roe* and *Planned Parenthood v. Casey* recognized a right to choose abortion before survival is possible outside the womb, usually around twenty-four weeks. Viability outside the womb is a moving target, affected by hospitals' capabilities and advancing technology—but no one was putting it as early as fifteen weeks.[53]

The relatively early limit was by design. Mississippi lawmakers believed viability was a weakness in the *Roe* framework and wanted to test the Court's commitment to it. Jackson Women's Health Organization, the only abortion provider in Mississippi, challenged the law, and both the district court and the Fifth Circuit Court of Appeals ruled that it could not stand. The Supreme Court agreed to hear the most explosive question in Mississippi's certiorari petition: whether all pre-viability abortion bans were unconstitutional.[54]

While *Dobbs* was pending, Bryan Hughes tried to take Mark Dickson's experiment to the state level. Here, Hughes and Mitchell relied on the Eleventh Amendment, which limited the circumstances under which plaintiffs could sue the state in federal court. The Supreme Court had carved out an exception in 1908 in *Ex parte Young*, allowing people to sue state officials charged with enforcing potentially unconstitutional laws. But if the state passed a bill that allowed only private citizens to sue, Mitchell and Hughes argued, there was no state official charged with enforcing the law, and the state could not be forced into federal court. Texas lawmakers had considered passing a version of Janet Porter's heartbeat bill in 2019 but had hesitated because, if they lost, they would have to fork over hundreds of thousands of dollars in attorneys' fees. Hughes and Mitchell instead proposed a heartbeat bill that expanded on the sanctuary city laws Mark Dickson had championed. The bill, SB8, would be enforced not by the state but by private citizens, who could sue anyone who performed or "aided or abetted" an abortion six weeks after a person's last menstrual period. SB8 passed in May 2021.[55]

Abortion providers immediately filed suit against a range of state lawmakers and judges as well as Dickson (who responded that he had no intention of filing a lawsuit). A district court blocked the law from going into effect, but the defendants appealed to the Fifth Circuit, which put a hold on proceedings and allowed SB8 to be enforced. After abortion providers filed an emergency appeal, the Supreme Court voted 5–4 that providers had not shown that they had identified the right people to sue. Texas began enforcing SB8, and in October, the Court decided to hear two cases—one asking whether the federal Department of Justice could challenge the constitutionality of Texas's law, and a second questioning whether abortion providers could rely on *Ex parte Young* to seek relief in federal court. Bryan Hughes and Mark Lee Dickson, who had been largely unknown outside of Texas, were soon all over the news.[56]

With the Court preparing to hear argument in *Dobbs*, many right-to-lifers suggested that the relationship between *Roe* and religious liberty should determine whether the Court preserved a right to abortion. The Becket Fund for Religious Liberty, one of the leading public interest law firms focused on religious freedoms, insisted that *Roe* had done more than anything else to undermine those freedoms in America. "Attempts to eliminate religious dissent," Becket's brief explained, are "meant to build a protective hedge around *Roe* and *Casey*."[57] The conservative Jewish Coalition for Religious Liberty likewise argued that the right to abortion guaranteed by *Roe* infringed rather than protected religious liberty: the ruling did not ensure that women can "fully participate in society without compromising their religious exercise" but instead sought "to yoke the rest of society to [the] theological preferences" of those who supported *Roe*.[58]

Roe's supporters described it not only as a guarantor of equality for women but also as a crucial safeguard for religious liberty. The Freedom from Religion Foundation argued that *Roe* was significant partly because it prevented the passage of bills "motivated by religious ideology."[59] Americans United for the Separation of Church and State simply argued that *Roe* (and the viability standard in particular) safeguarded religious liberty by showing "respect for everyone's right of conscience." These arguments reflected the conclusion that some people seeking abortion did so not because of indifference to matters of religion but because in their own interpretation of their faith, abortion was sometimes the right choice.[60]

The decision to take *Dobbs* suggested that the justices were ready to take another look at *Roe*. They also seemed ready to revise the jurisprudence of religious liberty. During the height of the COVID-19 pandemic, they had granted several emergency petitions brought by churches challenging restrictions on in-person worship. In November, a five-justice majority blocked New York from enforcing its attendance limits on places of worship in COVID red zones because the state had "singled out houses of worship for especially harsh treatment." In February, in *South Bay United Pentecostal Church v. Newsom*, the Court blocked limits on in-person worship put in place by California, while allowing the state to limit services to 25 percent capacity in high-risk areas. Then, in April, the Court again weighed in on California's COVID limits on in-person worship, holding that courts should strictly scrutinize such orders "whenever they treat any comparable secular activity more favorably than religious exercise."[61]

In theory, in these cases, the Court was applying a rule from *Employment Division v. Smith* (1990), a case involving two Native Americans who had lost their jobs because they consumed peyote during a religious ceremony and then were disqualified from receiving unemployment insurance. The employees argued that their disqualification violated the free exercise clause of the First Amendment, but the Court disagreed. As long as a law was neutral and generally applicable, said the majority opinion, it did not violate the free exercise clause. Under *Smith*, both the New York and California restrictions would have been allowable if they were "generally applicable," but in the Court's view they were not: religious services were singled out for disadvantageous treatment. Critics responded that the Court was second-guessing public health authorities who believed that religious services posed a greater risk of infection, but for many conservatives, that was beside the point. By 2021, conservative Christians were ready to ask the Court to get rid of *Smith* altogether.[62]

They made that request on behalf of Catholic Social Services (CSS), which had been cut out of Philadelphia's foster care program because CSS refused to place children with same-sex couples. In *Fulton v. City of Philadelphia*, CSS argued that the city's decision was unconstitutional under *Smith* but also invited the Court to reverse that opinion. To the surprise of many, the Court declined, holding that Philadelphia's policy was unconstitutional under *Smith* because it created discretionary exemptions. *Smith* required a generally applicable rule, and by giving the city so much discretion, Philadelphia had failed to create one. Writing in dissent, Justices Clarence Thomas, Samuel Alito, and Neil Gorsuch urged that *Smith* be reversed immediately; Justices Stephen Breyer, Brett Kavanaugh, and Amy Coney Barrett expressed grave doubts about *Smith* but stayed their hand because they were not sure they had a better standard to replace it.[63]

In December 2021, the Court's approaches to abortion and religious liberty diverged again. In oral argument in the Mississippi case *Dobbs v. Jackson Women's Health Organization*, the justices seemed ready to declare an end to abortion rights. *Roe* and *Casey* recognized a right to choose abortion until viability, but Chief Justice Roberts, who seemed to want to stop short of repudiating *Roe*, suggested that there was no connection between constitutional self-determination and the viability standard. Roberts's conservative colleagues, however, seemed uninterested in anything but an outright reversal. Brett Kavanaugh, who held a key vote in the case, suggested that the Constitution was scrupulously neutral on the issue, recognizing neither a right to abortion nor a right to life. Amy Coney Barrett, another potential swing justice, implied that reversing *Roe* would not damage the cause of women's equality.[64]

The week after the *Dobbs* argument, the Court allowed abortion providers' challenge to Texas's SB8 to proceed (the Court dismissed the challenge brought by the Justice Department as improvidently granted). But it held that providers could sue only four state licensing officials, not the clerks who filed lawsuits or the attorney general. This restriction made it much harder for anyone to block the law, and it forced providers to defend themselves from one suit after another. Moreover, the justices suggested that the only reason providers *could* sue the licensing officials was that there had been a slip-up by Texas lawmakers.

SB8 stated that nothing in it forbade the state to enforce "other abortion laws." Licensing officials were charged with enforcing the state health and safety code—a statute that included SB8—so in theory, the state had not prohibited those officials from enforcing SB8. The Court handed other states a roadmap: if they closed this loophole and simply stated that no official could enforce the law, they could protect themselves against suit in federal court. The Texas Supreme Court put an end to remaining challenges to SB8 in March 2022, ruling that the law did not give licensing officials "any authority to enforce the Act's requirements."[65]

The Court also seemed intent on expanding religious liberty in *Carson v. Makin*, a challenge to Maine's rules on school funding. The state constitution guaranteed every child a free public education, but not every district had its own school. To solve this problem, Maine allowed these state units to either contract with another school or pay the tuition at an approved public or private school to which a student was accepted. But the state excluded "sectarian" schools—an exception that religious parents considered unconstitutional. At oral argument, the justices seemed to agree. Even as it created a more capacious idea of religious liberty, the Court's conservative majority looked ready to erase the right recognized in *Roe*.[66]

The justices seemed to have charted a controversial course. Polling suggested that many Americans favored some abortion restrictions and were uncomfortable with the procedure later in pregnancy, but a majority opposed reversing *Roe* or criminalizing the procedure. In 2021, polls also suggested a deep partisan divide on religious liberty. In 2021, the Public Religion Research Institute published a study showing that the nation was evenly divided between those who believed religious liberty claims threatened vulnerable minorities and those who thought religious liberty was itself at risk. Another 2021 poll, from the Associated Press and the University of Chicago, showed

that although large majorities described themselves as strong supporters of freedom of conscience, white evangelicals and conservatives
cared much more about it—and felt it was more at risk—than did
other communities. Conflicting arguments about *Roe* and religious
liberty reflected a complicated view of what freedom of conscience
should look like. *Roe* could stand for the freedom to follow one's own
conscience, or for the government's brute power to enforce an outcome that conflicted with believers' deepest convictions. Neither argument explored what true religious pluralism would look like.
Debates about *Roe* showed the extent to which partisanship had
transformed religious liberty into another front in the culture wars.[67]

Janet Folger Porter spent 2021 almost constantly on the road, encouraging lawmakers across the country to pass a statewide version of
the ordinance that Dickson was still championing in rural counties
inside and outside Texas. After President Biden announced a vaccine
mandate for businesses with more than one hundred employees, Porter began giving speeches denouncing "Biden's forced vaccinations."[68]
She was also working on what she called a high-quality Christian sitcom, based on *What's a Girl to Do?*, her book about her single days. She
had lined up a cast and urged supporters to help fund production of
the first episodes. "We can make people laugh," she wrote, "while putting God and His Truths in a positive light once again."[69]

But right-to-lifers were increasingly convinced that defenders of
abortion rights were willing to dismantle Christians' religious liberty
and free speech in order to save *Roe*. Porter was ready for whatever
came next in this conflict. She sent her supporters an email declaring
that *Roe v. Wade* would soon be gone, but she thought her work was
only beginning. The next step was to persuade states to criminalize
abortion. "What must we do to bring the killing to an end?" she
wrote. "The answer remains, whatever it takes."[70]

Epilogue: *Roe* After the Overruling

As I wrote this, at the start of 2022, the Supreme Court seemed ready to reverse *Roe* in just months. Reporters across the world questioned why the United States was inching closer to allowing states to criminalize abortion even as countries from Mexico to Thailand moved in the other direction. New legal issues loomed: could states punish people for traveling out of state to have abortions in places where the procedure was still legal? Would state limits on the mailing or possession of abortion pills unconstitutionally interfere with interstate commerce? When states' laws clashed, which one's law would apply?[1]

It may be a bit of mystery why we care so much about *Roe*. The Court has issued other blockbuster opinions, and they have mostly faded into obscurity. Debates about gun violence rage on but do not consistently focus on *District of Columbia v. Heller*, the 2008 opinion recognizing an individual right to bear arms. The Court's recent decisions on voting rights, including *Shelby County v. Holder* and *Brnovich v. Democratic National Committee*, have opened the door to a wide range of new restrictions on voting. While voter rights—and election subversion—are hot topics, few Americans structure these discussions around *Shelby County*. The Court's decision on corporate campaign spending, *Citizens United v. Federal Election Commission*, is recognizable to many Americans and has sparked protests of its own. But *Citizens United* is no *Roe v. Wade*. It has not been at the center of the same intense social movement conflict or figured as centrally in judicial nominations or national elections.[2]

Perhaps the difference lies in our deepening partisan divides. Partisan affiliation is now one of the best predictors of one's attitude toward abortion. Political polarization may explain the toxicity of our abortion politics, especially as Americans hold increasingly negative attitudes about the opposing political party. Still, even in this environment, the abortion issue seems uniquely polarized. It divides the United States by region, religion, and race. Perhaps it is not *Roe* that is unique but abortion itself.[3]

It is true, of course, that abortion touches on deeply held convictions about sex, sexuality, the role of physicians, religion, and the beginning of human life. Sociologists have shown how attitudes about abortion correlate with beliefs about everything from motherhood to science. But *Roe* is not the Supreme Court's only abortion decision. It does not even define the Court's current approach, which is laid out in *Planned Parenthood of Southeastern Pennsylvania v. Casey*. Our unique fascination with *Roe* goes beyond our national fracture on abortion.[4]

This interest in *Roe* is even more puzzling given the scholarly criticism the decision has received. Almost from the start, commentators across the ideological spectrum have questioned the opinion's reasoning, which did not draw on constitutional text, history, or other conventional sources of interpretation. Ruth Bader Ginsburg, who would become the Supreme Court's most vocal defender of abortion rights, often argued that *Roe* went too far too fast and undermined the pro-choice movement's earlier progress. Feminists like Catharine MacKinnon described it as paternalistic and unconvincing. Originalists, starting with Robert Bork, have found it little short of horrifying. It is surprising that we care so much about a decision that is criticized by so many.[5]

A handful of other judicial decisions also occupy a central place in constitutional discourse. *Brown v. Board of Education*, the Court's desegregation opinion, is the most canonical decision in constitutional law, an opinion virtually everyone agrees was correctly decided. There are also decisions that everyone despises, from *Dred Scott v. Sandford* on slavery to *Plessy v. Ferguson* on segregation. But *Roe* does not fit well in either the canon or the anti-canon. To be sure, like *Brown*, it is used to mean many things. And like *Brown*, it gets drawn into debates about the values that are fundamental to the nation's identity. But *Roe*'s hold on us stems not from what it reveals about our shared values but from what it says about the things that divide us. *Roe* is a captivating symbol of disagreements that seem as simple as they are intractable.[6]

But *Roe* also compels us because it reveals how our disagreements are rarely black and white, even in a time of intense polarization. We often think of it as a stand-in for the most divisive subjects in our cultural wars, but it has also become a vault where we store the ambiguities and contradictions of our abortion politics. When we talk about *Roe*, we often articulate views that do not fit within a conventional pro-life/pro-choice framework, and that touch on questions we are tempted to push aside. We talk about *Roe* so much because we have made it a symbol of the nuances the Supreme Court has supposedly made it harder to discuss.

In the 1970s and '80s, new arguments framing *Roe* as a decision involving choice for women reflected the work both of a feminist anti-rape movement that had changed state law on sexual assault, and of abortion rights supporters who worked to activate what they saw as a silent majority of pro-choice voters. Evangelical Protestants, who were beginning to join the anti-abortion movement, happily connected *Roe* and choice to selfishness and hedonism. The national conversation about choice and consent showed that recognizing a right to make reproductive (or sexual) decisions did not mean that people would believe women's stories.

In the 1980s, the New Right and the Republican Party wove *Roe* into older attacks on judicial overreaching. Right-to-lifers, who wanted to shore up a then-fragile relationship with the GOP, likewise stressed that *Roe* was anti-democratic. But these conversations raised much harder questions about when the judiciary should bow to popular opinion—and how the courts could protect crucial rights without undermining the nation's commitment to democracy.

By the 1990s, as record numbers of women went to college, joined the workforce, and moved beyond "pink collar" jobs, *Roe* had come to embody differing views about the opportunities available to working parents. While pro-choice attorneys argued that the decision had made it easier for women to balance family and careers, right-to-lifers argued that abortion harmed women's health. These debates exposed how new opportunities for working parents were not equally available to all women. Fights about *Roe* also brought to light how little had changed in the division of labor at home, the availability of government support for working parents, or sexual harassment at work.

From the mid-1990s to the late 2000s, *Roe* was at the center of a tug-of-war about the relationship between politics and science. In fights about partial-birth abortion, groups like the National Right to Life Committee positioned *Roe* as part of a much bigger problem: that the media and the medical establishment were biased against conservatives. Abortion rights supporters responded that the prejudice ran the other way: abortion opponents, they said, ignored science by excluding a health exception from partial-birth abortion bans, passing laws tying abortion to breast cancer without evidence, and claiming, also without proof, that abortion caused something akin to post-traumatic stress disorder. These debates raised questions that were already familiar in controversies ranging from climate change to vaccine safety. But the back-and-forth made it clear that neither side had worked out a consistent approach to the proper role of moral norms in scientific disputes.

Between the 2000s and the 2010s, the dialogue about *Roe* and race took on new urgency. Right-to-lifers asserted that the movement to legalize abortion had been inspired by racism, even as an increasingly influential reproductive justice movement positioned *Roe* as part of a comprehensive approach to reproductive health care and racial justice. But while anti-abortion activists focused on the supposed biases of individual bigots, the debate flushed out questions about structural obstacles facing people of color. And while abortion rights supporters made *Roe* a symbol of a broader reproductive justice agenda, they also had to wrestle with the messy history of movements for eugenics, family planning, and abortion rights.

The decade of the 2010s saw escalating struggles over *Roe* and religious liberty. The introduction of a contraceptive mandate in the Affordable Care Act, the recognition of same-sex marriage, and a perception that Christianity was demographically declining reinforced some conservative Christians' sense that their views were no longer welcome in the public square. Anti-abortion leaders equated *Roe* with the denigration of freedom of conscience and the marginalization of people of faith. Pro-choice and reproductive justice groups responded that *Roe* protected religious liberty by allowing everyone to follow the dictates of their own faith. It became increasingly difficult to see religious liberty as just another partisan issue.

The repurposing of *Roe* offers a valuable example of how competing movements at times dictate one another's arguments. Framing, which helps the public make sense of a conflict and its place in the broader culture, can be central to campaigns to change the law or the broader society. Scholars like Suzanne Staggenborg, Doug McAdam, Reva Siegel, and William Eskridge have stressed the extent to which movements articulate their demands in dialogue with the opposition. In the case of *Roe*, this chess match often followed a specific pattern: each movement often acknowledged the importance of the issue raised by an opponent—getting the role of the judiciary right in democracy, for example, or ensuring justice for people of color—but would turn that argument upside down. While one side insisted that *Roe* (and legal abortion) protected that value, the other responded that *Roe* embodied everything that undermined it.[7]

At times, each side did present the other's argument as irrelevant. Anti-abortion activists, for example, sometimes suggested that claims about a right to choose were unimportant compared to the protection of human life. Abortion rights supporters at times suggested that concerns about judicial activism were overblown. But more often, each movement accepted the importance of the issue raised by the opposition but suggested that they, not their adversaries, had a better sense of how to address it. Pro-choice groups responded to arguments connecting *Roe* to threats of religious liberty by arguing that *Roe* protected freedom of conscience. Anti-abortion advocates reacted to arguments about abortion access and equality for women by suggesting that abortion made women ill. The more each movement focused on responding to the other, the harder it seemed to change the terms of the debate.

But the history of arguments made around *Roe* suggests that these limits reached only so far. The pro-choice and pro-life movements raised novel issues even when nominally replying to one another—and even when tying their points to *Roe*. When addressing pro-choice arguments about the needs of people of color, anti-abortion activists addressed race in an entirely different way, spinning the history of movements around eugenics, family planning, and abortion. When accusing their opponents of endorsing judicial activism, pro-choice groups offered a different idea of what the judiciary should do, suggesting that judicial modesty required some deference to popular opinion. While the movements studied here did feel compelled to respond to one another, advocates proved to be remarkably creative in working around the limits this involved.

This history is even more important now that the reversal of *Roe* seems to be a matter of when, not if. There is a better-than-even chance that it has happened by the time you read these words. Some suggest that the Court's decision will not make a difference for those in many states. Access to abortion has varied widely for decades depending on an individual's zip code. Conservative legislatures have passed dozens of restrictions on the reasons people can end pregnancies and the procedures doctors can use, and have mandated the information given to patients before a doctor performs a procedure. In the states most committed to eliminating legal abortion, access is already almost impossible for some patients. Reversing *Roe* might not mean much to those for whom the right to choose already means very little.[8]

In practical terms, however, overturning *Roe* will matter. Entire regions are likely to eliminate access to abortion. What "abortion" means will surely be contested by those with clashing views about how emergency contraception, intrauterine devices, or the morning after pill work. Travel distances to clinics will likely grow. While studies have established the safety of telehealth abortion, the risks of abortion medication are higher when patients take the pill without a doctor's supervision, especially later in pregnancy. Desperate patients may be more likely to misuse abortion pills, or to suffer adverse effects without seeking medical help, if they fear criminal prosecution. If it is difficult to find an abortion provider in large swathes of the United States, we might expect that eliminating *Roe* will make it that much harder.

But the history of how we talk about *Roe* shows that something equally important is at stake. For many, the decision stands not just for a right to abortion but for a broader idea of autonomy and equality. Advocates have invoked *Roe* in discussions of LGBTIQ rights and birth control. Whatever the justices intend, a decision reversing *Roe* will signal that the Court might be open to revisiting other rights. Undoing precedents recognizing same-sex marriage or protecting birth control might produce an even bigger backlash than overturning *Roe*. But for political as well as jurisprudential reasons, it will be hard to explain how *Roe*'s perceived flaws are not also present in *Obergefell v. Hodges* or *Griswold v. Connecticut*. In amicus briefs in *Dobbs*, some right-to-lifers noted this possibility and invited the justices to reconsider their rulings in *Obergefell* and *Lawrence v. Texas*, a case striking down criminal laws against same-sex intercourse. If the justices are willing to reconsider *Roe,* it may mean that other constitutional rights are no longer safe.[9]

Some may think that by reversing *Roe*, the Court will have taken a step toward ending the debate over abortion. If it allows states to reach their own conclusions, the argument goes, then the stakes of the conflict will be lower, and both the pro-choice and pro-life movements may be more willing to have a reasonable conversation. The history of struggles around *Roe* casts serious doubt on this idea. First, the movements contesting the abortion wars began their fight before 1973. Both sides have deeply held beliefs about equality, autonomy, and fetal life that predate the original *Roe* opinion. The Supreme Court did not create those beliefs, and it cannot resolve them.

A reversal of *Roe* will upend a half century of jurisprudence and forever define the current Court's legacy. What it will not do is stop us from talking about *Roe*. Americans certainly care about the decision because it has limited the extent to which states can restrict or ban abortion, but that is hardly the only reason. The way we talk about *Roe* is a window on our definitions of liberty and equality. Our conversations about it have a bearing on struggles over marriage, birth control, and civil rights. If the Court no longer recognizes a right to choose, *Roe* will almost certainly remain a rallying cry for those with different views about everything from race to religion.

The history I have described here does not suggest a clear path forward in our civil war over abortion. The reasons for our divisions are complicated and long-standing, and history supplies no easy answers.

But more often than we realize, our conversations about abortion have reached beyond what Harvard professor Laurence Tribe famously called the clash of absolutes. This dialogue suggests that we have begun a more robust popular constitutional practice when it comes to abortion than our fixation on *Roe* would suggest. That we make a single judicial decision stand for so much assigns the Court a central role in our constitutional culture. Using *Roe* as a symbol suggests real deference to and reliance on the Court. In practice, our many reinterpretations of *Roe* suggest a disconnect between the importance we rhetorically assign the Court and the way we behave when discussing, claiming, and questioning constitutional rights. The more the Court's popularity declines, and the more backlash greets the elimination of *Roe*, the more conscious and overt these popular interpretive practices may become. Many already interpret *Roe* with little regard for what the Court has said. In a post-*Roe* America, many may do so openly and deliberately.

When we talk about *Roe*, we contradict ourselves and one another. We bring to the surface nuances for which our politics leaves little room: the inconvenient questions that characterize so many of our views on abortion. In short, ideas that *Roe* supposedly put off limits have forced their way back into our discussions of it. So I ask again: why *Roe*? Because we have always needed a richer conversation about abortion than the courts make room for, and sometimes, without even knowing it, we have had one all along.

Abbreviations

ACCL   American Citizens Concerned for Life, Inc., Records, Gerald R. Ford Presidential Library and Museum, University of Michigan, Ann Arbor

ACF   Arthur Culvahouse Jr. Files, Ronald Reagan Presidential Library, Simi Valley, California

AUS   Americans United for the Separation of Church and State Subject Files, Rare Book and Manuscript Library, Columbia University, New York, New York

CUR   Choice USA Records, Smith College Special Collections, Smith College, Northampton, Massachusetts

FSP   Frederick T. Steeper Papers, Gerald R. Ford Memorial Library and Museum, University of Michigan, Ann Arbor

FWHC   Feminist Women Health Center Records, David M. Rubenstein Rare Book and Manuscript Library, Duke University, Durham, North Carolina

JBP   James Bopp Jr. Papers, Terre Haute, Indiana

JFP   Jerry Falwell/Falwell Ministry Papers, Jerry Falwell Library, Liberty University, Lynchburg, Virginia

JGR   John G. Roberts Papers, Ronald Reagan Presidential Library, Simi Valley, California

JRS   Dr. Joseph Stanton Human Life Issues Library and Resource Center, Our Lady of New York Convent, Bronx, New York

KKP   Kathryn Kolbert *Planned Parenthood v. Casey* Papers, Archives and Special Collections, Barnard College, New York, New York

LWP   Linda Wharton Papers, on file with the author

MBP   Morton Blackwell Papers, Ronald Reagan Presidential Library, Simi Valley, California

MFJ   Mildred F. Jefferson Papers, Schlesinger Library, Radcliffe Institute, Harvard University, Cambridge, Massachusetts

MGP   Myrna Gutiérrez Papers, on file with the author

NAPAWR National Asian and Pacific American Women's Forum Records, Smith College Special Collections, Smith College, Northampton, Massachusetts

NARAL   National Abortion Rights Action League Papers, Schlesinger Library, Radcliffe Institute, Harvard University, Cambridge, Massachusetts

PAW   People for the American Way Collection of Conservative Political Ephemera, Bancroft Library, University of California, Berkeley

PKF   Peter Keisler Files, Ronald Reagan Presidential Library, Simi Valley, California

PLN   Pro-Life Newsletters Collection, Schlesinger Library, Radcliffe Institute, Harvard University, Cambridge, Massachusetts

PWP   Paul Weyrich Papers, University of Wyoming, American Heritage Archive Center, Laramie

RCD   Robin Chandler Lynn Duke Papers, David M. Rubenstein Rare Book and Manuscript Library, Duke University, Durham, North Carolina

RCP   Richard Coleson Papers, Terre Haute, Indiana

RHS   Reproductive Health Services Papers, University of Missouri, St. Louis

RJN   Richard John Neuhaus Papers, American Catholic History Research Center and University Archives, Catholic University of America, Washington, DC

SBL   Southern Baptists for Life Records, Southern Baptist Historical Library and Archives, Nashville, Tennessee

SSR   SisterSong Women of Color Reproductive Justice Collective Records, Smith College Special Collections, Smith College, Northampton, Massachusetts

ABBREVIATIONS

VRP   Victor G. Rosenblum Papers, Northwestern Archival and Manuscript Collections, Northwestern University, Evanston, Illinois

WBF   William Barr Files, Ronald Reagan Presidential Library, Simi Valley, California

WCX   Wilcox Collection of Contemporary Political Movements, Kenneth Spencer Research Library, University of Kansas, Lawrence

Notes

Preface

1. A word on terminology is required here. I use the word *woman* at times to reflect historical debates about abortion and its effects on cisgender women. Obviously, the battles studied here had implications for transmen and other people who can get pregnant, but as a historical matter, using "woman" or "women" better captures the terms of the some of the debates described in this book. To refer to the movements contesting the abortion wars, I at times follow the Associated Press style guide and use "anti-abortion" or "abortion rights." At other times, I use the language that movements apply to themselves, such as "pro-choice," "pro-life," "right-to-life," and "reproductive justice." As a historian, I hope to make sense of how movements understand themselves and help readers to do the same, and borrowing movements' language can make this easier. On *Dobbs v. Jackson Women's Health Organization*, see Mary Ziegler, "This Could Be the Supreme Court Case That Takes Down *Roe v. Wade*," *CNN*, May 18, 2021, https://www.cnn.com/2021/05/17/opinions/abortion-mississippi-supreme-court-dobbs-v-jackson-womens-health-ziegler/index.html, accessed October 11, 2021; Leah Litman and Melissa Murray, "The Supreme Court's Conservative Supermajority Is about to Show Us Its True Colors," *Washington Post*, May 17, 2021, https://www.washingtonpost.com/opinions/2021/05/17/supreme-court-mississippi-abortion-restrictions-roe-v-wade/, accessed October 11, 2021. For an overview of claims about the importance of *Roe*, see Joshua Prager, *The Family Roe: An American Story* (New York: Norton, 2021), 1–21. For the South Korea decision, see Sayuri Umeda, "South Korea: Abortion Decriminalized since January 1, 2021," Library of Congress (March 2021), https://www.loc.gov/item/global-legal-monitor/2021–03–18/south-korea-abortion-decriminalized-since-january-1–2021/, accessed December 23, 2021. On developments in Argentina, see Taylor Boas et al., "Argentina Legalized Abortion. Here's How It Happened and What It Means for Latin America," *Washington Post*, January 18, 2021, https://www.washingtonpost.

com/politics/2021/01/18/argentina-legalized-abortion-heres-how-it-happened-what-it-means-latin-america, accessed December 23, 2021. On changes to abortion law in Kenya, see Nita Bhala and Humphrey Malalo, "Rape Survivors Win Right to Abortion in Landmark Court Ruling," *Reuters*, June 12, 2019, https://www.reuters.com/article/us-kenya-abortion-ruling/kenyas-rape-survivors-win-right-to-abortion-in-landmark-court-ruling-idUSKCN1TD2HG, accessed December 23, 2021. On developments in Mexico, see Natalie Kitroeff and Oscar Lopez, "Abortion Is No Longer a Crime in Mexico. But Most Women Still Can't Get One," *New York Times*, September 8, 2021, https://www.nytimes.com/2021/09/08/world/americas/mexico-abortion-access.html, accessed March 28, 2022.

2. For the Court's decision on *Dred Scott*, see *Dred Scott v. Sandford*, 60 U.S. 393 (1857). For the Court's decision in *Brown*, see *Brown v. Board of Education*, 347 U.S. 483 (1954). For a sample of work on the canon and the political reinterpretation of precedent, see Jamal Greene, "The Anticanon," *Harvard Law Review* 125 (2011): 379–425; Kenneth Kersch, "The Talking Cure: How Constitutional Argument Drives Constitutional Development," *Boston University Law Review* 94 (2014): 1083–1108; Jack M. Balkin and Sanford Levinson, "Commentary: The Canons of Constitutional Law," *Harvard Law Review* 111 (1998): 963–1024; Richard A. Primus, "Canon, Anti-Canon, and Judicial Dissent," *Duke Law Journal* 48 (1998): 243–303.

3. See *Planned Parenthood of Southeastern Pennsylvania v. Casey*, 505 U.S. 833 (1992) (plurality decision).

4. On the Court's declining popularity, see Jeffrey M. Jones, "Approval of Supreme Court Down to 40 Percent, a New Low," *Gallup*, September 23, 2021, https://news.gallup.com/poll/354908/approval-supreme-court-down-new-low.aspx, accessed December 20, 2021. For more on the history and current practice of popular constitutionalism, see Larry Kramer, *The People Themselves: Popular Constitutionalism and Judicial Review* (New York: Oxford University Press, 2004); Mark Tushnet, *Taking Back the Constitution: Activist Judges and the Next Age of American Law* (New Haven, CT: Yale University Press, 2020).

5. Anne Escacove, "Dialogic Framing: The Framing/Counter-framing of 'Partial-Birth Abortion,' " *Sociological Inquiry* 74 (2004): 70; Doug McAdam, "Tactical Innovation and the Pace of Insurgency," *American Sociological Review* 48 (1983): 735–754. For more examples of work on social movement framing across various disciplines, see William N. Eskridge, "Channeling: Identity-Based Social Movements and Public Law," *University of Pennsylvania Law Review* 150 (2001): 419–500; Suzanne Staggenborg and David S. Meyer, "Opposing Movement Strategies in U.S. Abortion Politics," *Research in Social Movements, Conflicts, and Change* 28 (2008): 207–238;

Deana Rohlinger, "Framing the Abortion Debate: Organizational Resources, Media Strategies, and Movement-Countermovement Dynamics," *Sociological Quarterly* 43 (2002): 479–507; Reva B. Siegel, "Constitutional Culture, Social Movement Conflict, and Constitutional Change: The Case of the De Facto Era," *California Law Review* 94 (2006): 1323–1400.

Chapter 1. The Making of *Roe*

1. See Leslie Reagan, *When Abortion Was a Crime: Women, Medicine, and Law in the United States, 1867–1973* (Berkeley: University of California Press, 1997), 22–25; Brief Amicus Curiae of the American Historical Association and the Organization of American Historians, 5–30, *Dobbs v. Jackson Women's Health Organization*, 2021 WL 4311852 (2022) (No. 19-1392). For disagreement on the relevance of quickening, see Joseph Dellapenna, *Dispelling the Myths of Abortion History* (Durham, NC: Carolina Academic Press, 2006).

2. See Reagan, *When Abortion Was a Crime*, 26–30; Janet Farrell Brodie, *Contraception and Abortion in Nineteenth-Century America* (Ithaca, NY: Cornell University Press, 1994), 265–274.

3. See Reagan, *When Abortion Was a Crime*, 26–30; Rickie Solinger, "Pregnancy and Power Before *Roe v. Wade*, 1950–1970," in *Abortion Wars: A Half-Century of Struggle, 1950–2000*, ed. Rickie Solinger (Berkeley: University of California Press, 2000), 17; Brodie, *Contraception and Abortion*, 254.

4. On maternal mortality from abortion in the 1930s, see Irving Loudon, "Maternal Mortality in the Past and Its Relevance to Developing Countries Today," *American Journal of Clinical Nutrition* 71 (2000): 241–246; Rachel Benson Gold, "Lessons from Before *Roe*: Will Past Be Prologue?" *Guttmacher Policy Review*, March 1, 2003, https://www.guttmacher.org/gpr/2003/03/lessons-roe-will-past-be-prologue, accessed November 10, 2021.

5. Marguerite Marshall, "A Serious Report on a Serious Subject: Baby Killers," *El Paso Times*, October 26, 1941, 52.

6. Reagan, *When Abortion Was a Crime*, 193–194; Rickie Solinger, " 'A Complete Disaster:' Abortion and the Politics of Hospital Abortion Committees," *Feminist Studies* 19 (1993): 241–252.

7. See David Garrow, *Liberty and Sexuality: The Right to Privacy and the Making of* Roe v. Wade (Berkeley: University of California Press, 1998), 142–199; "Reform," in *Before* Roe v. Wade: *Voices That Shaped the Debate Before the Supreme Court Decision*, ed. Linda Greenhouse and Reva Siegel (New York: Kaplan, 2010), 7–35. On the Clergy Consultation Service, see Gillian Frank, *Making Choice Sacred: Liberal Religion*

and the Struggle for Reproductive Rights Before Roe (Chapel Hill: University of North Carolina Press, forthcoming).

8. Eugene Quay, "Justifiable Abortion: Medical and Legal Foundations," *Georgetown Law Journal* 49 (1961): 395–425.

9. On NRLC, see Daniel K. Williams, *Defenders of the Unborn: The Pro-Life Movement Before* Roe v. Wade (New York: Oxford University Press, 2016), 131–190; Mary Ziegler, *After* Roe: *The Lost History of the Abortion Debate* (Cambridge, MA: Harvard University Press, 2015), 32–48.

10. See Mary Ziegler, "Originalism Talk," *Brigham University Law Review* 2014 (2014): 869–890; Mary Ziegler, *Abortion and the Law in America:* Roe v. Wade *to the Present* (New York: Cambridge University Press, 2020), 45–90.

11. See Donald Critchlow, *Intended Consequences: Birth Control, Abortion, and the Federal Government in Modern America* (New York: Oxford University Press, 1999); Matthew J. Connelly, *Fatal Misconception: The Struggle to Control World Population* (Cambridge, MA: Harvard University Press, 2008).

12. See Ziegler, *After* Roe, 107–120.

13. "Do Anti-Abortion Laws Curb Women's Rights?" *Miami Herald*, July 15, 1970, 15. For more on feminist pro-choice work before *Roe*, see "Repeal," in Greenhouse and Siegel, *Before* Roe v. Wade, 36–46, 49–55; Ziegler, *After* Roe, 120–145; Suzanne Staggenborg, *The Pro-Choice Movement: Organization and Activism in the Abortion Conflict* (New York: Oxford University Press, 1991), 10–56.

14. On the repeal movement, see Greenhouse and Siegel, "Repeal," 36–69; Staggenborg, *The Pro-Choice Movement*, 20–45; Garrow, *Liberty and Sexuality*, 100–145.

15. For the Court's decision in *Griswold*, see *Griswold v. Connecticut*, 381 U.S. 479, 500–504 (1965).

16. *United States v. Vuitch*, 402 U.S. 62 (1971).

17. Morris Kaplan, "State Abortion Law Upheld on Appeal," *New York Times*, February 26, 1972, 1. On the *Byrn* litigation, see *Byrn v. New York City Health and Hospitals Corporation*, 286 N.E.2d 887 (N.Y. 1972); *Byrn v. New York City Health and Hospitals Corporation*, 38 A.2d 316 (N.Y. App. Div. 1972).

18. *Eisenstadt v. Baird*, 405 U.S. 438, 446–455 (1972). On the connection between *Eisenstadt* and *Roe*, see Bob Woodward and Scott Armstrong, *The Brethren: Inside the Supreme Court* (New York: Simon and Schuster, 1979), 210–211.

19. See Garrow, *Liberty and Sexuality*, 200–290; Linda Greenhouse, *Becoming Justice Blackmun: Harry Blackmun's Supreme Court Journey* (New York: Henry Holt, 2005), 111–136.

20. *Roe v. Wade*, 410 U.S. 113, 137–145 (1973).

21. See ibid., 143–157.

22. On the debates about originalism and abortion, see Jack Balkin, "Abortion and Original Meaning," *Constitutional Commentary* 24 (2007): 297–361; Joshua Craddock, "Protecting Prenatal Persons: Is Abortion Unconstitutional?" *Harvard Journal of Law and Public Policy* 40 (2017): 539–561; Ed Whelan, "Doubts about Constitutional Personhood," *First Things*, April 3, 2021, https://www.firstthings.com/web-exclusives/2021/04/doubts-about-constitutional-personhood, accessed January 19, 2021; John Finnis, "Abortion Is Unconstitutional," *First Things*, April 2021, https://www.firstthings.com/article/2021/04/abortion-is-unconstitutional, accessed January 19, 2021.

23. See *Roe v. Wade*, 410 U.S. 113, 143–157 (1973).

24. On the history of the viability standard, see David Garrow, "How *Roe v. Wade* Was Written," *Washington and Lee Law Review* 71 (2014): 893–913. On the effects of *Roe*, see Ziegler, *Abortion and the Law*, 12–34; Garrow, *Liberty and Sexuality*, 342–367; Williams, *Defenders of the Unborn*, 201–213.

25. See Gayle White, "*Roe v. Wade* Role Just a Page in a Rocky Life Story," *Atlanta Journal-Constitution*, January 22, 2003, A1; Bill Rankin, "1973 Plaintiff Seeks Reversal of Abortion Law," *Atlanta Journal-Constitution*, September 23, 2003, B4; Jacinthia Jones, "Famous Plaintiffs Disavow Abortion 3 Decades Later," *Commercial Appeal*, November 9, 2001, DS1.

26. White, "*Roe v. Wade*," A1.

27. Linda Greenhouse, "Harry Blackmun, Author of Abortion Right, Dies," *New York Times*, March 5, 1999, https://www.nytimes.com/1999/03/05/us/justice-blackmun-author-of-abortion-right-dies.html, accessed October 6, 2021. For more on Blackmun, see Greenhouse, *Becoming Justice Blackmun*, 134–183.

28. On McCorvey's life, see Joshua Prager, *The Family Roe: An American Story* (New York: Norton, 2021).

Chapter 2. Choice and Consent

1. Karen Mulhauser, interview with Mary Ziegler, March 31, 2021; Karen Mulhauser, interview with Mary Ziegler, April 3, 2021; Karen Mulhauser, email interview with Mary Ziegler, May 21, 2021; Karen Mulhauser, email interview with Mary Ziegler, May 22, 2021.

2. Mulhauser, March 31 interview; Mulhauser, April 3 interview; Mulhauser, May 21 email interview; Mulhauser, May 22 email interview.

3. Mulhauser, March 31 interview; Mulhauser, April 3 interview; Mulhauser, May 21 email interview; Mulhauser, May 22 email interview.

4. On the early years of the National Right to Life Committee, see Daniel K. Williams, *Defenders of the Unborn: The Pro-Life Movement Before* Roe v. Wade (New York: Oxford University Press, 2016), 3–10, 94–95; Mary Ziegler, *After* Roe: *The Lost History of the Abortion Debate* (Cambridge, MA: Harvard University Press, 2015), 37–45; Jennifer Holland, *Tiny You: A Western History of the Anti-Abortion Movement* (Berkeley: University of California Press, 2020).

5. On NRLC's meeting, see Meeting Minutes, NRLC Ad Hoc Strategy Meeting (February 11, 1973), ACCL, Box 4, 1973 NRLC Folder 1. On the importance of an anti-abortion constitutional amendment, see Williams, *Defenders of the Unborn*, 213–245; Ziegler, *After* Roe, 23–45.

6. On the Blair House, see Helene Cooper, "Sorry, We're Booked, White House Tells Obamas," *New York Times*, December 12, 2008, https://thecaucus.blogs.nytimes.com/2008/12/12/sorry-were-booked-white-house-tells-obamas/?_r=0, accessed August 12, 2021.

7. Lee Gidding to NARAL Board of Directors et al. (February 5, 1973), NARAL, Carton 1, 1973–1974 Executive Committee Folder. On NARAL's interest in appealing to the elites, see Ziegler, *After* Roe, 178–184.

8. Abortion Part I: Testimony on S. 119 and S. 130: Before the Senate Subcommittee Judiciary Subcommittee, 93rd Congress, 2nd Sess. (1974), 8–9 (Statement of Dr. Mildred Jefferson). For more on Jefferson, see Joshua Prager, *The Family Roe: An American Story* (New York: Norton, 2021), 130–156; Mary Ziegler, *Abortion and the Law:* Roe v. Wade *to the Present* (New York: Cambridge University Press, 2020), 60–74.

9. For Jefferson's statement: Nils Bruzelius, "Impact: Legal, Psychological," *Boston Globe*, December 18, 1976, 8. Claims about the ethics of abortion providers had a longer history. See Rickie Solinger, *The Abortionist: A Woman against the Law* (Berkeley: University of California Press, 1996).

10. On the marginalization of feminists in NARAL in the late 1960s and early 1970s, see Ziegler, *After* Roe, 178–184. For an overview of some of the feminist arguments made before *Roe*, see Reva Siegel, "*Roe's* Roots: The Women's Rights Claims That Engendered *Roe*," *Boston University Law Review* 30 (2010): 1875–1900.

11. Mulhauser, March 31 interview; Mulhauser, April 3 interview; Mulhauser, May 21 email interview; Mulhauser, May 22 email interview. On other feminists leading major abortion rights organizations in the period, see Ziegler, *After* Roe, 199–202.

12. See Willard Cates Jr., "Legal Abortion: Are American Black Women Healthier Because of It?" *Phylon* 38 (1977): 267–281; Jacqueline Darroch Forrest, Christopher Tietze, and Ellen Sullivan, "Abortion in the United States, 1976–1977," *Family Planning Perspectives* 10 (1978): 271–279.

13. On the Hyde Amendment and veto override, see Donald T. Critchlow, "When Republicans Became Revolutionaries: Conservatives in Congress," in *The American Congress: The Building of Democracy*, ed. Julian E. Zelizer (New York: Houghton Mifflin Harcourt, 2004), 703–725; "Ford Makes a Point of Supporting Hyde Provision in Veto Message," *National Right to Life News*, September 1976, 4, JRS, 1976 National Right to Life News Box.

14. On the increasing number of abortions and the rising abortion rate, see Rachel Benson Gold, "After the Hyde Amendment: Public Funding for Abortion in FY 78," *Family Planning Perspectives* 12 (1980): 131–134; James Trussell, Jane Menken, Barbara Lindheim, and Barbara Vaughan, "The Impact of Restricting Medicaid Financing for Abortion," *Family Planning Perspectives* 12 (1980): 122–130. On the importance NARAL attached to the Hyde Amendment and power in Congress, see Carol Werner to NARAL Board of Directors (June 30, 1976), NARAL, Box 41, Folder 10. On the abortion rate at the time, see Jacqueline Darroch Forrest, Ellen Sullivan, and Christopher Tietze, "Abortion in the United States, 1977–1978," *Family Planning Perspectives* 11 (1979): 329–341.

15. NARAL, Model Letter to Congress (January 1977), NARAL, Box 46, Folder 10.

16. "Freedom Is the Right to Choose: Rally for Abortion Rights" (n.d., ca. 1978), RHS, Box 1, Folder 16; "Freedom to Choose Is the American Way" (n.d., ca. 1978), RHS, Box 1, Folder 16. For NARAL's statement about the rights of the poor: Draft, Statement of Carol Werner (August 4, 1977), NARAL, Box 46, Folder 10.

17. On the history of rape law, see Estelle B. Freedman, *Redefining Rape: Sexual Violence in the Era of Suffrage and Segregation* (Cambridge, MA: Harvard University Press, 2013); Danielle L. McGuire, *At the Dark End of the Street: Black Women, Rape, and Resistance—A New History of the Civil Rights Movement from Rosa Parks to the Rise of Black Power* (New York: Vintage, 2011). For the Model Penal Code provision, see 1962 Model Penal Code § 213.4. On the ERA, see Serena Mayeri, "A New ERA or a New Era? Amendment Advocacy and the Reconstitution of Feminism," *Northwestern Law Review* 103 (2009): 1223–1240; Jane Mansbridge, *Why We Lost the ERA* (Chicago: University of Chicago Press, 1986).

18. Susan Griffin, "Rape: The All-American Crime," *Ramparts*, January 1971, 10, 26; see also Susan Griffin, *Rape and the Politics of Consciousness* (New York: Harper and Row, 1986).

19. Susan Brownmiller, *Against Our Will: Men, Women, and Rape* (New York: Fawcett, 1975). On the anti-rape movement of the 1970s, see Maria Bevacqua, *Rape on the Public Agenda: Feminism and the Politics of Sexual Assault* (Boston: Northeastern University Press, 2000).

20. "Court Limits Rape Testimony," *Daily Press*, October 11, 1978, 9.

21. Mulhauser, March 31 interview. On the new laws, see Grace Lichtenstein, "Rape Laws Undergoing Changes to Aid Victims," *New York Times*, June 4, 1975, 1. For a sample of MacKinnon's work, see Catharine A. MacKinnon, *The Sexual Harassment of Working Women* (New Haven, CT: Yale University Press, 1979), 7. For Farley's work, see Lin Farley, *Sexual Shakedown: The Sexual Harassment of Women on the Job* (New York: McGraw-Hill, 1978).

22. For the physicians' argument in *Singleton*, see Brief for Respondents, *Singleton v. Wulff*, 428 U.S. 106 (1976) (No. 74-1393). For the Court's decision in *Singleton*, see *Singleton v. Wulff*, 428 U.S. 106, 112–116 (1976).

23. *Maher v. Roe*, 428 U.S. 464, 473–476 (1977).

24. Karen Mulhauser to NARAL Members (July 1976), NARAL, Box 46, Folder 10. On the reaction of NARAL and other pro-choice groups to the Hyde Amendment, see Ziegler, *Abortion and the Law*, 42–47; Ziegler, *After* Roe, 138.

25. On the rise of freestanding abortion clinics, see Stanley Henshaw, Jacqueline Darroch Forrest, and Elaine Blaine, "Abortion Services in the United States, 1981–1982," *Family Planning Perspectives* 16 (1984): 119–124. On the feminist women's health movement, see Jennifer Nelson, *More Than Medicine: A History of the Feminist Women's Health Movement* (New York: New York University Press, 2015); Sandra Morgen, *Into Our Own Hands: The Women's Health Movement in the United States, 1970–1990* (New Brunswick, NJ: Rutgers University Press, 2002). On the dip in hospital abortions and the rise of abortion clinics, see Barbara Lindheim, "Services, Policies, and Costs in U.S. Abortion Facilities," *Family Planning Perspectives* 11 (1979): 283–289.

26. On the changes to health care delivery in the 1970s, see John C. Burnham, *Health Care in America: A History* (Baltimore, MD: Johns Hopkins University Press, 2015), 416–423; David Charles Sloane and Beverlie Conant Sloane, *Medicine Moves to the Mall* (Baltimore, MD: Johns Hopkins University Press, 2003); Gordon T. Moore, "The Case of the Disappearing Generalist: Does It Need to Be Solved?" *Millbank Quarterly* 70 (1992): 361–379.

27. On Carter's and Ford's positions on abortion, see Laurence H. Tribe, *Abortion: The Clash of Absolutes* (New York: Norton, 1992), 148; Raymond Tatalovich, *The Politics of Abortion in the United States and Canada: A Comparative Study* (New York: Routledge, 1997), 168; Rickie Solinger, *Pregnancy and Power: A Short History of Reproductive Politics in America* (New York: New York University Press, 2005), 20.

28. On Downey, see Tom Shales, "Shriek Chic! It's Morton Downey!" *Washington Post*, July 6, 1988, D1; Robert Hilburn, "Morton Downey Jr.: The Mouth Goes on the

Record," *Los Angeles Times*, April 4, 1989, 12; John Herbert, "Abortion Foes Target 5 Senators," *Atlanta Journal-Constitution*, December 13, 1978, 7A. On Paul Brown, see Nathaniel Sheppard Jr., "Group Fighting Abortion Planning to Step Up Its Drive," *New York Times*, July 3, 1978, 20; Leslie Bennetts, "Anti-Abortion Group Asks Defeat of Javits and Five Others at Polls," *New York Times*, January 19, 1980, 11. On Sassone, see Dorothy Townsend, "Pro and Con Protestors Scuffle at Closed Abortion Facility," *Los Angeles Times*, March 22, 1970, A1; "Lawyer Denied 'Guardian of the Unborn' Plea," *Los Angeles Times*, June 3, 1971, D8; Sheppard, "Group Fighting," 20.

29. On Clark, see Murrey Marder, "US Silence Bolsters Report of Aid to Portugal and Angola," *Washington Post*, September 26, 1975, A7; Leslie Gelb, "U.S. Aides Tell Senators of Arms Aid to Angolans," *New York Times*, November 7, 1975, 3.

30. See Margaret Ann Latus, "Ideological PACs and Political Action," in *The New Christian Right: Mobilization and Legitimation*, ed. Robert C. Liebman and Robert Wuthnow (Piscataway, NJ: Transaction, 1983), 45–54. On the history of the New Right, see Anne Nelson, *Shadow Network: Media, Money, and the Secret Hub of the Radical Right* (London: Bloomsbury, 2019); Daniel K. Williams, *God's Own Party: The Making of the Christian Right* (New York: Oxford University Press, 2010), 167–172.

31. "Heavy Rural Vote Works for Republicans," *Des Moines Register*, November 9, 1978, 16A; see also Doug Kneeland, "Clark Defeat in Iowa Laid to Abortion Issue," *New York Times*, November 13, 1978, https://www.nytimes.com/1978/11/13/archives/clark-defeat-in-iowa-laid-to-abortion-issue-national-help.html, accessed August 13, 2021.

32. "Heavy Rural Vote," 16A.

33. For examples of LAPAC's courting of the media, see Bill Peterson, "Foes of Abortion Aim at 'Deadly Dozen,'" *Washington Post*, February 11, 1979, A3; "Abortion Foe Will Seek Presidential Nomination," *New York Times*, June 8, 1979, A21.

34. For Mulhauser's statement: Karen Mulhauser to Joe Napolitan (January 23, 1980), NARAL, Box 45, Folder 6. The spread of ultrasound and fetal images also contributed to the stigma surrounding abortion. See Sara Dubow, *Ourselves Unborn: A History of the Fetus in Modern America* (New York: Oxford University Press, 2010), 50–71.

35. NARAL, 1977 Letter to Members of Congress, 1.

36. On Harrold: Karon Harrold, interview with Mary Ziegler, June 2, 2021. On Booth: Heather Booth, interview with Mary Ziegler, April 19, 2021. On Weinberg: Jean Weinberg, interview with Mary Ziegler, August 13, 2021.

37. Peterson, "Foes of Abortion," A3.

38. Marlene Perrin, "Pro-Choice Advocate Talks to Majority," *Iowa Press-Citizen*, November 30, 1979, 20; Weinberg, interview.

39. On various strategies for an anti-abortion constitutional amendment and the response of pro-choice groups, see Tribe, *Abortion*, 150–151; Ziegler, *After* Roe, 141–143.

40. On the spread of incremental abortion restrictions, see Ziegler, *Abortion and the Law*, 42–65; Ziegler, *After* Roe, 43–62.

41. On the influence of Catholics on the early pro-life movement, see Williams, *Defenders of the Unborn*, 4–15; Holland, *Tiny You*, 3–30.

42. See Williams, *God's Own Party*, 115–119; Neil J. Young, *We Gather Together: The Religious Right and the Problem of Interfaith Politics* (New York: Oxford University Press, 2016), 105–112.

43. On the founding of Christian Voice and the Moral Majority, see Darren Dochuk, *From Bible Belt to Sunbelt: Plain-Folk Religion, Grassroots Politics, and the Rise of Evangelical Conservatism* (New York: Norton, 2011), 348–359; Paul Boyer, "The Evangelical Resurgence in 1970s American Protestantism," in *Rightward Bound: Making America Conservative in the 1970s*, ed. Julian Zelizer and Bruce Schulman (Cambridge, MA: Harvard University Press, 2008), 48–54; Williams, *God's Own Party*, 165–182.

44. On the SBC's changing position on abortion, see Andrew R. Lewis, *The Rights Turn in Conservative Christian Politics: How Abortion Transformed the Culture Wars* (New York: Cambridge University Press, 2017), 18–89; Young, *We Gather Together*, 98–112; Frances FitzGerald, *The Evangelicals: The Struggle to Shape America* (New York: Simon and Schuster, 2017), 114–121.

45. On the evangelical vogue of the 1970s, see Daniel K. Williams, *The Election of the Evangelical: Jimmy Carter, Gerald Ford, and the Presidential Contest of 1976* (Lawrence: University Press of Kansas, 2020), 43–84, 123; FitzGerald, *The Evangelicals*, 43–87; Sean P. Cunningham, *American Politics in the Postwar Sunbelt: Conservative Growth in a Battleground Region* (New York: Cambridge University Press, 2014), 173–182. For the Gallup poll on evangelicals, see "Half of U.S. Protestants Are 'Born Again' Christians," Gallup Poll, September 26, 1976, 1–10, on file with the author. For the *Newsweek* story, see "Born Again," *Newsweek*, October 28, 1976, 68–78.

46. For Falwell's references to abortion on demand, see Jerry Falwell Jr., "Enforcing God's Law in the Voting Booth," *Los Angeles Times*, September 7, 1980, E5; Jim Auchmutey, "Falwell Sees Abortion as Similar to Killing Jews," *Atlanta Journal-Constitution*, March 24, 1982, B1. On the history of arguments about abortion on demand, see Williams, *Defenders of the Unborn*, 132–154.

47. Jerry Falwell, "The Healing of America," *Old-Time Gospel Hour*, May 22, 1983, 1–14, JFP, Box 8, Folder 6.

48. Jerry Falwell, "Abortion on Demand: Is It Murder?" *Old-Time Gospel Hour*, February 26, 1978, JFP, Box 8, Folder 6.

49. For the Court's decision in *Danforth*, see *Planned Parenthood of Central Missouri v. Danforth*, 428 U.S. 52 (1976).

50. On the Akron bill and the strategy it reflected, see Reginald Stuart, "Akron Divided by Heated Abortion Debate," *New York Times*, February 1, 1978, A10.

51. Memorandum, Informed Consent (n.d., ca. 1978), 4, 8, 11, JBP, Matter Box 143.

52. Mulhauser, March 31 interview; Mulhauser, April 3 interview.

53. Mulhauser, May 21 email interview; Mulhauser, May 22 email interview.

54. "Maine Folks Misled on Abortion," *Desert Sun*, March 2, 1978, B20. On the back-and-forth about a rape and incest exception in Congress, see Michael Putzel, "Government Clears Abortion Funding for Rape, Incest Victims," *Washington Post*, January 27, 1978, A9; "Senate Holds Firm on Abortion Funds," *Atlanta Journal-Constitution*, September 25, 1979, 6A; Marjorie Hunter, "House Acts to Allow States to Bar Abortion Financing," *New York Times*, December 12, 1979, A22.

55. Labor and Department of Health, Education, and Welfare Subcommittee of the Senate Appropriations Committee, 96th Congress, 1st Sess. (March 1979) 232–245 (Statement of Karen Mulhauser).

56. On Judie Brown's career in the anti-abortion movement, see, e.g., Carol Mason, *Killing for Life: The Apocalyptic Narrative of Pro-Life Politics* (Ithaca, NY: Cornell University Press, 2002), 15; Judie Brown, *It Is I Who Have Chosen You: An Autobiography* (Stafford, VA: American Life League, 1997), 7, 15, 41.

57. See Judy Mann, "A Woman Is Raped—And the Hurt Goes On," *Washington Post*, February 18, 1981, https://www.washingtonpost.com/archive/local/1981/02/18/a-woman-is-raped-and-the-hurt-goes-on/cf2a4d80-dc35-4fa8-979f-e07c6973082c/, accessed August 18, 2021.

58. Ibid.

59. On Reagan's 1976 primary run, see Rick Perlstein, *Reaganland: America's Right Turn, 1976–1980* (New York: Simon and Schuster, 2020), 398; Ziegler, *After Roe*, 15; Williams, *Defenders of the Unborn*, 231–239.

60. Bill Peterson, "Abortion Aid Faces Further Cut," *Washington Post*, March 20, 1981, A1.

61. Paul West, "Switch by 5 Democrats Enabled Passage of Stringent Abortion Ban," *Atlanta Journal-Constitution*, May 24, 1981, 25A.

62. On polling about a rape and incest exception, see Gallup, "Abortion in Depth," https://news.gallup.com/poll/1576/abortion.aspx, accessed August 18, 2021.

63. Mulhauser, April 3 interview; Mulhauser, May 22 email interview. For more on NARAL's plan for defeating an anti-abortion constitutional amendment, see Karen Mulhauser to NARAL Media Committee, "NARAL's Plan for the Hatch Amendment" (September 3, 1981), NARAL, Box 53, Folder 6; Emergency Appeal (October 23, 1981), NARAL, Box 53, Folder 6.

64. Mulhauser, March 31 interview; Mulhauser, May 22 email interview; Harrold, interview; Weinberg, interview.

65. See Jim Adams, "Robert McCoy Never Feared Controversy," *Star Tribune*, June 1, 2010, https://www.startribune.com/robert-mccoy-never-feared-controversy/95284089/, accessed August 18, 2021. For more on McCoy's work with NARAL, see Garrow, *Liberty and Sexuality*, 259; Jim Klobuchar, "Abortion Reformist Feels That Living Come First," *Star Tribune*, January 21, 1970, 1; "Abortion Referral Service Keeps Man Busy," *Star Tribune*, March 20, 1969, 1.

66. Mulhauser, March 31 interview; Mulhauser, April 3 interview; Mulhauser, May 21 email interview; Mulhauser, May 22 email interview.

67. Mulhauser, March 31 interview; Mulhauser, April 3 interview; Mulhauser, May 21 email interview; Mulhauser, May 22 email interview; Weinberg, interview.

68. On the award offered by the Women's Information Network and Mulhauser's career, see "Karen Mulhauser," WomenWerk (2021), https://www.womenwerk.com/karen-mulhauser, accessed October 8, 2021. On the watch party, see Petula Dvorak, " 'I Never Told Anyone': Christine Blasey Ford Has Unleashed a Torrent of Sexual-Assault Stories," *Washington Post*, September 27, 2018, https://www.washingtonpost.com/local/i-never-told-anyone-christine-blasey-ford-has-unleashed-a-torrent-of-sexual-assault-stories/2018/09/27/f877cb3a-c287–11e8–97a5-ab1e46bb3bc7_story.html, accessed October 8, 2021. On Mulhauser's move and downsizing party, see Petula Dvorak, " 'Anything You Want, Take It': A Downsizing Party After 45 Years in the Same House," *Washington Post*, November 14, 2019, https://www.washingtonpost.com/local/anything-you-want-take-it-a-downsizing-party-after-45-years-in-the-same-house/2019/11/13/02147fde-064e-11ea-8292-c46ee8cb3dce_story.html, accessed October 8, 2021.

69. Mulhauser, March 31 interview; Mulhauser, April 3 interview; Mulhauser, May 21 email interview; Mulhauser, May 22 email interview. On the harassment findings, see David Peterson, "McCoy Quits in Wake of Harassment Findings," *Star Tribune*, September 10, 1983, 1.

70. See Adams, "Robert McCoy."

Chapter 3. The Judiciary in American Democracy

1. On Rosenblum's relationship with his family and students: Warren Rosenblum, interview with Mary Ziegler, March 4, 2021; Peter Rosenblum, interview with Mary Ziegler, March 19, 2021; Susan Rabens, interview with Mary Ziegler, March 30, 2021; Ellen Rosenblum, interview with Mary Ziegler, March 20, 2021; Laura Rosenblum Peterson, email interview with Mary Ziegler, October 31, 2021; Mindy Roseman, interview with Mary Ziegler, March 26, 2021.

2. Warren Rosenblum, interview. On Warren's career, see Jim Newton, *Justice for All: Earl Warren and the Nation He Made* (New York: Penguin, 2007); Geoffrey Stone and Davis Strauss, *Democracy and Equality: The Enduring Constitutional Vision of the Warren Court* (New York: Oxford University Press, 2020).

3. On Rosenblum's upbringing: Warren Rosenblum, interview; Peter Rosenblum, interview.

4. On Rosenblum's time in Berkeley and later career: Warren Rosenblum, interview; Peter Rosenblum, interview; Susan Rabens, interview; Ellen Rosenblum, interview.

5. For Rosenblum's 1969 statement: John Cardinal Wright, "Crisis in Morality: The Vatican Speaks Out," *Philadelphia Inquirer*, October 6, 1969, 1, 7; see also "Abortion Still Dramatic Issue," *San Bernardino County Sun*, June 14, 1973, A1. On the Cradle in Evanston, see Susan Nelson, "Rocking the Cradle's Image," *Chicago Tribune*, October 8, 1972, L10; John Drury, "Three Thousand Babies Are Graduated from 'Cradle' to Homes of a Chicago Suburb," *Dayton Daily News*, May 22, 1936, 6.

6. On Stanton, see Hadley Arkes, "Life Watch: Remembering Joe Stanton," *Crisis*, December 1, 1997, https://www.crisismagazine.com/1997/life-watch-remembering-joe-stanton, accessed August 19, 2021. On Ratner, see Donald DeMarco, "Herbert Ratner: Apostle for the Culture of Life," *National Catholic Register*, July 22, 1997, https://www.crisismagazine.com/1997/life-watch-remembering-joe-stanton, accessed August 19, 2022. For examples of Rosenblum's work in AUL, see Marjory Mecklenberg to Victor Rosenblum (May 24, 1977), VRP, Box 6, Folder 7; Victor Rosenblum to Lore Maier (July 6, 1977), VRP, Box 6, Folder 7.

7. The Southern Manifesto of 1956 (March 12, 1956), https://history.house.gov/Historical-Highlights/1951-2000/The-Southern-Manifesto-of-1956/, accessed December 20, 2021.

8. On Frankfurter and other progressives' criticism of judicial activism, see Noah Feldman, *Scorpions: The Battles and Triumphs of FDR's Great Supreme Court Justices* (New York: Hachette, 2010), 130–163; Damon Root, *Overruled: The Long War for Control of the U.S. Supreme Court* (New York: St. Martin's 2014), 51–64. On Nixon and the politics of judicial activism, see Laura Kalman, *The Long Reach of the Sixties:*

LBJ, Nixon, and the Making of the Contemporary Supreme Court (New York: Oxford University Press, 2017), 101–157.

9. For Horan's speech, see Dennis J. Horan, "Abortion and the Conscience Clause: Current Status," *Catholic Lawyer* 20 (1974): 289–302. On Horan's life and personality, see Dolores Horan, "Acceptance of *Linacre Quarterly* Award," *Linacre Quarterly* 57 (1990): 13–16; Eugene F. Diamond, "Eulogy Given at the Funeral of Dennis J. Horan," *Linacre Quarterly* 55 (1988): 4–5; Kenan Heise, "Dennis Horan, 56, Led Chicago Law Firm," *Chicago Tribune*, May 2, 1988.

10. Clarke Forsythe, interview with Mary Ziegler, March 25, 2021.

11. For more on Rosenblum's arguments about the vulnerable, see "Choose Life over Death, Prof Urges," *Detroit Free Press*, May 14, 1981, 7 (Rosenblum arguing that protecting life from the moment of fertilization "ought to be among our highest common priorities"); Bob Womack, "Abortion Foe Believes Gender Shouldn't Disqualify Opinions," *Arizona Star*, September 29, 1983, 2F (Rosenblum describing his abortion work in service of "supporting everyone in living out his or her life to the fullest").

12. See Press Release, "Northwestern Professors Share Expertise Arguing before the Supreme Court and a Website with Arguments from *Roe v. Wade*," January 22, 1998, https://www.newswise.com/articles/northwestern-professors-on-roe-v-wade, accessed October 8, 2021. On the earlier litigation of *Zbaraz*, see *Zbaraz v. Quern*, 469 F.Supp. 1212 (N.D. Ill. 1979).

13. Brief of Intervening Appellants James L. Buckley, Jesse A. Helms, Henry J. Hyde, and Isabella Pernicone, *Harris v. McRae*, 448 U.S. 297 (1980) (No. 79-1268); see also Brief of Intervening Defendants-Appellants, 42, *Williams v. Zbaraz*, 448 U.S. 358 (1980) (No. 79-4) (arguing that "there is neither a constitutional right of indigents to receive nor a constitutional obligation on the states or federal government to pay the medical expenses of indigents").

14. Brief of Intervening Appellants, 15.

15. Robert Shogan, "Reagan Attacks High Court on Abortion Funding," *Los Angeles Times*, February 22, 1980, B3. On the 1980 GOP platform, see Douglas Kneeland, "Forecast of Snowy Iowa: A Flurry of Candidates," *New York Times*, February 19, 1979, A13; Republican Party Platform of 1980, July 15, 1980, https://www.presidency.ucsb.edu/documents/republican-party-platform-1980, accessed March 29, 2022.

16. "High Court Restores Full Abortion Funding," *Human Events*, March 1980, 3.

17. *Harris v. McRae*, 448 U.S. 297, 318 (1980). For the Court's decision in *Zbaraz*, see *Williams v. Zbaraz*, 448 U.S. 358, 369 (1980).

18. Lee Sobel and Joseph Sjostrom, "State Set to End Abortion Aid; Court Decision Hailed, Attacked," *Chicago Tribune*, July 1, 1980, 7.

19. On Potter Stewart, see Bob Woodward and Scott Armstrong, *The Brethren: Inside the Supreme Court* (New York: Simon and Schuster, 1979), 9–10, 328–359; David Garrow, *Liberty and Sexuality: The Right to Privacy and the Making of* Roe v. Wade (Berkeley: University of California Press, 1998), 353–382.

20. Patrick Buchanan, "Reagan's Historic Opportunity," *Chicago Tribune*, June 27, 1981, 8.

21. On Reagan's strategy considerations surrounding the judiciary, see Gil Troy, *Morning in America: How Ronald Reagan Invented the 1980s* (Princeton, NJ: Princeton University Press, 2005), 77–80; David Alistair Yalof, *Pursuit of Justices: Presidential Politics and the Selection of Judicial Nominees* (Chicago: University of Chicago Press, 1999), 135–142.

22. Hedrick Smith, "Reagan's Court Choice: A Deft Maneuver," *New York Times*, July 9, 1981, A17. For more on anti-abortion opposition to O'Connor, see "Sandra Day O'Connor," in *A Documentary History of Abortion*, ed. Neal Devins and Wendy Garland (New York: Garland, 1995), 3–6; Yalof, *Pursuit of Justices*, 140–142.

23. On the fight about desegregation, see Matthew Delmont, *Why Busing Failed: Race, Media, and the National Resistance to Integration* (Berkeley: University of California Press, 2016), 3–45; Ronald P. Formisano, *Boston against Busing: Race, Class, and Ethnicity in the 1960s and 1970s* (Chapel Hill: University of North Carolina Press, 2004), 2–35. On changing white attitudes about "busing," see Gary Orfield, "School Desegregation After Two Generations: Race, Schools, and Opportunity in Urban Society," in *Race in America*, ed. Herbert Hill and James Jones (Madison: University of Wisconsin Press, 1993), 245.

24. See Hermine Herta Meyer, "Court Stripping or Constitution Stripping?" (1982), MBP, Box 19, Folder 6; Steve Gerstel, "Senate Launches Double-Barrel Attack on Busing," *Chicago Defender*, June 24, 1981, 10; Albert Hunt and James M. Perry, "The Machine That Helms Built: How His Conglomerate Spreads 'Real' Conservatism," *Washington Post*, July 26, 1981, D5.

25. For a sample of scholarship on the constitutionality of court stripping, see Akhil Reed Amar, "*Marbury*, Section 13, and the Original Jurisdiction of the Supreme Court," *University of Chicago Law Review* 56 (1989): 443–499; Steven Calabresi and Gary Lawson, "The Unitary Executive, Jurisdiction Stripping, and the *Hamdan* Opinions: A Textualist Response to Justice Scalia," *Columbia Law Review* 102 (2007): 1002–1047. For the Court's opinion in *Martin*, see *Martin v. Hunter's Lessee*, 14 U.S. 304 (1816).

26. Stuart Taylor Jr., "Bar Leader Fears Crisis over Curbs on Courts," *New York Times*, November 12, 1981, A24; see also "The Court Strippers," *New York Times*, February 8, 1982, A18.

27. On the failure of an anti-abortion constitutional amendment in the early 1980s, see Judie Brown, "Senator Hatch, No!" *ALL about News*, January 1982, 1, WCX, ALL about News Folder; Christopher Wolfe, "The Human Life Bill—Yes!" *ALL about News*, February 1982, 6, WCX, 1982 ALL about News Folder; "Senate Panel OKs Antiabortion Amendment," *Chicago Tribune*, December 17, 1981, A5. On Rosenblum's advisory role with the American Family Institute, see Frank Van Der Linden, "Pressure for Pro-Family Judges," *Lebanon Daily News*, December 20, 1980, 10; "Governor James Reports," *Abbeville Herald*, December 4, 1980, 2.

28. For Rosenblum's statement about the possibility of a pro-life majority, see "Choose Life over Death," 1.

29. On the benefits of arguments about judicial activism, see Mary Ziegler, *Dollars for Life: The Anti-Abortion Movement and the Fall of the Republican Establishment* (New Haven, CT: Yale University Press, 2022), 23–45. On the existence of a pro-choice majority—and arguments about it—see Mary Ziegler, *After* Roe: *The Lost History of the Abortion Debate* (Cambridge, MA: Harvard University Press, 2015), 140–162. On polling in the 1980s, see Gallup, "Abortion" (2021), https://news.gallup.com/poll/1576/abortion.aspx, accessed November 24, 2021.

30. For Rosenblum's statement: Morton Kondracke, "Rights of Handicapped Babies Deserve Protection," *Corpus Christi Caller Times*, December 1, 1983, 1. On the Baby Doe battle, see John D. Lantos and William L. Meadow, *Neonatal Bioethics: The Moral Challenges of Medical Innovation* (Baltimore, MD: Johns Hopkins University Press, 2006), 70–75.

31. On Rosenblum's work in Baby Doe cases, see Womack, "Abortion Foe Believes"; Kondracke, "Rights of Handicapped Babies," 1.

32. Stuart Taylor Jr., "Attorney General Outlines Campaign to Rein in the Courts," *New York Times*, October 30, 1981, A1; see also "Attorney General Urges 'Judicial Restraint,'" *New York Times*, November 1, 1981, E8. For Meese's statement, see Fred Barbash, "Meese Questions Efforts to Curb the Federal Courts," *Washington Post*, August 12, 1981, A9.

33. Fred Barbash, "High Court's School Ruling Fuels Debate on Judicial Authority," *Washington Post*, June 17, 1982, A3. On the campaign for judicial recognition of an individual right to bear arms, see Adam Winkler, *Gunfight: The Battle over the Right to Bear Arms in America* (New York: Norton, 2011). On the litigation led by right-to-lifers, see Mary Ziegler, "Originalism Talk," *Brigham Young University Law Review* 2014 (2014): 869–879.

34. See Michael Uhlmann and Stephen Galebach to Edwin Harper (August 23, 1982), WBF, Box 16, Chronological File, 08/25/1982–08/31/1982.

35. Ibid., 2–6; see also Stephen Galebach to Michael Uhlmann (June 13, 1983), WBF, Box 16, Chronological Files, 06/14/1983–06/30/1983.

36. On the Akron ordinance, see Judith Adamek to Akron City Council (January 16, 1978), JBP, Matter Boxes, File 306.

37. *City of Akron v. Akron Center for Reproductive Health, Inc.*, 462 U.S. 416, 458 (1983) (O'Connor, J., dissenting). On the significance that anti-abortion leaders attached to O'Connor's dissent, see Americans United for Life Board of Minutes, Legal Report (July 1984), MFJ, Box 13, Folder 8.

38. See Fundraising Letter, Americans United for Life (July 21, 1984), MFJ, Box 13, Folder 6; Americans United for Life, Board of Directors Meeting Minutes (March 30, 1984), MFJ, Box 13, Folder 6; Americans United for Life Report of the Education Division (March 30, 1984), MFJ, Box 13, Folder 6; E. R. Shipp, "Foes of Abortion Examine Strategies of N.A.A.C.P.," *New York Times*, April 2, 1984, A15.

39. Steven Baer, "It's Time for a Pro-Life Backlash," *Chicago Tribune*, July 12, 1983, 15. On AUL's strategy: Fundraising Letter, 2; Legal Report, 1–4; Maura K. Quinlan, "Abortions Are Legal through the Full Nine Months of Pregnancy for Any Reason Relevant to the Woman's Emotional Wellbeing" (September 1987), on file with the author; Victor Rosenblum and Dennis J. Horan, eds., *Reversing* Roe *through the Courts* (Washington, DC: Georgetown University Press, 1987). For Rosenblum's statements: "Pro-Lifers Plot Strategy to Reverse 1973 Ruling Legalizing Abortion," *Catholic Advance*, April 5, 1984, 3.

40. Stuart Taylor Jr., "High Court to Hear 2 Abortion Cases," *New York Times*, November 6, 1985, A22; see also Philip Hager, "Justices Take Up States' Abortion Curbs, Give No Sign of Heeding Administration Plea to Void '73 Decision," *Los Angeles Times*, November 6, 1985, 5. On Rosenblum's testimony on the Hatch proposal, see "Abortion Foes, Backers Clash over Hatch Proposal," *Tucson Citizen*, April 3, 1985, 7B.

41. For the Court's decision in *Charles*, see *Diamond v. Charles*, 476 U.S. 54 (1986). For the Court's decision in *Thornburgh*, see *Thornburgh v. American College of Obstetricians and Gynecologists*, 476 U.S. 747, 751–759 (1986). On the significance of the Court's *Thornburgh* decision, see Garrow, *Liberty and Sexuality*, 652, 657, 662.

42. Fred Fielding, Memorandum for Patrick Buchanan (April 22, 1985), JGR, Box 65, Chronological File, 04/20/1985–04/30/1985. For Roberts's statement: John G. Roberts, Memorandum for Fred Fielding (April 22, 1985), JGR, Box 65, Chronological File, 04/20/1985–04/30/1985.

43. See Steven Teles, *The Rise of the Conservative Legal Movement: The Battle for Control of the Law* (Princeton, NJ: Princeton University Press, 2008); Amanda Hollis-Brusky, *Ideas with Consequences: The Federalist Society and the Conservative Counterrevolution*

(New York: Oxford University Press, 2015). On the founding of the Federalist Society, see Michael Kruse, "The Weekend at Yale That Changed American Politics," *Politico*, September/October 2018, https://www.politico.com/magazine/story/2018/08/27/federalist-society-yale-history-conservative-law-court-219608, accessed September 10, 2020.

44. See Stuart Taylor Jr., "Liberals Portray Scalia as Threat but Bar Group Sees Him as Open," *New York Times*, August 7, 1986, A19; David M. O'Brien, "Scalia and the Court: Pulling Consensus to the Right," *Los Angeles Times*, June 29, 1986, F1. On Scalia's confirmation vote, see Linda Greenhouse, "Senate, 65 to 33, Votes to Confirm Rehnquist as 16th Chief Justice," *New York Times*, September 18, 1986, A1.

45. See Bork Candidate Notebook (n.d., ca. 1987), 2, 10–11, ACF, OA 15149, Bork Notebook File. On Bork's opposition to the *Roe* decision, see Jack M. Balkin, "Introduction: *Roe v. Wade*: Engine of Controversy," in *What* Roe v. Wade *Should Have Said: The Nation's Top Legal Experts Rewrite America's Most Controversial Decision*, ed. Jack M. Balkin (New York: New York University Press, 2005), 13–14; H. L. Pohlman, *Constitutional Debate in Action: Civil Rights and Liberties*, 2nd ed. (Lanham, MD: Rowman and Littlefield, 2005), 116; Andrew Hartman, *A War for the Soul of America: A History of the Culture Wars* (Chicago: University of Chicago Press, 2015), 153–155. For Bork's comments on the right to privacy and *Roe*, see Ruth Marcus, "Bork on 'Judicial Imperialism,' " *Washington Post*, July 2, 1987, https://www.washingtonpost.com/archive/politics/1987/07/02/bork-on-judicial-imperialism/60fb83a3-f529-4751-8066-7a9806883f0e/, accessed April 9, 2020. For the statements in the Biden Report: Response Prepared to the White House's Statement on Judge Bork's Record (September 2, 1987), 3, 18, PKF, Box 23, Biden Report File.

46. On the Bork confirmation vote, see David Lauter, "Senate Rejects Bork, 58-42," *Los Angeles Times*, October 23, 1987, 1; Linda Greenhouse, "Judge Bork Is Stepping Down to Answer Critics and Reflect," *New York Times*, January 15, 1988, A1. On Horan's passing, see "Dennis M. Horan, 56, a Lawyer and Author," *New York Times*, May 3, 1988, https://www.nytimes.com/1988/05/03/obituaries/dennis-m-horan-56-a-lawyer-and-author.html, accessed August 20, 2021; "Dennis Horan, 56; Led Chicago Law Firm," *Chicago Tribune*, May 3, 1988, https://www.chicagotribune.com/news/ct-xpm-1988-05-03-8803130903-story.html, accessed August 20, 2021.

47. On Rosenblum's speech: Catherine Warren and Kendra Ensor, "Law Professor Says Meese Isn't Sincere about Constitutional Interpretation," *Casper Star Tribune*, March 15, 1986, 3.

48. David Hoffman, "Bush Draws Contrast with Rival," *Washington Post*, November 2, 1988, A1. On Bush's early primary struggles, see Bill Peterson, "Robertson Defeats Bush for GOP's Second Place," *Washington Post*, February 9, 1988, A1. On Trump's hints

about running, see "A Trump Presidential Bid?" *New York Times*, July 14, 1987, A13; Jon Margolis, "Grass Roots Casts a Vote for Trump," *Chicago Tribune*, July 14, 1987, A10.

49. See Cynthia Gorney, "Beyond the *Webster* Case: Abortion Arguments and Predictions," *Washington Post*, April 9, 1989, W25; Chris Bull, "Feminists Gear Up for DC Action," *Gay Community News*, March 5–11, 1989, 10.

50. Victor Rosenblum, draft editorial, "Should the States Decide for Themselves about Abortion?" (n.d., ca. 1989), VRP, Box 6, Folder 8. For the statement from AUL's newsletter: Americans United for Life Special Report (September 1989), 1–3, SBL, Box 1, Folder 2. For Missouri's statement: Appellant's Reply Brief, 1, *Webster v. Reproductive Health Services*, 492 U.S. 490 (1989) (No. 88-605). For the statement from AUL's brief, see Brief of Certain State Legislators as Amicus Curiae in Support of Appellants, 30, *Webster v. Reproductive Health Services*, 492 U.S. 490 (1989) (No. 88-605).

51. For the argument that overruling *Roe* would jeopardize other constitutional rights, see Brief of Appellees, 9–11, *Webster v. Reproductive Health Services*, 492 U.S. 490 (1989) (No. 88-605). For Missouri's response, see Brief of Appellants, 12–18, *Webster v. Reproductive Health Services*, 492 U.S. 490 (1989) (No. 88-605).

52. "In the Wake of *Webster*: The Pro-Life Movement One Year Later," *AUL Forum*, Fall 1990, SBL, Box 1, Folder 2. For the Court's conclusion in *Webster*, see *Webster v. Reproductive Health Services*, 492 U.S. 490, 517–519 (1989). For the statute challenged in *Webster*, see Mo. Rev. Stat. §§ 1.205.1(1), (2) (1986); § 188.029; §§ 188.205, 188.210, 188.215.

53. William Grady, "Professor Straddles Two Political Platforms," *Chicago Tribune*, June 24, 1992, C1.

54. For the statement about Rosenblum: "Noted Legal Scholar Victor Rosenblum Dies at 80," *Northwestern Now*, March 15, 2006, https://www.northwestern.edu/newscenter/stories/2006/03/rosenblum.html, accessed April 8, 2022.

55. Clarke Forsythe and Stephen Presser, "The Tragic Failure of *Roe v. Wade*," *Texas Review of Law and Politics* 10 (2005): 85–170.

Chapter 4. Women Who Have It All

1. Elizabeth Snead, "Hillary's Hair Band: Zippy or Just Dippy?" *USA Today*, February 7, 1992, 8D.

2. On women's increasing rates of college enrollment and graduation in the 1990s, see Jennifer Flashman, "A Cohort Perspective on Gender Gaps in College Attendance and Completion," *Research in Higher Education* 54 (2013): 545–570; Donghun Cho, "The Role of High School Performance in Explaining Women's Rising College Enrollment," *Economics of Education Review* 26 (2007): 450–462; Lynn

White and Stacey J. Rodgers, "Economic Circumstances and Family Outcomes: A Review of the 1990s," *Journal of Marriage and Family* 62 (2000): 1035–1051. On shifting patterns of workforce participation for women in the 1990s, see Cynthia Coline, Arline Geronimus, and Maureen Phillips, "Getting a Piece of the Pie? The Economic Boom of the 1990s and Declining Teen Birth Rates in the United States," *Social Science and Medicine* 63 (2006): 1531–1545; Maureen Perry-Jenkins, Rena Repetti, and Ann Crouter, "Work and Family in the 1990s," *Journal of Marriage and Family* 62 (2000): 981–998. On the popularity of *Murphy Brown*, see Bonnie J. Dow, *Prime-Time Feminism: Television, Media Culture, and the Women's Movement since 1970* (Philadelphia: University of Pennsylvania Press, 1996), 145.

3. Linda Wharton, interview with Mary Ziegler, May 25, 2021. On the history of RCA in Camden, see Jefferson Cowie, *Capital Moves: RCA's Seventy-Year Quest for Cheap Labor* (Ithaca, NY: Cornell University Press, 1999).

4. Wharton, interview; Linda Wharton, interview with Mary Ziegler, November 3, 2018.

5. Wharton, 2021 interview.

6. Myrna Gutiérrez, interview with Mary Ziegler, March 2021; Myrna Gutiérrez, email interview with Mary Ziegler, November 2021; Myrna Gutiérrez, interview with Mary Ziegler, 2018.

7. Gutiérrez, March 2021 interview; Gutiérrez, 2018 interview.

8. Gutiérrez, March 2021 interview; Gutiérrez, 2018 interview; Gutiérrez, November 2021 email interview.

9. On the early organization of Operation Rescue, see Jim Risen and Judy Thomas, *Wrath of Angels: The American Abortion War* (New York: Basic Books, 1998), 181–182, 258–261; Daniel K. Williams, *God's Own Party: The Making of the Christian Right* (New York: Oxford University Press, 2010), 223–224; Karissa Haugeberg, *Women against Abortion: Inside the Largest Moral Reform Movement of the Twentieth Century* (Champaign: University of Illinois Press, 2017), 80–143; Faye Ginsburg, "Rescuing the Nation: Operation Rescue and the Rise of Anti-Abortion Militance," in *Abortion Wars: A Half-Century of Struggle*, ed. Rickie Solinger (Berkeley: University of California Press, 1998), 227–251.

10. On the spread of blockades in 1989, see "Operation Rescue New York City," *Rescue News Brief*, January–February 1989, 1, FWHC, Box 8, Operation Rescue Folder; "Las Vegas Rescue Saves Three Babies," *Rescue News Brief*, March 1989, 3, FWHC, Box 8, Operation Rescue Folder. On the Republican Study Committee, see "Republican Committee Task Force," *Rescue News Brief*, March 1989, 6, FWHC, Box 8, Operation Rescue Folder.

11. Randall Terry, "*Webster*: A Faltering Step in the Right Direction," *Rescue News Brief*, June 1989, 6, FWHC, Box 51, Operation Rescue Folder.

12. Wharton, 2021 interview; *Roe v. Operation Rescue*, 710 F.Supp. 577, 580–591 (E.D. Pa. 1989).

13. See *Roe v. Operation Rescue*, 710 F.Supp. 577, 580–591 (E.D. Pa. 1989).

14. For Bush's statement: *Proclamation 6170: Women's Equality Day, 1990* (August 1990), https://www.presidency.ucsb.edu/documents/proclamation-6170-womens-equality-day-1990, accessed August 25, 2021. On the gender pay gap, see Council of Economic Advisors, "Explaining Trends in the Gender Wage Gap" (June 1998), https://clintonwhitehouse2.archives.gov/WH/EOP/CEA/html/gendergap.html, accessed August 25, 2021; Elise Gould, Jessica Schieder, and Kathleen Geier, "What Is the Gender Pay Gap, and Is It Real?" *Economic Policy Institute*, October 20, 2016, https://www.epi.org/publication/what-is-the-gender-pay-gap-and-is-it-real/, accessed November 11, 2021. On changing patterns of education and career options for women, see Flashman, "A Cohort Perspective," 545–570; Cho, "The Role of High School Performance," 450–462; White and Rodgers, "Economic Circumstances and Family Outcomes," 1035–1051, Coline, Geronimus, and Phillips, "Getting a Piece of the Pie?"

15. Planned Parenthood, Operation Rescue Strategy Meeting (May 23, 1989), 1–3, 5, FWHC, Box 51, Operation Folder.

16. See Harrison Hickman to Loretta Ucelli and Kate Michelman, "Re: Parental Consent/ Notification Update" (February 12, 1991), FWHC, Box 63, Parental Notification Talking Points Folder; see also National Abortion Federation and National Women's Law Center, "The Judicial Bypass Procedure Fails to Protect Young Women" (1990), FWHC, Box 63, Parental Notification Talking Points Folder.

17. Belle Taylor-McGhee to Editorial Writers et al. (July 17, 1998), NARAL, Box 220, Folder 1.

18. See Carol Sanger, *About Abortion: Terminating Pregnancy in Twenty-First-Century America* (Cambridge, MA: Harvard University Press, 2017), 170–201; Helena Silverstein, *Girls on the Stand: How Courts Fail Pregnant Minors* (New York: New York University Press, 2007). For the Court's earlier decisions on parental involvement, see *Planned Parenthood of Central Missouri v. Danforth*, 428 U.S. 74 (1976); *Bellotti v. Baird*, 443 U.S. 662 (1979); *H.L. v. Matheson*, 450 U.S. 398 (1981); *City of Akron v. Akron Center for Reproductive Health*, 462 U.S. 416 (1983).

19. See Brief of Petitioners, 9, 20–22, *Hodgson v. Minnesota*, 497 U.S. 417 (1990) (No. 88-1125). For the statute challenged in *Hodgson*, see Minn. Stat. §§ 144.343(2)–(7).

20. Clarke Forsythe to State Pro-Life Legislators and Other Interested Parties (August 23, 1989), RJN, Box 33, Folder 2. On Forsythe's path to AUL, see Deanna Silberman, "They're in It for Life," *Student Lawyer* 18 (1989): 30–35.

21. Dan Balz, "Antiabortion Forces Seek to Shift Debate," *Washington Post*, December 21, 1989, A8.

22. *Hodgson v. Minnesota*, 497 U.S. 417, 451 (1990); see *Ohio v. Akron Center for Reproductive Health et al.*, 497 U.S. 502, 523–535 (1990). For the lower court's decision in *Casey*, see *Planned Parenthood of Southeastern Pennsylvania v. Casey*, 822 F.Supp. 227 (E.D. Penn. 1993).

23. Sandy Banisky, "Bowie Family Condones Anti-Abortion Violence," *Baltimore Sun*, October 9, 1994, 1A. For more on Jayne Bray, see Jennifer Jefferis, *Armed for Life: The Army of God and Anti-Abortion Terror in the United States* (New York: ABC-CLIO, 2011), 68–80; Eleanor Bader and Patricia Baird-Windle, *Targets of Hatred: Anti-Abortion Terrorism* (New York: St. Martin's, 2015), 72–87.

24. See Ruth Marcus, "Justices to Review Limits on Antiabortion Protestors," *Washington Post*, February 26, 1991, A4. On the Souter nomination, see Jack Nelson, Robert Shogan, and Ronald Brownstein, "Bush May Avoid Bitter Confirmation Struggle," *Washington Post*, July 24, 1990, A1. For the lower court's decision in *Bray*, see *National Organization for Women v. Operation Rescue*, 914 F.2d 582 (4th Cir. 1990).

25. Guy Condon to Richard John Neuhaus (October 23, 1991), RJN, Box 2, Folder 34.

26. Americans United for Life Conceptual Meeting (March 21, 1990), RJN, Box 2, Folder 33.

27. Neil A. Lewis, "Law Professor Accuses Thomas of Sexual Harassment in the '80s," *New York Times*, October 7, 1991, A1. On the Thomas nomination, see Terry Atlas, "Bush Chooses Conservative for the Supreme Court," *Chicago Tribune*, July 2, 1991. For the details of Hill's story, see Ruth Marcus, "Hill Describes Details of Alleged Harassment," *Washington Post*, October 12, 1991, A1.

28. On the prevalence of sexual harassment experienced by working women, see Marjorie Williams, "From Women, an Outpouring of Anger," *Washington Post*, October 9, 1991, A1; Elizabeth Kolbert, "The Thomas Nomination: Sexual Harassment at Work Is Pervasive, Study Finds," *New York Times*, October 11, 1991, A1. On the confirmation vote, see "The Thomas Confirmation: How the Senate Voted on Thomas," *New York Times*, October 16, 1991, https://www.nytimes.com/1991/10/16/us/the-thomas-confirmation-how-the-senators-voted-on-thomas.html, accessed April 13, 2020.

29. On racial differences among women in economic mobility in the period, see Melissa S. Kearney, "Intergenerational Mobility for Women and Minorities in the

United States," *The Future of Children* 16 (2006): 37–53. On the struggles of women in two-career marriages, see Rosanna Hertz, *More Equal Than Others: Women and Men in Dual-Career Marriages* (Berkeley: University of California Press, 1986). On the obstacles preventing women from securing leadership positions, see Sarah Hardesty and Nehama Jacobs, *Success and Betrayal: The Crisis of Women in Corporate America* (New York: Franklin Watts, 1986); Judith Warner and Danielle Corley, "The Women's Leadership Gap" May 21, 2017, https://www.hernewstandard.com/wp-content/uploads/2018/11/The-Women%E2%80%99s-Leadership-Gap-Center-for-American-Progress-copy.pdf, accessed August 26, 2021. On the backlash facing feminism in the 1990s, see Susan Faludi, *Backlash: The Undeclared War against American Women* (New York: Crown, 1991).

30. "Federal Court Approves Strict Pa. Abortion-Control Law," *Baltimore Sun*, October 22, 1991, A7. For the Third Circuit's decision, see *Planned Parenthood of Southeastern Pennsylvania v. Casey*, 947 F.2d 682 (3d Cir. 1991).

31. See Kitty Kolbert and Linda Wharton to Amicus Organizing Team (December 10, 1991), KKP, Box 1, *Casey* Notes and Memoranda Folder; Kitty Kolbert to Reproductive Freedom Project Attorneys (September 26, 1991), KKP, Box 1, *Casey* Notes and Memoranda Folder; Kitty Kolbert and Lynn Paltrow to Nadine Strossen et al., "Re: *Casey* Campaign" (December 24, 1991), KKP, Box 1, *Casey* Notes and Memoranda Folder.

32. Brief for Petitioners/Cross-Respondents, 33–34, *Planned Parenthood of Southeastern Pennsylvania v. Casey*, 505 U.S. 833 (1992) (No. 91-744, 91-902). On Kolbert and Wharton's predictions, see Kathryn Kolbert and Linda Wharton to Supporters of Reproductive Freedom (June 12, 1992), LWP, on file with the author.

33. For a sample of anti-abortion briefs in this vein, see Brief of Catholics United for Life et al., 3, *Planned Parenthood of Southeastern Pennsylvania v. Casey*, 505 U.S. 833 (1992) (No. 91-744, 91-902); Brief for Focus on the Family et al., 7, *Planned Parenthood of Southeastern Pennsylvania v. Casey*, 505 U.S. 833 (1992) (No. 91-744, 91-902); Brief of the Rutherford Institute et al., 25–26, *Planned Parenthood of Southeastern Pennsylvania v. Casey*, 505 U.S. 833 (1992) (No. 91-744, 91-902).

34. *Planned Parenthood of Southeastern Pennsylvania v. Casey*, 505 U.S. 833, 857–870 (1992) (plurality opinion).

35. See ibid., 853–857.

36. Ibid.

37. Ibid., 881–882.

38. Talking Points, "Abortion and Women's Equality" (n.d., ca. 1994), MGP.

39. Gutiérrez, March 2021 interview; Gutiérrez, 2018 interview; Gutiérrez, November 2021 interview. For more on Gutiérrez's work at AUL, see Americans

United for Life, Press Release (June 30, 1994), MGP; Americans United for Life, Media Guide (n.d., ca. 1994), MGP; Americans United for Life, "Women's Views on the RU 486 Trauma" (n.d., ca. 1994), MGP.

40. See "Guy Condon Takes the Helm at CAC," *Action Line*, January/February 1993, 1, PAW, Box 15, Folder 11. On AUL's financial troubles, see Mary Ziegler, *Abortion and the Law in America: Roe v. Wade to the Present* (New York: Cambridge University Press, 2020), 117–121.

41. Gutiérrez, March 2021 interview. On the impact of the abortion issue on the 1992 election, see Market Strategies, "1992 Post-Election Report for RNC," 2–10 (January 10, 1993), FSP, Box 36, Post-Election Folder 1; see also Post-Election Survey Result (1992), 1, 17, 36, FSP, Box 36, Post-Election Folder 1. On the sweep of Clinton's win, see Robin Toner, "The 1992 Elections: The Overview—Clinton Captures Presidency with Huge Electoral Margin," *New York Times*, November 4, 1992, https://www.nytimes.com/1992/11/04/us/1992-elections-president-overview-clinton-captures-presidency-with-huge.html, accessed August 26, 2021.

42. Brief for Respondents, 8, *Bray v. Alexandria Women's Health Clinic*, 506 U.S. 263 (1993) (No. 90-985).

43. Ibid., 28.

44. See Elizabeth Williamson, "Trump's Other Personal Lawyer: Close to the Right, but Far from Giuliani," *New York Times*, December 1, 2019, https://www.nytimes.com/2019/12/01/us/politics/trump-sekulow-impeachment.html, accessed August 28, 2021. On Sekulow's work with Operation Rescue, see Paul Geitner, "Criminal Charges Filed for Presenting Aborted Fetus to Clinton," *AP*, August 12, 1992, https://apnews.com/article/0cb442baf575647f079e600786257ce2, accessed August 26, 2021; Tracy Thompson, "Operation Rescue Denies Blocking D.C. Clinics," *Washington Post*, January 25, 1992, https://www.washingtonpost.com/archive/politics/1992/01/25/operation-rescue-denies-blocking-dc-clinics/634f1bb6-1822-45fa-8991-1965fd2f30e0/, accessed August 26, 2021.

45. Brief for Petitioners, 23–24, *Bray v. Alexandria Women's Health Clinic*, 506 U.S. 263 (1993) (No. 90-985).

46. *Bray v. Alexandria Women's Health Clinic*, 506 U.S. 263, 270–271 (1993).

47. On Cunningham, see Silberman, "They're in It for Life," 30–35; see also Paige Comstock Cunningham, "Unborn Child Is Treated as Property," *Chicago Tribune*, December 22, 1993, 1.

48. See Americans United for Life, Board of Directors Meeting Minutes (April 24, 1993), MFJ, Box 13, Folder 6.

49. On Gunn's murder, see Deana A. Rohlinger, *Abortion Politics, Mass Media, and Social Movements in America* (New York: Cambridge University Press, 2015), 70, 235; Jefferis, *Armed for Life*, 108, 138–140; Risen and Thomas, *Wrath of Angels*, 340–355.

50. Americans United for Life, April Board Meeting Minutes, 3.

51. Wharton, 2021 interview; Wharton, 2020 interview.

52. Linda J. Wharton, Susan Frietsche, and Kathryn Kolbert, "Preserving the Core of *Roe:* Reflections on *Planned Parenthood v. Casey*," *Yale Law and Feminism* 18 (2006): 308–323.

53. See CHOICE, "An Unacceptable Burden: The Effects of Pennsylvania's Restrictions on Medical-Assistance Funded Abortions," KKP, Box 1, Casey Notes and Memoranda Folder; see also Kolbert, Frietsche, and Wharton, "Preserving the Core of *Roe*," 321–323.

54. See *Planned Parenthood of Southeastern Pennsylvania v. Casey*, 812 F.Supp. 541 (E.D. Pa. 1993); *Planned Parenthood of Southeastern Pennsylvania v. Casey*, 822 F. Supp. 227 (E.D. Pa. 1993); *Casey v. Planned Parenthood of Southeastern Pennsylvania*, 14 F.3d 848 (3d Cir. 1994). For Justice Souter's conclusion, see *Planned Parenthood of Southeastern Pennsylvania v. Casey*, 114 S.Ct. 909 (1994) (denying stay). For Wharton's argument on the importance of reopening the record, see Linda Wharton, Notes, "Reopening the Record" (n.d., ca. 1993), LWP.

55. Myrna Gutiérrez, "Abortion No Solution for Poor Women," *Chicago Tribune*, August 24, 1994, D16.

56. See Robert Pear, "Health Initiative Tilting toward Price Regulation," *New York Times*, February 16, 1993, A14; Robert Pear, "2 Dozen New Taxes Weighed to Pay for Health Care Plans," *New York Times*, February 17, 1993, A1.

57. Adam Clymer, "State of the Union: The Republicans: In Response to Clinton, Dole Denies There Is a 'Crisis,' " *New York Times*, January 26, 1994, https://www.nytimes.com/1994/01/26/us/state-union-republicans-gop-response-clinton-dole-denies-there-crisis-health.html, accessed August 26, 2021.

58. On the dueling welfare proposals offered by Clinton and the Republicans, see Michael Meeropol, *Surrender: How the Clinton Administration Completed the Reagan Revolution* (Ann Arbor: University of Michigan Press, 2000), 248–252; Arline Geronomis, "Teenage Childbearing and Personal Responsibility: An Alternative View," in *Race, Poverty, and Domestic Policy*, ed. C. Michael Henry (New Haven, CT: Yale University Press, 2004), 480–500.

59. On the Contract with America, see David E. Rosenbaum, "Republicans Offer Voters a Deal for Takeover of the House," *New York Times*, September 28, 1994,

https://www.nytimes.com/1994/09/28/us/republicans-offer-voters-a-deal-for-takeover-of-house.html, accessed August 26, 2021; Maureen Dowd, "Americans Like GOP Agenda but Split on How to Reach Goals," *New York Times*, December 15, 1994, https://www.nytimes.com/1994/12/15/us/americans-like-gop-agenda-but-split-on-how-to-reach-goals.html, accessed August 26, 2021.

60. Gutiérrez, March 2021 interview; Gutiérrez, November 2021 email interview; Gutiérrez, 2018 interview.

61. Wharton, 2021 interview.

62. John Danforth, *Resurrection: The Confirmation of Clarence Thomas* (New York: Viking, 1994), 175.

63. Richard Cohen, "Entitled to Lie? Thomas May Have Had No Other Choice," *Washington Post*, December 8, 1994, A23.

Chapter 5. Simply a Scientific Question

1. Martin Haskell, interview with Mary Ziegler, April 5, 2021. On the history of Birmingham's founding family, see Thomas McAdory Owen, *History of Alabama and Dictionary of Alabama* (Ann Arbor: University of Michigan Press, 1921), 125–126. On Alabama's Jim Crow, see C. Vann Woodward, *The Strange Career of Jim Crow* (New York: Oxford University Press, 1955), 85–99. On Birmingham's color line, see Debbie Elliott, "Remembering Birmingham's 'Dynamite Hill' Neighborhood," *NPR*, July 6, 2013, https://www.npr.org/sections/codeswitch/2013/07/06/197342590/remembering-birminghams-dynamite-hill-neighborhood, accessed September 7, 2021.

2. Haskell, interview. On Schweitzer, see James Brabazon, *Albert Schweitzer: A Biography*, 2nd ed. (Syracuse, New York: Syracuse University Press, 2000).

3. Haskell, interview.

4. Ibid.

5. Ibid.

6. Ibid. For more on the actions taken against Haskell's clinics, see Carrie Labroia, "Abortion Clinics Feeling Pressure," *Dayton Daily News*, March 24, 1986, 4.

7. Peter Skerry, "The Class Conflict over Abortion," *Public Interest* 52 (1978): 69–84.

8. For more on the neoconservative critique of science, see Kenneth Kersch, "Neoconservatives and the Court: *The Public Interest*, 1965–1980," in *Ourselves and Our Posterity: Essays in Constitutional Originalism*, ed. Bradley Watson (Lanham, MD: Lexington, 2009), 247–297.

9. On the scientific scandals of the 1970s, see Mary Ziegler, *Abortion and the Law in America: Roe v. Wade to the Present* (New York: Cambridge University Press, 2020),

170–174. For more on the politics of science in the period, see Sheila Jasanoff, *The Fifth Branch: Science Advisors as Policymakers* (Cambridge, MA: Harvard University Press 1998); Andrew Jewett, *Science under Fire: Challenges to Scientific Authority in Modern America* (Cambridge, MA: Harvard University Press, 2020), 15–20, 227–256.

10. On McMahon and the history of dilation and extraction, see Johanna Schoen, *Abortion After Roe* (Chapel Hill: University of North Carolina Press, 2015), 257–273. On the early days of the partial-birth abortion campaign, see ibid., 247–256; Sara Dubow, *Ourselves Unborn: A History of the Fetus in Modern America* (New York: Oxford University Press, 2010), 153–180.

11. National Right to Life Committee, "Partial-Birth Abortion: A Look behind the Disinformation" (July 19, 1995), JBP, Matter Boxes, Folder 1275. On the backstory of the bill, see Debra Rosenberg, "Chipping Away at *Roe*," *Newsweek*, March 16, 2003, https://www.newsweek.com/chipping-away-roe-133053, accessed September 7, 2021; Reva B. Siegel, "Dignity and the Politics of Protection: Abortion Restrictions under *Casey/Carhart*," *Yale Law Journal* 117 (2008): 1694–1723.

12. For Romer's testimony: Partial-Birth Abortion Act: Testimony before the Senate Judiciary Committee, 104th Congress, 1st Sess. (1995), 110 (Statement of Dr. Nancy Romer).

13. See Brief of Plaintiffs-Appellees, 14–36, *Women's Medical Professional Corporation v. Voinovich*, 130 F.3d 187 (6th Cir. 1997) (Nos. 96-3157, 96-3159).

14. For Canady's statement: Charles Canady, "Abortion Ban Protects Health of Mothers," *New York Times*, November 24, 1995, A24. On the veto, see Ann Devroy, "Late-Term Abortion Ban Vetoed," *Washington Post*, April 11, 1996, A1.

15. On the exorcism, see Carol Biliczky, "Ohio Doctor Is at the Center of Controversy," *Akron Beacon Journal*, October 15, 2000, A1. On Haskell's unwillingness to testify before Congress, see Ann Gerhart and Annie Groer, "The Reliable Source," *Washington Post*, March 21, 1996, D3.

16. On Tiller, see Judy Thomas and David Klepper, "The Complex Life of George Tiller," *Kansas City Star*, June 7, 2009, https://www.kansascity.com/news/state/kansas/article230986418.html, accessed September 7, 2021; "Doctor Refused to Quit: 'I Know They Need Me,' " *NBC News*, June 2, 2009, https://www.nbcnews.com/id/wbna31060234, accessed September 7, 2021. For more on Tiller's significance, see Stephen Singular, *Death in Wichita: The Death of George Tiller and the Battle over Abortion* (New York: St. Martin's, 2011); David S. Cohen and Krysten Connen, *Living in the Crosshairs: The Untold Stories of Anti-Abortion Terrorism* (New York: Oxford University Press, 2015).

17. Haskell, interview.

18. "CBS 60 Minutes on Partial-Birth Abortion: A Critique" (June 10, 1996), JBP, Matter Boxes, File 1325.

19. Pamphlet, PHACT, "Your Conscience Tells You This Is Wrong" (1996), PWP, Box 80, Folder 2. For the district court's decision in *Voinovich*, see *Women's Medical Corporation v. Voinovich*, 911 F. Supp. 1051 (S.D. Ohio 1995).

20. "Just the PHACTs, Ma'am," *Life Insight*, July–August 1996, JBP, Matter Boxes, File 1325.

21. On the effort to publicize a connection between abortion and breast cancer, see "Breast Cancer Emerges as Major Weapon in Fight against Abortion," *AUL Forum*, September 2000, 1, PLN, AUL Forum Boxes; "AUL Focuses on Women's Right to Know, Abortion–Breast Cancer Link," *AUL Forum*, Spring 1998, RCP, AUL Folder. On the campaign around RU 486, see Ziegler, *Abortion and the Law*, 157–158. For the *New England Journal of Medicine Study*, see Mads Melbye et al., "Induced Abortion and the Risk of Breast Cancer," *New England Journal of Medicine* 36 (1997): 81–85.

22. Emily J. Minor, "The Children of Operation Rescue," *Palm Beach Post*, July 20, 1997, 1A. On the 1996 election, see Adam Nagourney and Elizabeth Kolbert, "How Bob Dole's Dream Was Dashed," *New York Times*, November 8, 1996, https://www.nytimes.com/1996/11/08/us/how-bob-dole-s-dream-was-dashed.html, accessed April 12, 2022.

23. National Right to Life Committee, Fundraising Letter (May 30, 1997), JBP, Matter Boxes, Folder 1395. On the Return to Truth, see Minor, "The Children of Operation Rescue." On the Shannon shooting, see James Risen, "Anti-Abortion Zealot's Gun May Have Wounded Allies," *Los Angeles Times*, April 18, 1994, A1; "Abortion Foe Who Shot a Doctor Is Convicted of Attempted Murder," *New York Times*, March 26, 1994, 1. For the Sixth Circuit's decision on appeal in *Voinovich*, see *Women's Professional Medical Corporation v. Voinovich*, 130 F.3d 187, 203–217 (6th Cir. 1997). For ACOG's 1997 statement: ACOG Executive Committee, "ACOG Policy Statement: Partial-Birth Abortion" (January 13, 1997), https://www.politico.com/pdf/PPM154_memos21_22.pdf, accessed January 26, 2022. For the AMA's statement: American Medical Association, "Late-Term Pregnancy Termination Techniques" (1997), https://policysearch.ama-assn.org/policyfinder/detail/*?uri=%2FAMADoc%2FHOD.xml-0-4533.xml, accessed January 26, 2021.

24. National Foundation for Life, Brochure, "The Global Project" (n.d., ca. 1997), PWP, Box 80, Folder 2; see also Harold Cassidy to Karen Deeds (November 14, 1997), PWP, Box 80, Folder 2.

25. On the radicalization of Operation Rescue, see Ana Puga, "Radicalizing Right to Life," *Boston Globe*, October 30, 1994, 26; Sara Rimer, "Abortion Foes in Boot

Camp Mull Doctor's Killing," *New York Times*, March 19, 1993, A12. On the significance of the FACE Act, see Ziegler, *Abortion and the Law*, 136, 139, 144. For the text of the FACE Act, see 18 U.S.C. §248.

26. Life Forum Meeting Minutes (July 10, 1998), PWP, Box 80, Folder 2; see also National Foundation for Life, "The Global Project," 1–3; Cassidy to Deeds, 1–2.

27. For the district court decision in *Stenberg*, see *Carhart v. Stenberg*, 11 F.Supp. 1099 (D. Neb. 1998); *Carhart v. Stenberg*, 11 F.Supp. 1134 (D. Neb. 1998). For the appellate court decision in the case, see *Carhart v. Stenberg*, 192 F.3d 1142 (8th Cir. 1999).

28. Brief Amici Curiae of the Association of American Physicians and Surgeons et al., 23, *Stenberg v. Carhart*, 530 U.S. 914 (2000) (No. 99-830).

29. Brief Amici Curiae of the American College of Obstetricians and Gynecologists et al., 22, *Stenberg v. Carhart*, 530 U.S. 914 (2000) (No. 99-830).

30. *Stenberg v. Carhart*, 530 U.S. 914, 935–937 (2000).

31. Ibid., 961.

32. National Right to Life Committee, Member Update, November 29, 1999, JBP, Matter Boxes, Folder 1934.

33. Brochure, "The Global Project." On McCorvey's change of heart, see " 'Jane Roe' Shifts Stance on Abortion: After Baptism, She Joins Operation Rescue," *Chicago Tribune*, August 11, 1994, D4; Lynn Smith, "A Woman's Right to Change Her Mind," *Los Angeles Times*, August 15, 1995, E1.

34. Virginia Norton, "Attorney Outlines Anti-Abortion Plan," *Augusta Chronicle*, January 17, 2001, C8. On Parker's work on school choice, see Laura Litvan, "A School Voucher Test Case?" *Investors' Business Daily*, January 21, 1999, A1.

35. NRLC, Member Update, 2.

36. NARAL Foundation, "Choice for America" (1999), 1–3, RCD, Box 2, NARAL Folder.

37. Howard Kurtz, "Limbaugh, Post Clinton, Dining Happily on What's Left," *Washington Post*, May 7, 2001, C1; see also Bob Baker, "What's the Rush? Loudmouth Rush Limbaugh Harangues Feminazis, Environmentalist Wackos, and Commie-Libs While His Ratings Soar," *Los Angeles Times*, January 20, 1991, A18; Peter Carlson, "It's All the Rage: America Has Made the Breathless Harangue into a Screaming Success," *Washington Post*, February 13, 2003, C1. For more on the politics of climate change in the period, see Paul R. Brewer and Andrew Pease, "Federal Climate Change Politics in the United States: Polarization and Paralysis," in *Turning Down the Heat: The Politics of Climate Policy in Affluent Societies,* ed. Hugh Compston and Ian Bailey (New York: Palgrave-Macmillan, 2008), 80–92.

38. On the vaccine hearings, see J. B. Orenstein, "A Look at . . . Fear of Vaccines," *Washington Post*, April 16, 2000, B3; Anita Manning, "Public Confidence in Vaccines at Risk," *USA Today*, December 2, 2002, D8. On the history of the anti-vaccine movement, see Paul A. Offit, *Deadly Choices: How the Anti-Vaccine Movement Threatens Us All* (New York: Basic Books, 2011), 60–72; Susan Jacoby, *The Age of American Unreason* (New York: Knopf, 2008), 219–223; Mark A. Largent, *Vaccine: The Debate in Modern America* (Baltimore, MD: Johns Hopkins University Press, 2012).

39. On perceived media bias about climate change, see Kurtz, "Limbaugh, Post-Clinton," C1; Howard Kurtz, "The Sky Is Falling, Friday at Five: On the Environment, a Record of Extremes," *Washington Post*, June 24, 2002, C1. See also James Glassman, "It's No Time to Go Wobbly on Kyoto," *Wall Street Journal*, May 11, 2001, A14. For examples of anti-abortion perceptions of bias on the part of scientific and medical organizations, see National Right to Life Committee Fundraising Letter (March 17, 1997), JBP, Matter Box 1395; National Right to Life Committee, Press Release, "US House Overrides Veto of Partial-Birth Abortion Ban" (July 22, 1998), JBP, Matter Box 1931.

40. Biliczky, "Ohio Doctor," A1.

41. "Operation Rescue West: Nation's Leading Partial-Birth Abortionist Days Away from Prosecution," *US Newswire*, March 13, 2003, 1. On Tiller's offer of free abortions, see Roxana Hegeman, "Free Abortions Draw Protests," *Chicago Tribune*, January 20, 2002, 14; Stephanie Simons, "The Nation: Protestors Who Push the Limits," *Los Angeles Times*, February 17, 2004, A1. On the signing of the bill, see "President Bush Signs Partial-Birth Abortion Ban Act" (November 5, 2003), https://georgewbush-whitehouse.archives.gov/news/releases/2003/11/20031105-1.html, accessed September 7, 2021.

42. On the litigation around Haskell's license, see *Women's Professional Medical Corporation v. Baird*, 277 F.Supp.2d 862 (S.D. Ohio 2003). For Haskell's arguments in the case, see Plaintiff's Motion on Remand from the Sixth Circuit for Preliminary Injunction and Memorandum in Support, *Women's Professional Medical Corporation v. Baird*, 2008 WL 545015 (S.D. Ohio 2008) (Civil Action 03-00162); Plaintiff's Reply to Memorandum Opposing Motion on Remand from Sixth Circuit for Preliminary Injunction, *Women's Professional Medical Corporation v. Baird*, 2008 WL 545015 (S.D. Ohio 2008) (Civil Action 03-00162). For the Sixth Circuit's decision on Ohio's partial-birth abortion ban, see *Women's Professional Medical Corporation v. Taft*, 353 F.3d 436 (6th Cir. 2003).

43. On Newman's haranguing of Tiller, see Simons, "Protestors Who Push the Limits." For more on Newman and the Truth Truck, see Kimberley Sevcik, "One Man's God Squad," *Rolling Stone*, August 19, 2004, 108–112.

44. See Elisabeth Bumiller and Carl Hulse, "Bush Picks U.S. Appeals Judge to Take O'Connor's Court Seat," *New York Times*, November 1, 2005, A1; Sheryl Gay Stolberg and Elizabeth Bumiller, "Congress Confirms Roberts as 17th Chief Justice," *New York Times*, September 30, 2005, A1; Adam Liptak, "Alito Vote May Be Decisive in Marquee Cases This Term," *New York Times*, February 1, 2006, A1. For the lower court litigation in the case, see *Carhart v. Ashcroft*, 331 F.Supp.2d 805 (D. Neb. 2004); *Carhart v. Ashcroft*, 413 F.3d 791 (8th Cir. 2005); *Planned Parenthood Federation of America v. Ashcroft*, 320 F.Supp.2d 957 (N.D. Cal. 2004); *Planned Parenthood Federation of America v. Ashcroft*, 435 F.3d 1163 (9th Cir. 2006).

45. Brief Amici Curiae of American Women's Medical Association et al., 25, *Gonzales v. Carhart*, 550 U.S. 124 (2007) (No. 05-1382).

46. Brief of the American College of Obstetricians and Gynecologists as Amicus Curiae Supporting Respondents, 3, *Gonzales v. Carhart*, 550 U.S. 124 (2007) (No. 05-1382).

47. Brief for the Petitioners, 27, *Gonzales v. Carhart*, 550 U.S. 124 (2007) (No. 05-1382).

48. Amicus Brief for the American Center for Law and Justice in Support of Petitioner, 9, *Gonzales v. Carhart*, 550 U.S. 124 (2007) (No. 05-1382).

49. Brief of the Thomas More Law Society, Inc. as Amicus Curiae Supporting Petitioner, 12, *Gonzales v. Carhart*, 550 U.S. 124 (2007) (No. 05-1382).

50. Brief of Sandra Cano, the former "Mary Doe" of *Doe v. Bolton*, and 180 Women Injured by Abortion as Amici Curiae in Support of Petitioner, 29, *Gonzales v. Carhart*, 550 U.S. 124 (2007) (No. 05-1382).

51. *Gonzales v. Carhart*, 550 U.S. 124, 137–139 (2007).

52. Ibid., 159–162.

53. Ibid., 162–164.

54. Robin Toner, "Abortion Foes See Validation for New Tactic," *New York Times*, May 22, 2007, A1. For the text of the South Dakota law: S.D. Cod. Law 34-23A-10.1. For Cassidy's argument about the constitutionality of the South Dakota law, see Brief on Appeal of Intervenors Alpha Center et al., 36–63, *Planned Parenthood of Minnesota, South Dakota, North Dakota v. Rounds*, 530 F.3d 724 (8th Cir. 2008) (No. 05-3093)

55. On Haskell's transfer battle, see Tom Beyerlein, "Abortion Clinic's Situation Political, Attorney Says," *Dayton Daily News*, February 29, 2008, A6; Tom Beyerlein, "State Allows Area's Sole Abortion Clinic to Stay Open," *Dayton Daily News*, March 5, 2008, A4.

56. See National Right to Life Committee, Press Release, "Pain Capable Unborn Children Protected in Nebraska" (October 15, 2010), www.nrlc.org/communications/

releases/2010/release101510, accessed September 27, 2017; Pam Belluck, "Complex Science at Issue in Politics of Fetal Pain," *New York Times*, September 17, 2013, A1; Erik Eckholm, "Theory on Pain Is Driving Rules on Abortion," *New York Times*, August 1, 2013, 1.

57. Liz Szabo, "Thimerosal Vaccine Didn't Cause Autism," *USA Today*, March 12, 2010, http://usatoday30.usatoday.com/news/health/2010–03–12-autism-vaccines_N.htm, accessed September 8, 2021. For more on the *Cedillo* litigation, see *Cedillo v. Secretary of Health and Human Services*, 617 F.3d 1328 (D.C. App. 2010); Donald McNeil Jr., "3 Rulings Find No Link to Vaccine and Autism," *New York Times*, March 12, 2009, A16.

58. Barbara Hollingsworth, "Going to a Tea Party in Fairfax County," *Washington Examiner*, July 19, 2009, 16. For more on Obama's early climate change policy, see Christopher J. Bailey, *U.S. Climate Change Policy* (London: Routledge, 2016), 113–128.

59. On the grand jury process, see Judy Peres, "Abortion Foes Put Grand Jury on Case," *Chicago Tribune*, February 11, 2008, 1; "The Nation: Grand Jury Can't Get Abortion Files," *Los Angeles Times*, February 6, 2008, A13; Monica Davey, "Grass-Roots Grand Juries Becoming the Latest Abortion Battlefield," *New York Times*, June 17, 2008, A1. On the misdemeanor charges, see Robin Abcarian, "The Nation: Abortion Provider's Trial Opens," *Los Angeles Times*, March 24, 2009, A12. On Tiller's unwillingness to give up his practice, see "Kan. Doctor Refused to Quit: 'I Know They Need Me,' " *Gainesville Sun*, June 2, 2009, 2.

60. Haskell, interview. On Roeder, see Nicholas Riccardi, "Slaying Suspect Tied to Militias," *Los Angeles Times*, June 2, 2009, A1; Susan Saulny and Monica Davey, "Seeking Clues on Suspect in Shooting of Doctor," *New York Times*, June 2, 2009, A1; Peter Slevin, "Slaying Raises Fears on Both Sides of Abortion Debate," *Washington Post*, June 2, 2009, A1.

61. Dale Byrom, "Letter to the Editor," *Dayton Daily News*, December 15, 1989, 18. On Tillerisms, see Cecile Richards, *Making Trouble Young: Standing Up, Speaking Out, and Finding the Courage to Lead* (New York: Simon and Schuster, 2019), 174; Haskell, interview.

62. Haskell, interview.

Chapter 6. *Roe* and Race

1. Catherine Davis, interview with Mary Ziegler, March 24, 2021; Catherine Davis, interview with Mary Ziegler, April 2, 2021.

2. Davis, March 24, 2021 interview; Davis, April 2, 2021 interview.

3. Davis, March 24, 2021 interview; Davis, April 2, 2021 interview.

4. Davis, March 24, 2021 interview; Davis, April 2, 2021 interview.

5. Davis, March 24, 2021 interview; Davis, April 2, 2021 interview. For the book that changed Davis's perspective, see George Grant, *Grand Illusions: The Legacy of Planned Parenthood*, 2nd ed. (Tyler, TX: Institute for Christian Economics, 1996).

6. Kierra Johnson, interview with Mary Ziegler, April 8, 2021.

7. Ibid.; Kierra Johnson, email interview with Mary Ziegler, December 6, 2021.

8. Johnson, April 8, 2021 interview; Johnson, December 6, 2021 interview.

9. Johnson, April 8, 2021 interview; Johnson, December 6, 2021 interview.

10. Johnson, April 8, 2021 interview; Johnson, December 6, 2021 interview.

11. On the declining support for legal abortion in the mid-2000s, see Laura Sessions Stepp, "For Abortion Rights, a Changing of the Guard," *Washington Post*, April 24, 2004, C1; see also Alec Gallup and Frank Newport, eds., *The Gallup Poll: Public Opinion 2005* (Lanham, MD: Rowman and Littlefield, 2005), 150–175. For more on the organization of the march, see Lynette Clemetson, "For Abortion Rights Cause, a New Diversity," *New York Times*, April 24, 2004, A14; Elizabeth Williamson, "Women's Marchers, City Gear Up for Mega-Rally," *Washington Post*, April 22, 2004, B1.

12. Karen Mulhauser to Gloria Steinem (February 7, 2002), 1, SSR, Box 10, March for Women's Lives Folder.

13. "Choice USA Reveals New Image at 10th Anniversary Celebration" (February 25, 20020, CUR, Box 10, Choice USA Press Releases 2004 Folder. For more on the people of color leading reproductive justice organizing in the early 2000s, see Laura Flanders, *Blue Grit: Making Impossible, Improbable, and Inspirational Political Change in America* (New York: Penguin, 2008), 145; Jael Silliman, Marlene Gerber Fried, Loretta Ross, and Elena Gutiérrez, *Undivided Rights: Women of Color Organizing for Reproductive Justice* (Chicago: Haymarket, 2004), 110–153.

14. "Choice USA Reveals," 2.

15. Loretta Ross, "Notes on Analytical Perspectives" (February 4, 2004), SSR, Box 10, March for Women's Lives Folder.

16. Strategy Notes, The Color of Choice: Women of Color and the March for Women's Lives (2004), SSR, Box 10, March for Women's Lives Folder.

17. On the influence of reproductive justice arguments and activists of color on the march, see Zakiya Luna, "Marching toward Reproductive Justice: Coalitional (Re-) Framing of the March for Women's Lives," *Sociological Inquiry* 80 (2010): 554–578.

18. Ibid.

19. Clemetson, "For Abortion Rights." For more on the women of color who shaped the march, see Julian Bond, "It's Time to March for Women's Lives," *Sacramento Observer*, March 25, 2004, C6; Williamson, "Women's Marchers," B1; Cassie

M. Chew, "Black Women Shape Their Own Message at March for Women's Lives," *Crisis*, July/August 2004, 14–15.

20. Randall K. O'Bannon, "Margaret Sanger's Eugenic Legacy," *National Right to Life News*, April 1, 2005, 22; see also Mary Meehan, "Why Liberals Should Defend the Unborn," *Human Life Review*, Summer 2011, 15; Rebecca Messall, "Margaret Sanger and the Eugenics Movement," *Human Life Review*, Spring 2010, 98. For the study, see Stanley K. Henshaw and Kathryn Kost, "Trends in the Characteristics of Women Obtaining Abortions, 1974–2004," *Guttmacher Institute*, August 2008. For coverage of the story, see Rob Stein, "Study Finds Major Shift in Abortion Demographics," *Washington Post*, September 23, 2008, A3.

21. Davis, March 24, 2021 interview; Davis, April 2, 2021 interview.

22. On Davis's failed campaigns for political office, see "The South Has Risen Again as the #1 Battleground for Control of the Senate," *Roll Call*, May 17, 2004, 1; Mae Gentry, "Anti-McKinney Vote Up for Grabs in Congress Race," *Atlanta Journal-Constitution*, June 15, 2004, B1; Ernie Suggs and Sonji Jacobson, "Third Time's the Charm, Davis Insists," *Atlanta Journal-Constitution*, August 10, 2006, B1.

23. Messaging on Reproductive Rights and Health Prepared for the David and Lucile Packard Foundation (Spring 2005), NAPAWR, Box 11, Reproductive Justice Messaging Folder.

24. Memo, Women Donors Network to Interested Parties (January 2007), NAPAWR, Box 11, Reproductive Justice Messaging Folder.

25. For examples of the ongoing emphasis put on arguments about choice, see Press Release, "NARAL Pro-Choice America: Alito Does Not Refute His Opposition to *Roe v. Wade*," *U.S. Newswire*, January 10, 2006, 1; David Garrow, "The Battles over Abortion," *Chicago Tribune*, June 18, 2006, 14. At other times, NARAL embraced arguments about personal responsibility. See, for example, Frances Kissling and Kate Michelman, "Abortion's Battle of Messages," *Los Angeles Times*, January 22, 2008, A19.

26. Laura Flanders, "Not by Spin Alone," *In These Times* 36 (2006): 18–19. For Kissling and Michelman's argument, see Kissling and Michelman, "Abortion's Battle of Messages," A19.

27. Nancy Keenan, Address, 2008 Democratic National Convention Day 1, August 25, 2008, https://www.c-span.org/video/?280553-1/2008-democratic-convention-day-1, accessed September 24, 2021. On the NARAL endorsement, see Katharine Q. Seelye, "NARAL Picks Obama, and Uproar Breaks Out," *New York Times*, May 16, 2008, https://www.nytimes.com/2008/05/16/us/politics/16campaign.html, accessed September 24, 2021. On Obama's record on abortion, see Bill Adair, "Barack Obama Voted Consistently for Abortion Rights," *Politifact*, February 6, 2008, https://www.

politifact.com/factchecks/2008/feb/06/barack-obama/obama-voted-consistently-for-abortion-rights/, accessed September 24, 2021.

28. "Black Pastor Jailed for Speaking Up against Genocidal Abortion," *New York Beacon*, March 26, 2009, 4. For more on the controversy surrounding Hoye's arrest, see Robert Artigo, *Black and Pro-Life in America: The Incarceration and Exoneration of Walter P. Hoye III* (San Francisco: Ignatius, 2018). For more on Black right-to-lifers, see Angela K. Lewis, *Conservatism in the Black Community: To the Right and Misunderstood* (New York: Routledge, 2013), 25–52; Louis G. Prisock, *African-Americans in Conservative Movements: The Inescapability of Race* (New York: Palgrave-Macmillan, 2018), 92–120. On the background of the Oakland ordinance, see Puck Lo, "City Buffer Zone, Separating Abortion Patients from Protestors, Faces Lawsuit in Federal Court," *Oakland North*, November 7, 2009, https://oaklandnorth.net/2009/11/07/city-buffer-zone-separating-abortion-patients-from-protesters-faces-lawsuit-in-federal-court/, accessed April 12, 2022.

29. Sheryl Gay Stolberg, "A Pregnant Pause: For a Whole Generation, Abortion Has Been a Personal Choice and Not a Political Cause. That Worries Members of the Menopausal Militia and Their Sisters in Congress," *New York Times*, November 29, 2009, A21. On the debate about the Stupak Amendment, see Josh Blackman, *Unraveled: Obamacare, Religious Liberty, and Executive Power* (New York: Cambridge University Press, 2016), 33–37; Rickie Solinger, *Reproductive Politics: What Everyone Needs to Know* (New York: Oxford University Press, 2013), xlix; William D'Antonio, Steven Tuch, and Josiah R. Baker, *Religion, Politics, and Polarization: How Religiopolitical Conflict Is Changing Congress and American Democracy* (Lanham, MD: Rowman and Littlefield, 2013), 66–73.

30. Shaila Dawan, "To Court Blacks, Foes of Abortion Make Racial Case," *New York Times*, February 27, 2010, A1. For more on the billboards, see Errin Haines, "Anti-Abortion Billboards Lobby for Black Support," *Charleston Gazette*, February 15, 2010, B7; Shaila Dawan, "Anti-Abortion Billboards on Race Split Atlanta," *New York Times*, February 6, 2010, A9.

31. On *Maafa 21*, see Dewan, "To Court Blacks," A10; Lynnette Holloway, "Some Black Pro-Lifers Say Abortion Is Genocide," *The Root*, March 15, 2010.

32. On Rose's "sting," see Lila Rose, James O'Keefe, and Sean Hannity, "Planned Parenthood: Cleaner Race by 'Helping' Blacks," *UCLA Buzzfeed News*, April 3, 2008, 3. On the political response to the videos, see Erik Eckholm, "Budget Feud Ropes in Planned Parenthood," *New York Times*, February 18, 2011, A16; Mary Ziegler, "Sexing *Harris*: The Law and Politics of Defunding Planned Parenthood," *Buffalo Law Review* 60 (2012): 720–731.

33. Ernie Suggs, "Senate Oks No Coercion Abortion Bill," *Atlanta Journal-Constitution*, March 27, 2010, A10.

34. On Americans for Prosperity, see Jane Mayer, *Dark Money: The Hidden History of The Billionaires behind the Radical Right* (New York: Penguin, 2016), 221–225, 265. On FreedomWorks, see Theda Skocpol and Vanessa Williamson, *The Tea Party and the Remaking of Republican Conservatism* (New York: Oxford University Press, 2012), 83; Theda Skocpol, "The Elite and Popular Roots of Contemporary Republican Extremism," in *Upending American Politics: Polarizing Parties, Ideological Elites, and Citizen Activists from the Tea Party to the Anti-Trump Resistance*, ed. Theda Skocpol and Catherine Tervo (New York: Oxford University Press, 2020), 3–29.

35. Dana Milbank, "More Than Just White Tea?" *Washington Post*, September 15, 2010, A23. On the Contract from America, see Teddy Davis, "Tea Party Activists Craft 'Contract from America,'" *ABC News*, February 3, 2010, https://abcnews.go.com/Politics/tea-party-activists-craft-contract-america/story?id=9740705, accessed September 24, 2021; Kate Zernike, "Tea Party Avoids Divisive Social Issues," *New York Times*, March 12, 2010, https://www.nytimes.com/2010/03/13/us/politics/13tea.html, accessed September 24, 2021; Chris Good, "Tea Party Releases Document of Principles," *Atlantic*, April 14, 2010, https://www.theatlantic.com/politics/archive/2010/04/tea-partiers-release-document-of-principles/38922/, accessed September 24, 2021. On racism within the Tea Party, see Kirk A. Johnson, *African American Tea Party Supporters: Explaining a Political Paradox* (Lanham, MD: Rowman and Littlefield, 2019), viii, 160–172; Christopher Parker and Matt Barretto, *Change They Can't Believe In: The Tea Party and Reactionary Politics in America* (Princeton, NJ: Princeton University Press, 2014), 3–8. On the NAACP study and surveys, see Kate Zernike, "N.A.A.C.P. Report Raises Concerns about Racism within Tea Party Groups," *New York Times*, October 21, 2010, A23.

36. Caitlin Coakley, "After Lengthy Debate, Arizona House Committee Passes Abortion Bill 'We All Can Agree On,'" *Arizona Capitol Times*, February 9, 2011; see also "Arizona: Abortion Banned for Race Selection," *New York Times*, March 31, 2011, https://www.nytimes.com/2011/03/31/us/31brfs-ABORTIONBANN_BRF.html, accessed April 4, 2022. On the laws defunding Planned Parenthood, see Jennifer Skalka, "Abortion Opponents Have a New Voice," *Christian Science Monitor*, August 13, 2011, http:// www.csmonitor.com/USA/society/2011/0813/Abortion-opponents-have-a-new-voice, accessed September 24, 2021; Cheryl Wetzstein, "GOP Has 'Blueprint for Action' on Planned Parenthood," *Washington Times*, July 14, 2011, http://washingtontimes.com/news/2011/jul/14/gop-has-blueprint-for-action-on-planned-parenthood, accessed September 24, 2021.

37. Johnson, April 8, 2021 interview.

38. See Sabrina Tavernise, "Squalid Abortion Clinic Escaped State Oversight," *New York Times*, January 23, 2011, A25; Larry Miller, "Poor, Minorities, Abortion Victims," *Philadelphia Inquirer*, January 21, 2011, 1A, 6A; Larry Miller, "Gosnell Case Fuels Abortion Debate," *Philadelphia Inquirer*, February 13, 2011, 1A, 12A; Chelsea Conaboy, "Doctor's Long Tumble to Jail," *McClatchy-Tribune Business News*, January 23, 2011.

39. See Miller, "Gosnell Case." On the spread of the billboards, see Stacey Patton, "Soho Billboard: Womb Is 'Most Dangerous Place' for an African-American," *Sun Reporter*, March 3, 2011, 5; Natasha Hemley, "Pro-Life Billboards Stir Controversy," *Windy City Times*, April 6, 2011, 10; Dawn Turner Trice, "Debate over Black Abortion Disparity," *Chicago Tribune*, April 20, 2011, 1. On the Pence Amendment, see Mahalet Dejene, "Planned Parenthood, Supporters Unite against Pence Amendment," *Amsterdam News*, March 3, 2011, 1; Erik Eckholm, "Budget Feud Ropes in Planned Parenthood," *New York Times*, February 18, 2011, A16.

40. Miller, "Gosnell Case"; see also Kathryn Smith, "Gosnell Fallout: Focus on Clinic Regs," *Politico*, May 13, 2013; Linda Feldmann, "The Gosnell Trial: Will It Affect Abortion Rights?" *Christian Science Monitor*, April 15, 2013, 11.

41. Smith, "Gosnell Fallout"; see also Feldmann, "The Gosnell Trial."

42. Smith, "Gosnell Fallout."

43. See Mary Spaulding Balch to Whom It May Concern (June 2011), JBP, Digital Records, Pain-Capable File; Doug Johnson to David N. O'Steen (April 27, 2012), JBP, Digital Records, Pain-Capable File.

44. See Peter Loftus and Louise Radnofsky, "Abortion Doctor Convicted of Murder in Baby Deaths," *Wall Street Journal*, May 13, 2013, A1.

45. On the history of redlining, see Richard Rothstein, *The Color of Law: A Forgotten History of How Our Government Segregated America* (New York: Liveright, 2017), 2–10, 82–124; Mehra Baradaran, *The Color of Money: Black Banks and the Racial Wealth Gap* (Cambridge, MA: Harvard University Press, 2019), 105–106; Keeanga-Yamahtta Taylor, *Race for Profit: How Banks and the Real Estate Industry Undermined Black Homeownership* (Chapel Hill: University of North Carolina Press, 2019). On the history of redlining in Mantua, see Amy Hillier, "Spatial Analysis of Historical Redlining: A Methodological Exploration," *Journal of Housing Research* 14 (2003): 137–142; Joseph Puckett, "Mantua and the Great Migration," University of Pennsylvania, West Philadelphia Collaborative History, https://collaborativehistory.gse. upenn.edu/stories/mantua-and-great-migration, accessed September 27, 2021.

46. Press Release, "Americans United for Life: Applauds Life-Saving Law, Championed by Texas House, Senate, and Governor Rick Perry," July 13, 2013, https://aul.

org/2013/07/13/americans-united-for-life-applauds-life-saving-law-championed-by-the-texas-house-senate-and-governor-rick-perry/, accessed April 4, 2022; see also Americans United for Life, "Women's Health Protection Act," in *Legislative and Policy Guide for the 2013 Legislative Year* (Washington, DC: Americans United for Life, 2013), 1–6.

47. See Monica Simpson, "Reproductive Justice and 'Choice:' An Open Letter to Planned Parenthood" (August 5, 2014), https://rewirenewsgroup.com/article/2014/08/05/reproductive-justice-choice-open-letter-planned-parenthood/, accessed September 27, 2021.

48. "Letter to the Editor: *Roe v. Wade* Anniversary," *Massachusetts Daily Collegian*, January 22, 2014.

49. See Maya Roden, "What We Stand to Lose," *Essence*, May 2014, 68. For more on reproductive justice organizing on college campuses, see Patricia Zavella, *The Movement for Reproductive Justice: Empowering Women of Color through Social Activism* (New York: New York University Press, 2019).

50. Press Release, Statement of Planned Parenthood in Honor of the 50th Anniversary of the Civil Rights Act of 1964, *Targeted News Service*, July 2, 2014.

51. The Restoration Project, "The Selma Project" (2015), https://www.therestorationproject.life/the-selma-project.html, accessed September 27, 2021. On the spread of "reasons bans," see "Bans on Abortion in Cases of Race or Sex Selection or Fetal Anomaly" (January 2020), https://www.guttmacher.org/evidence-you-can-use/banning-abortions-cases-race-or-sex-selection-or-fetal-anomaly, accessed September 27, 2021. On the ban proposed by Representative Franks, see Representative Trent Franks, Press Release, "This Is the Civil Rights Struggle That Will Define Our Generation," *Congressional Documents and Publications*, April 14, 2016.

52. See *Planned Parenthood of Greater Texas Surgical Health Services v. Abbott*, 951 F.Supp. 2d 891 (W.D. Tex. 2013); *Planned Parenthood of Greater Texas Surgical Health Services v. Abbott*, 734 F.3d 406 (5th Cir. 2013); *Planned Parenthood of Greater Texas Surgical Services v. Abbott*, 748 F.3d 583, 593–601 (5th Cir. 2014).

53. Brief Amici Supporting Petitioners National Advocates for Pregnant Women et al., 2–3, *Whole Woman's Health v. Hellerstedt*, 136 S.Ct. 2292 (2016) (No. 15-274).

54. Brief of Amici Curiae National Women's Law Center et al., 1–4, 22–25, *Whole Woman's Health v. Hellerstedt*, 136 S.Ct. 2292 (2016) (No. 15-274).

55. Brief of Twelve Organizations Dedicated to the Fight for Reproductive Justice as Amici Curiae Supporting Petitioners, 16, *Whole Woman's Health v. Hellerstedt*, 136 S.Ct. 2292 (2016) (No. 15-274).

56. Brief Amici Curiae of the American Association of Pro-Life Obstetricians and Gynecologists et al., 21, *Whole Woman's Health v. Hellerstedt*, 136 S.Ct. 2292 (2016) (No. 15-274).

57. See Brief Amicus Curiae of 3,348 Women Injured by Abortion and the Justice Foundation as Amicus Curiae, 3–4, *Whole Woman's Health v. Hellerstedt*, 136 S.Ct. 2292 (2016) (No. 15-274).

58. Samantha Lachman, "Hillary Spoke about Reproductive Justice in a Truly Intersectional Way," *Huffington Post*, June 10, 2016. On Trump's racist comments, see Richard Fording and Sanford Schram, *Hard White: The Mainstreaming of Racism in American Politics* (New York: Oxford University Press, 2020), 1–13. On Trump's early interactions with the anti-abortion movement, see Mary Ziegler, *Dollars for Life: The Anti-Abortion Movement and the Fall of the Republican Establishment* (New Haven, CT: Yale University Press, 2022), 200–215.

59. *Whole Woman's Health v. Hellerstedt*, 136 S.Ct. 2292, 2309–2314 (2016).

60. See ibid.

61. Davis, March 24, 2021 interview; Davis, April 2, 2021 interview.

62. Davis, March 24, 2021 interview; Davis, April 2, 2021 interview. On Scalia's death and the blocking of Garland's nomination, see Eva Ruth Moravec, Sari Horvitz, and Jerry Markon, "The Death of Antonin Scalia: Chaos, Confusion and Conflicting Reports," *Washington Post*, February 14, 2016, www.washingtonpost.com/politics/texas-tv-station-scalia-died-of-a-heart-attack/2016/02/14/938e2170-d332–11e5–9823–02b905009f99_story.html, accessed April 30, 2019; Ron Elving, "What Happened with Merrick Garland and Why It Matters Now," *NPR*, June 29, 2018, www.npr.org/2018/06/29/624467256/what-happenedwith-merrick-garland-in-2016-and-why-it-matters-now, accessed April 30, 2019.

63. *Box v. Planned Parenthood of Indiana and Kentucky*, 139 S.Ct. 1780, 1793 (2019) (Thomas, J., concurring); Davis, March 24, 2021 interview; Davis, April 2, 2021 interview.

64. Davis, March 24, 2021 interview; Davis, April 2, 2021 interview.

65. Johnson, April 8, 2021 interview.

Chapter 7. Religious Liberty and Equal Treatment

1. Janet Folger Porter, interview with Mary Ziegler, September 17, 2021. For more on Porter's story, see Janet Folger, *True to Life: The Incredible Story of a Young Woman Who Spoke Up for the Unborn and Found Herself in the National Spotlight* (Bartonville, IL: Loyalty, 2000); Janet Folger, *What's a Girl to Do? While Waiting for Mr. Right* (New York: Random House, 2004).

2. Porter, interview; see also Janet Folger Porter, *A Heartbeat Away: How the Heartbeat Bill Will Pierce the Heart of* Roe v. Wade *and the Shocking Betrayal That No One Saw Coming* (Shippensburg, PA: Destiny Image, 2020), 34–68, 120–134.

3. Porter, interview. For more on the development of the heartbeat bill, see Porter, *A Heartbeat Away*, 3–34, 102–134. On Lally's career, see "Right to Life Lawyer Mark S. Lally Dies at 63," *Columbus Dispatch*, November 28, 2010, https://www.dispatch.com/story/news/2010/11/28/right-to-life-lawyer-mark/23532593007/, accessed October 4, 2021.

4. Porter, interview.

5. Ibid. For Porter's statement: Laurie Goodstein, "Architect of the 'Gay Conversion' Campaign," *New York Times*, August 13, 1998, https://www.nytimes.com/1998/08/13/us/the-architect-of-the-gay-conversion-campaign.html, accessed October 4, 2021. For more on Kennedy, see Robert Nolin and James D. Davis, "Ex-Dance Instructor Built Religious Empire," *Sun Sentinel*, August 29, 2007, https://www.sun-sentinel.com/news/fl-xpm-2007-08-29-0708280504-story.html, accessed October 4, 2021.

6. See Sarah Kliff, "Lawmakers Debate Contraceptive Mandate," *Washington Post*, February 17, 2012, A3; "Health, Faith, and Birth Control," *Los Angeles Times*, August 1, 2012, A16.

7. Fundraising Letter, "An Urgent Message from ADF" (1994), AUS, Box 1, Folder 14.

8. "ADL Hits Christian Fundamentalists," *Forward*, June 10, 1994, 4. For more on ADF and other conservative Christian litigators, see Daniel Bennett, *Defending Faith: The Politics of the Christian Conservative Legal Movement* (Lawrence: University Press of Kansas, 2017); Hans J. Hacker, *The Culture of Conservative Christian Litigation* (Lanham, MD: Rowman and Littlefield, 2005), 29, 106; Andrew Lewis, *The Rights Turn in Christian Politics: How Abortion Transformed the Culture Wars* (New York: Cambridge University Press, 2017), 156–159.

9. Alliance Defense Fund, Fundraising Letter, "White Hot and Getting Hotter" (2001), AUS, Box 1, Folder 14. For more on ADF, see Amanda Hollis-Brusky and Joshua Wilson, *Separate but Faithful: The Christian Right's Radical Struggle to Transform Law and Culture* (New York: Oxford University Press, 2020).

10. Jane Lampman, "For Evangelicals, A Bid to 'Reclaim America,' " *Christian Science Monitor*, March 16, 2005, 16; see also William Lobdell, "Conferences Debate Religion vs. Politics," *Los Angeles Times*, April 27, 2001, B3.

11. David Yonke, "Signs of the Digital Times; Thousands Sign Online Declaration," *McClatchy-Business Tribune*, December 12, 2009. For more on the significance of the Manhattan Declaration, see Douglas NeJaime and Reva Siegel, "Conscience

Wars in Transnational Perspective: Religious Liberty, Third-Party Harm, and Plural-ism," in *The Conscience Wars: Rethinking the Balance between Religion, Identity, and Equality*, ed. Michael Rosenfeld and Susanna Mancini (New York: Cambridge University Press, 2018), 196–197. For the Manhattan Declaration itself, see *The Manhattan Declaration: A Call of Christian Conscience*, November 20, 2009, https://www.manhattandeclaration.org/, accessed October 12, 2021.

12. See Press Release, "AUL's Legal Team Files 29th Brief Defending Conscience Rights of Americans Opposed to Life-Ending Drugs" (January 11, 2016), https://aul.org/2016/01/11/auls-legal-team-files-29thbrief-defending-conscience-rights-of-americans-opposed-to-life-ending-drugs, accessed November 5, 2018.

13. Rob Boston, "Catholic, Evangelical Declaration Signers Seek to Nuke the Church-State Wall," *Church and State*, January 2010, 4–6.

14. Porter, interview; Porter, *A Heartbeat Away*, 3–23. For more on the personhood movement, see Dan Becker, "National Personhood Alliance" (July 16, 2014), www.grtl.org/?q=nationalpersonhood-alliance, accessed July 31, 2018; see also "Who Is Personhood Alliance?" www.personhood.org/index.php/press/who-is-national-personhood-alliance, accessed July 31, 2018.

15. "The Pro-Life Heartbeat Bill: Questions and Answers" (n.d., ca. 2019), on file with the author.

16. David Forte, "Life, Heartbeat, Birth: A Medical Basis for Reform," *Ohio State Law Journal* 74 (2012): 142. On Porter's early travels to promote the heartbeat bill, see Erik Eckholm, "Anti-Abortion Groups Are Split on Legal Tactics," *New York Times*, December 4, 2011, A1.

17. David Forte, "Reply to Critics of the Heartbeat Bill" (2012), 4, on file with the author.

18. Porter, interview. On divisions within the anti-abortion movement about the heartbeat bill, see Eckholm, "Anti-Abortion Groups." On Porter's promotion of the birther theory, see Nina Liss-Schulz, "The Mastermind behind Ohio's New 'Heartbeat' Abortion Bill Is Too Extreme for Christian Talk Radio," *Mother Jones*, December 9, 2016, https://www.motherjones.com/politics/2016/12/ohio-heartbeat-abortion-janet-porter/, accessed October 4, 2021.

19. David Limbaugh, "There's Nothing 'Live and Let Live' about the Orwellian Pro-Abortion Left," *Washington Examiner*, March 24, 2014.

20. Editorial Review, "Crying Wolf on Religious Liberty," *New York Times*, March 23, 2012, SR12.

21. Brief of Thomas More Law Center as Amicus Curiae in Support of Hobby Lobby and Conestoga et al., 13–14, *Burwell v. Hobby Lobby Stores, Inc.*, 134 S.Ct. 2751 (2014) (Nos. 13-354, 13-356).

22. Brief of Life, Liberty, and the Law Foundation, 18, *Burwell v. Hobby Lobby Stores, Inc.*, 134 S.Ct. 2751 (2014) (Nos. 13-354, 13-356).

23. Brief for the National Women's Law Center et al., 24, *Burwell v. Hobby Lobby Stores, Inc.*, 134 S.Ct. 2751 (2014) (Nos. 13-354, 13-356).

24. Brief Amicus Curiae of Lambda Legal, 4, *Burwell v. Hobby Lobby Stores, Inc.*, 134 S.Ct. 2751 (2014) (Nos. 13-354, 13-356) (citation and quotation omitted).

25. *Burwell v. Hobby Lobby Stores, Inc.*, 134 S.Ct. 573 U.S. 682,721–723 (2014).

26. Ibid., 724–726.

27. On the history of the same-sex marriage struggle, see Michael J. Klarman, *From the Closet to the Altar: Courts, Backlash, and the Struggle for Same-Sex Marriage* (New York: Oxford University Press, 2013); Lillian Faderman, *The Gay Revolution: The Story of the Struggle* (New York: Simon and Schuster, 2015). For the decision in *Windsor*, see *United States v. Windsor*, 570 U.S. 744 (2013).

28. Oral Argument, *Obergefell v. Hodges*, 576 U.S. 644 (April 27, 2015), 69 (Statement of John J. Bursch).

29. Brief Amici Curiae Public Affairs Campaign et al., 7, *Obergefell v. Hodges*, 576 U.S. 644 (2015) (Nos. 14-556, 14-562, 14-571, 14-574).

30. Brief Amicus Curiae of United States Conference of Catholic Bishops in Support of Respondents, 23, *Obergefell v. Hodges*, 576 U.S. 644 (2015) (Nos. 14-556, 14-562, 14-571, 14-574).

31. *Obergefell v. Hodges*, 576 U.S. 644, 655 (2015). For Alito's dissent: ibid., 741.

32. Michael McManus, "Homosexual Agenda Becoming the '*Roe v. Wade* of Marriage,'" *El Dorado News-Times*, February 28, 2015, https://www.eldoradonews.com/news/2015/feb/28/homosexual-agenda-becoming-roe-v-wade-marriage/, accessed October 4, 2021. For the Pew findings, see Pew Research Center, "America's Changing Religious Landscape" (May 12, 2015), https://www.pewforum.org/2015/05/12/americas-changing-religious-landscape/, accessed October 4, 2021.

33. For Kasich's action, see Jason Slotkin, "Ohio Gov. Kasich Signs 20-Week Abortion Limit, Rejects 'Heartbeat Bill,'" *NPR*, December 13, 2016, https://www.npr.org/sections/thetwo-way/2016/12/13/505457437/ohio-gov-kasich-signs-20-week-abortion-limit-rejects-heartbeat-bill, accessed April 5, 2022. For Porter's statement: Porter, *A Heartbeat Away*, 145.

34. Ian Lovett, "Conservative Christian Leaders Praise President Trump's Pick for Supreme Court," *Wall Street Journal*, February 1, 2017.

35. On Trump's moves on religious liberty, see Juliet Eilperin, "Trump Moves to Expand Exemption from ACA Birth-Control Coverage," *Washington Post*, June 1,

2017, A3; Robert Pear and Jeremy Peters, "Trump Gives Health Workers New Religious Liberty Protections," *New York Times*, January 18, 2018.

36. Leada Gore, "Janet Porter, Spokesperson for Roy Moore, Alleges Plots and Lies in Combative Interviews," *Al.com*, March 7, 2019, https://www.al.com/news/2017/12/janet_porter_spokesperson_for.html, accessed October 4, 2021.

37. See Jeffrey Toobin, "Should Democrats Bother Fighting Brett Kavanaugh's Confirmation? History Says Yes," *New Yorker*, July 31, 2018, www.newyorker.com/news/daily-comment/should-democrats-bother-fighting-brett-kavanaughs-confirmation-history-suggests-yes, accessed July 31, 2018; Karlyn Bowman, "Brett Kavanaugh and Public Opinion on Supreme Court Nominations," *Forbes*, July 25, 2018, www.forbes.com/sites/bowmanmarsico/2018/07/25/brett-kavanaughand-public-opinion-on-supreme-court-confirmations/#70e5a4786001, accessed May 28, 2019. For a brief overview of the #MeToo Movement, see Jessica Bennett, "The #MeToo Moment: What's Next?" *New York Times*, January 5, 2018, www.nytimes.com/2018/01/05/us/the-metoo-moment-whats-next.html, accessed April 19, 2019.

38. See Mike Nowatzki, "Abortion Law Costs $245,000 in Legal Fees," *Bismarck Tribune*, April 12, 2016, https://bismarcktribune.com/news/state-and-regional/abortion-law-costs-north-dakota-245-000-in-legal-fees/article_7714f47f-0702-5624-aca1-bcd24f5e9ae1.html, accessed October 4, 2021. For more on the Civil Rights Attorney's Fees Act, see M. J. McNamara, "Judicial Discretion and the 1976 Civil Rights Attorney's Fees Award Act: What Special Circumstances Render an Award Unjust?" *Fordham Law Review* 51 (1982–83): 320–344.

39. See Jessica Campisi et al., "All the States Taking Up New Abortion Laws in 2019," *The Hill*, May 27, 2019, https://thehill.com/policy/healthcare/445460-states-passing-and-considering-new-abortion-laws-in-2019, accessed October 4, 2021.

40. Mark Lee Dickson, email interview with Mary Ziegler, November 8, 2021; Mark Lee Dickson, email interview with Mary Ziegler, October 19, 2021.

41. Mark Lee Dickson, interview with Mary Ziegler, September 9, 2021.

42. Dickson, September interview. On pro-life abolitionists, see Sophie Novack, "Meet the 'Abortion Abolitionists' Shaping Policy in the Texas GOP," *Texas Monthly*, July 17, 2019, https://www.texasobserver.org/meet-the-abortion-abolitionists-shaping-policy-in-the-texas-gop/, accessed October 4, 2021; Abolish Human Abortion, "The Difference between Pro-Lifers and Abolitionists" (2021), https://abolishhumanabortion.com/abolitionism/the-difference-between-pro-lifers-and-abolitionists/, accessed October 4, 2021.

43. Dickson, September interview. For the Court's decision in *June Medical*, see *June Medical Services v. Russo*, 140 S.Ct. 2103 (2020).

44. Adelle Banks, "Chick-fil-A to Draw Crowds—and Not for Its Food," *Washington Post*, July 31, 2012, https://www.washingtonpost.com/national/on-faith/chick-fil-a-to-draw-crowds-_-and-not-for-its-food/2012/07/31/gJQA3omfNX_story.html, accessed October 4, 2021.

45. For the text of the bill, see Act of September 1, 2019, 86th Leg., R.S., ch. 10, § 2400 et seq., 2019 Tex. Sess. Law Serv. 903. For more on the Save Chick-fil-A law, see Gwen Aviles, "Texas Gov. Greg Abbott Signs 'Save Chick-fil-A' Bill," *NBC News*, July 19, 2019, https://www.nbcnews.com/feature/nbc-out/texas-gov-greg-abbott-signs-save-chick-fil-bill-n1031786, accessed April 6, 2022; Hannah Denham, "Texas Signs 'Save Chick-fil-A' Bill into Law," *Washington Post*, July 19, 2019, https://www.washingtonpost.com/business/2019/07/19/chick-fil-a-inspires-new-texas-law-focused-protecting-religious-freedom/, accessed October 4, 2021.

46. For a detailed version of the standing argument, see "The Effort to Outlaw Abortion in Cisco, Texas, Factsheet" (August 2021), on file with the author.

47. *June Medical Services v. Russo*, 140 S.Ct. 2103, 2129–2136 (2020). For Roberts's concurrence, see ibid., 2134–2140 (Roberts, C.J., concurring).

48. "The Effort to Outlaw Abortion in Cisco, Texas, Factsheet."

49. See Sarah McCammon, "Ginsburg's Death a 'Pivot Point' for Abortion Rights, Advocates Say," *NPR*, September 19, 2020, https://www.npr.org/sections/death-of-ruth-bader-ginsburg/2020/09/19/914864867/ginsburgs-death-a-pivot-point-for-abortion-rights-advocates-say, accessed October 4, 2021.

50. Jerry Dunleavey, " 'The Dogma Lives Loudly': Amy Coney Barrett Emerges as Top Contender for Trump Supreme Court Pick," *Washington Examiner*, September 23, 2020, https://www.washingtonexaminer.com/news/the-dogma-lives-loudly-amy-coney-barrett-emerges-as-top-contender-for-trump-supreme-court-pick, accessed November 17, 2021.

51. Janet Folger Porter, Mass Email, "How to Overcome the Criminalization of Christianity" (March 4, 2021), on file with the author. On Trump's effort to overturn the election, see Philip Bump, "What We Know about Trump's Efforts to Subvert the 2020 Election," *Washington Post*, January 25, 2021, https://www.washingtonpost.com/politics/2021/01/25/what-we-know-about-trumps-efforts-subvert-2020-election/, accessed February 2, 2021; Jim Rutenberg et al., "77 Days: Trump's Campaign to Subvert the Election," *New York Times*, January 31, 2021, https://www.nytimes.com/2021/01/31/us/trump-election-lie.html, accessed February 2, 2021.

52. On the Lubbock vote, see Brittany Shammas, "Voters Declare Lubbock, Tex., a 'Sanctuary City for the Unborn' in Effort to Ban Abortions," *Washington Post*, May 5, 2021, https://www.washingtonpost.com/nation/2021/05/05/lubbock-texas-

abortion-ban/, accessed November 17, 2021. For the district court's decision on the ordinance, see *Planned Parenthood of Greater Texas Surgical Health Services v. City of Lubbock, Texas*, 542 F.Supp.3d 465, 477–478 (N.D. Tex. 2021).

53. On the research governing fetal pain, see Susan J. Lee et al., "Fetal Pain: A Systematic Multidisciplinary Review of the Evidence," *Journal of the American Medical Association* 294 (2005): 947–954. On the timing of viability, see American College of Obstetricians and Gynecologists, "Periviable Birth" (October 2017), https://www.acog.org/clinical/clinical-guidance/obstetric-care-consensus/articles/2017/10/periviable-birth, accessed October 4, 2021.

54. On the Court's grant of certiorari in *Dobbs*, see *Dobbs v. Jackson Women's Health Organization*, 141 S.Ct. 2619 (2021). On the lower court litigation, see *Jackson Women's Health Organization v. Currier*, 349 F.Supp.3d 536 (D. Miss. 2018); *Jackson Women's Health Organization v. Dobbs*, 945 F.3d 265 (5th Cir. 2019).

55. See Act of September 1, 2021, 87th Leg., Ch. 171, § 201, 2021 Tex. Gen. Laws 2882.

56. Dickson, September 2021 interview; Dickson, November 2021 interview. For more on Hughes and his work on SB8, see Patrick Svitek, "The Texas Lawmaker behind the GOP Abortion Ban, Voting Restrictions, and More," *Texas Tribune*, September 17, 2021, https://www.texastribune.org/2021/09/17/texas-abortion-ban-voting-bryan-hughes/, accessed December 21, 2021. For the Court's order on SB8, see *Whole Woman's Health v. Jackson*, 141 S.Ct. 2494 (2021). For an overview of the earlier litigation in the case, see Mark Tushnet, "Has the US Supreme Court Effectively Overruled *Roe v. Wade*?" *Verfassungsblog*, September 3, 2021, https://verfassungsblog.de/has-the-u-s-supreme-court-effectively-overruled-roe-v-wade/, accessed October 4, 2021.

57. Brief Amicus Curiae of the Becket Fund for Religious Liberty, 5–12, *Dobbs v. Jackson Women's Health Organization*, 2021 WL 4311852 (2022) (No. 19-1392).

58. Brief Amicus Curiae of the Jewish Coalition for Religious Freedom, 5, *Dobbs v. Jackson Women's Health Organization*, 2021 WL 4311852 (2022) (No. 19-1392).

59. Brief Amici Curiae of Freedom from Religion et al., 11, *Dobbs v. Jackson Women's Health Organization*, 2021 WL 4311852 (2022) (No. 19-1392).

60. Brief Amici Curiae of Americans United for Separation of Church and State et al., 20, *Dobbs v. Jackson Women's Health Organization*, 2021 WL 4311852 (2022) (No. 19-1392).

61. *Tandon v. Newsom*, 141 S.Ct. 1494 (2021) (per curiam). For the November order, see *Roman Catholic Diocese of New York v. Cuomo*, 141 S.Ct. 63, 66 (2021) (per curiam). For the order in *South Bay*, see *South Bay United Pentecostal Church v.*

Newsom, 141 S.Ct. 716 (2021). For analysis of the decisions, see Jim Oleske, "*Tandon* Steals *Fulton*'s Thunder," *Scotusblog*, April 15, 2021, https://www.scotusblog. com/2021/04/tandon-steals-fultons-thunder-the-most-important-free-exercise-decision-since-1990/, accessed October 4, 2021.

62. For the Court's decision in *Smith*, see *Employment Division v. Smith*, 494 U.S. 872 (1990).

63. For the Court's decision in *Fulton*, see *Fulton v. City of Philadelphia*, 141 S.Ct. 1868, 1878–1883 (2021). For the concurring opinion, see ibid., 1882–1885 (Barrett, J., concurring).

64. For analysis of the oral argument in *Dobbs*, see Mary Ziegler, "The End of *Roe* Is Coming, and It Is Coming Soon," *New York Times*, December 1, 2021, https:// www.nytimes.com/2021/12/01/opinion/supreme-court-abortion-mississippi-law. html, accessed December 13, 2021.

65. For the Court's decision on SB8, see *Whole Woman's Health v. Jackson*, 142 S.Ct. 522 (2021). For analysis of the decision, see "The Supreme Court Declines to Block Texas's Abortion Law," *Economist*, December 10, 2021, https://www.economist.com/ united-states/2021/12/10/the-supreme-court-declines-to-block-texass-abortion-law, accessed December 13, 2021. For the Texas Supreme Court's decision, see *Whole Woman's Health v. Jackson*, 65 Tex. Sup. Ct. J. 625 (Tex. 2022).

66. For analysis of the argument in *Makin*, see Adam Liptak, "Supreme Court Seems Wary of Ban on State Aid to Religious Schools," *New York Times*, December 8, 2021.

67. Public Religion Research Institute, "Is Religious Liberty a Shield or a Sword?" (February 10, 2021), https://www.prri.org/research/is-religious-liberty-a-shield-or-a-sword/, accessed October 4, 2021; Elana Schor and Hannah Fingerhut, "Religious Freedom: Popular and Polarizing," *AP*, August 5, 2020, https://apnews.com/article/ donald-trump-religion-u-s-news-virus-outbreak-reinventing-faith-535624d93b-8ce3d271019200e362b0cf, accessed October 4, 2021. For more on the transformation of religious liberty politics, see Andrew R. Lewis, "The Fight for Religious Freedom Isn't What It Used to Be," *Atlantic*, June 17, 2021, https://www.theatlantic.com/ideas/ archive/2021/06/fulton-and-polarization-religious-freedom/619158/, accessed November 15, 2021; Jeremiah Castle, "New Fronts in the Culture Wars? Religion, Partisanship, and Polarization on Religious Liberty and Transgender Rights in the United States," *American Politics Research* 47 (2019): 650–679. For polling on abortion, see Gallup, "Abortion: In Depth" (2021), https://news.gallup.com/poll/1576/ abortion.aspx, accessed December 13, 2021.

68. Janet Folger Porter, Mass Email, "Porter's Video Response to Biden's Forced Vaccinations," September 10, 2021, on file with the author.

69. Janet Porter, Mass Email, "Janet Porter Joins Dr. James Dobson Today," September 16, 2021, on file with the author.

70. Porter, *A Heartbeat Away*, 161; Porter, interview. For the email declaring *Roe* dead, see Letter to Faith2Action Partner, Mass Email, December 13, 2021.

Epilogue. *Roe* After the Overruling

1. On predictions that the Court would soon reverse *Roe*, see Adam Liptak, "Supreme Court to Hear Abortion Case Challenging *Roe v. Wade*," *New York Times*, October 7, 2011, https://www.nytimes.com/2021/05/17/us/politics/supreme-court-roe-wade.html, accessed October 11, 2021; Nina Totenberg, "Mississippi Is Trying to Get the Supreme Court to Reverse *Roe*," *NPR*, July 23, 2021, https://www.npr.org/2021/07/23/1019746478/on-abortion-mississippi-swings-for-the-fences-asks-the-supreme-court-to-reverse-, accessed October 11, 2021. On the women's marches around the *Dobbs* case, see Julia Manchester, "Women's March to Hold Nationwide Events to Respond to Texas Abortion Law," *The Hill*, September 3, 2021, https://thehill.com/homenews/campaign/570769-womens-march-to-hold-nationwide-mobilization-event-to-respond-to-texas, accessed October 11, 2021. On the Mexico Supreme Court's decision on abortion, see Vanessa Romo, "Mexico's Supreme Court Has Voted to Decriminalize Abortion," *NPR*, September 7, 2021, https://www.npr.org/2021/09/07/1034925270/mexico-abortion-decriminalized-supreme-court, accessed October 11, 2021. On the shift in policy in Thailand, see Muktita Sukhartono and Mike Ives, "Thailand Legalizes Abortion in First Trimester but Keeps Other Restrictions," *New York Times*, January 28, 2021, https://www.nytimes.com/2021/01/28/world/asia/thailand-abortion-rights.html, accessed October 11, 2021.

2. On the politics of gun rights and gun control, see Hana Bajramovic, *Whose Right Is It? The Second Amendment and the Fight over Guns* (New York: Henry Holt, 2020); Adam Winkler, *Gunfight: The Battle over the Right to Bear Arms in America* (New York: Norton, 2011). For the Court's decision in *Heller*, see *District of Columbia v. Heller*, 554 U.S. 570 (2008). For recent debate about voter suppression, election laws, and subversion, see Richard L. Hasen, "Republicans Aren't Done Messing with Elections," *New York Times*, April 23, 2021, https://www.nytimes.com/2021/04/23/opinion/republicans-voting-us-elections.html, accessed October 11, 2021; Paul Steinhauser, "Republican Party Launching a New Election Integrity Commission," Fox News, February 21, 2021, https://www.foxnews.com/politics/republican-party-launching-new-election-integrity-committee, accessed October 11, 2021. For the Court's decision in *Shelby County*, see *Shelby County v. Holder*, 570 U.S. 529 (2013). For the Court's decision in *Brnovich*, see *Brnovich v. Democratic National Committee*,

141 S.Ct. 2321 (2021). For the Court's decision in *Citizens United*, see *Citizens United v. Federal Election Commission*, 558 U.S. 310 (2010).

3. On the importance of partisanship in predicting abortion attitudes and political identity, see Michele Margolis, *From Politics to the Pews: How Partisanship and the Political Environment Shape Religious Identity* (Chicago: University of Chicago Press, 2018); see also Kelsey Dallas, "What We Misunderstand about the Role of Religion in Abortion Politics," *Deseret News*, May 22, 2019, https://www.deseret.com/2019/5/23/20674119/what-we-misunderstand-about-religion-s-role-in-the-abortion-debate#in-this-friday-jan-18–2019-file-photo-anti-abortion-activists-march-outside-the-u-s-supreme-court-building-during-the-march-for-life-in-washington-has-the-abortion-debate-moved-from-a-strictly-religious-sphere-to-a-partisan-and-political-one, accessed October 11, 2021. On the spread of negative partisanship, see Alan I. Abramowitz, *The Great Alignment: Race, Party Transformation, and the Rise of Donald Trump* (New Haven, CT: Yale University Press, 2018), 3–16; Lilliana Mason, *Uncivil Agreement: How Politics Became Our Identity* (Chicago: University of Chicago Press, 2018), 28, 94.

4. For a sample of leading sociological analyses of *Roe*, see Kristin Luker, *Abortion and the Politics of Motherhood* (Berkeley: University of California Press, 1984); Ziad Munson, *The Making of Pro-Life Activists: How Social Movement Mobilization Works* (Chicago: University of Chicago Press, 2008); Faye Ginsburg, *Contested Lives: The Abortion Debate in an American Community* (Berkeley: University of California Press, 1989).

5. For an overview of scholarly criticisms of *Roe*, see Mary Ziegler, *After* Roe*: The Lost History of the Abortion Debate* (Cambridge, MA: Harvard University Press, 2015), 3–15.

6. For the Court's decision in *Dred Scott*, see *Dred Scott v. Sandford*, 60 U.S. 393 (1857). For the Court's decision in *Plessy*, see *Plessy v. Ferguson*, 163 U.S. 537 (1896). For the Court's decision in *Brown*, see *Brown v. Board of Education*, 347 U.S. 483 (1954).

7. For examples of social movement scholarship, see Doug McAdam, "Tactical Innovation and the Pace of Insurgency," *American Sociological Review* 48 (1983): 735–754; William N. Eskridge, "Channeling: Identity-Based Social Movements and Public Law," *University of Pennsylvania Law Review* 150 (2001): 419–500; Suzanne Staggenborg and David S. Meyer, "Opposing Movement Strategies in U.S. Abortion Politics," *Research in Social Movements, Conflicts, and Change* 28 (2008): 207–238; Deana Rohlinger, "Framing the Abortion Debate: Organizational Resources, Media Strategies, and Movement-Countermovement Dynamics," *Sociological Quarterly* 43 (2002): 479–507; Reva B. Siegel, "Constitutional Culture, Social Movement Con-

flict, and Constitutional Change: The Case of the De Facto Era," *California Law Review* 94 (2006): 1323–1400.

8. On existing disparities in abortion laws, see Jordan Smith, "Millions of Women Already Live in a Post-*Roe* America," *Intercept*, January 18, 2019, https://theintercept.com/2019/01/18/abortion-roe-v-wade-reproductive-rights/, accessed October 11, 2021.

9. See Brief Amicus Curiae of Texas Right to Life, *Dobbs v. Jackson Women's Health Organization*, 2021 WL 4311852 (2022) (No. 19-1392).

Index

abortion: ACA coverage of, 111–112; dilation and evacuation technique for, 81, 82, 88; ethical dimensions of, 2, 80, 90, 94, 99, 168n9; global liberalization of, ix, 150; maternal mortality from, 2, 165n4; Medicaid funding for, 18–20, 30, 39, 49, 107, 113, 119; medication-induced, 1, 55, 85, 132, 156; pain-capable laws and, 97–98, 117, 143; parental involvement mandates for, 62–63; partial-birth, 81–97, 104, 127, 153, 189n10; political polarization over, x, xii, 151, 210n3; privacy rights and, x, 8–9; rates of, 2, 18, 107–108, 113, 123, 169n14; sanctuary city bans on, 139–144; sex-selection, 64, 114, 121; spousal notification laws and, 67, 73, 94; state restrictions on, xiv, 1–3, 6, 62–63; stigmatization of, 21, 22, 24, 171n34; undue burden test for restrictions on, 73–74, 123. *See also* criminalization of abortion; informed consent laws; pro-choice movement; pro-life movement; *specific court cases*

abortion clinics: blockades at, 60–65, 71–72, 85, 182n10; emergence of, 21, 170n25; legislative protection for, 87, 110–111; picketing at, 22, 32, 79;

unsafe practices at, 116, 122; violence at, 64, 72, 79, 83–85, 87, 111

abortion on demand, 27–28, 49, 172n46

abortion providers: AUL strategy on, 64, 65; civil enforcement actions against, 140–141, 144; federal protection of, 92; malpractice lawsuits against, 112; racism accusations against, 107, 113; referrals to, 4, 14; *Roe* on rights of, 17; stigmatization of, 21; violence against, 72, 79, 83–84, 87, 99–100, 111

ACLU. *See* American Civil Liberties Union

ACOG. *See* American College of Obstetricians and Gynecologists

Affordable Care Act of 2010 (ACA), 111–112, 115, 128–136, 154

African Americans. *See* Black Americans

Against Our Will: Men, Women, and Rape (Brownmiller), 19–20

Akron, City of v. Akron Reproductive Health Services (1983), 48, 179n37

Akron II decision. See *Ohio v. Akron Center for Reproductive Health* (1990)